For Jem

Semiotics:
The Basics

'This is the best introduction to semiotics I have read. Comprehensive, accessible and interesting, it is an invaluable resource for both beginners and more advanced students.'

Guy Cook, University of Reading, UK

'This book introduces a growing area of investigation with humour and insight. Eclectic rather than dogmatic, this is a book students should know about.'

Tony Thwaites, University of Queensland, Australia

'It is no small task to present semiotics in a manner that makes it accessible to the beginning student, and Chandler achieves this, describing difficult concepts clearly and thoroughly.'

Donald J. Cunningham, Indiána University, USA

Following the successful *Basics* format, this is the book for anyone coming to semiotics for the first time. Using jargon-free language and lively, up-to-date examples, *Semiotics: The Basics* demystifies this highly interdisciplinary subject. Along the way, the reader will find out:

- What is a sign?
- Which codes do we take for granted?
- What is a text?
- How can semiotics be used in textual analysis?
- Who are Saussure, Peirce, Barthes and Jakobson – and why are they important?

Features include a glossary of key terms and realistic suggestions for further reading. There is also a highly-developed and long-established online version of the book at: www.aber.ac.uk/media/Documents/S4B.

Daniel Chandler is a Lecturer in the department of Theatre, Film and Television Studies at the University of Wales, Aberystwyth.

Other titles in this series include:

Archaeology: The Basics
Clive Gamble

Language: The Basics (Second edition)
R. L. Trask

Philosophy: The Basics (Third edition)
Nigel Warburton

Politics: The Basics (Second edition)
Stephen D. Tansey

Shakespeare: The Basics
Sean McEvoy

Sociology: The Basics
Martin Albrow

Semiotics:

The Basics

■ Daniel Chandler

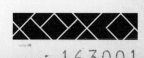

First published 2002 by Routledge
11 New Fetter Lane, London EC4P 4EE

Simultaneously published in the
USA and Canada
by Routledge
29 West 35th Street, New York, NY
10001

Reprinted 2003 (twice), 2004

*Routledge is an imprint of the Taylor &
Francis Group*

© 2002 Daniel Chandler

Typeset in Times New Roman by
Florence Production, Stoodleigh, Devon
Printed and bound in Great Britain by
Biddles Ltd, King's Lynn, Norfolk

*British Library Cataloguing in
Publication Data*

Chandler, Daniel Glen Joel, 1952–
Semiotics: the basics
1. Semiotics
I. Title II. Series
302.2'21   P99.C463   2002

*Library of Congress Cataloging in
Publication Data*

A catalog record for this book has is
available on request

ISBN 0–415–26593–2 (hbk)
ISBN 0–415–35111–1 (pbk)

Contents

List of figures   xi
List of tables   xiii
Preface   xv
Acknowledgements   xix

Introduction   1

Definitions   2
Traditions   5
Methodologies   7
Relation to linguistics   9
Langue and parole   12
Why study semiotics?   14

1 Models of the sign   17

The Saussurean model   18
Two sides of a page   21
The relational system   22
Arbitrariness   25
The Peircean model   32
Relativity   36
Symbolic mode   38
Iconic mode   39
Indexical mode   41

Modes not types	43
Changing relations	44
Digital and analogue	45
Types and takens	47
Rematerializing the sign	49
Hjelmslev's framework	53

2 Signs and things   55

Naming things	55
Referentiality	58
Modality	60
The word is not the thing	64
Empty signifiers	74

3 Analysing structures   79

Horizontal and vertical axes	79
The syntagmatic dimension	83
Conceptual relations	84
Spatial relations	86
Sequential relations	89
Structural reduction	92
The paradigmatic dimension	98
The commutation test	99
Oppositions	101
The language of opposition	102
Us and them	104
Alignment	106
Markedness	110
Valorizing Term B	115
The semiotic square	118

4 Challenging the literal   123

Rhetorical tropes	123
Metaphor	127
Metonymy	130
Synecdoche	132
Irony	134
Master tropes	137
Denotation and connotation	140
Myth	144

5 Codes 147

Types of codes 148
Perceptual codes 150
Social codes 154
Textual codes 157
Codes of realism 161
Invisible editing 166
Broadcast and narrowcast codes 170
Interaction of textual codes 171
Codification 172

6 Textual interactions 175

Models of communication 175
The positioning of the subject 179
Adopting a perspective 183
Modes of address 188
Reading positions 192
Intertextuality 194
Problematizing authorship 196
Reading as rewriting 197
No text is an island 199
Intratextuality 201
Bricolage 203
Types and degrees of intertextuality 203

7 Limitations and strengths 207

Imperialism 208
Form and function 209
Inescapable frames 211
Poststructuralist semiotics 213
Strengths of semiotic analysis 214
Mediation 215
The construction of meanings and subjects 217
Semiotic modes 218

Going further 221
Glossary 223
References 247
Index 263

Figures

1.1	Saussure's model of the sign	18
1.2	Concept and sound pattern	19
1.3	Planes of thought and sound	22
1.4	The relations between signs	23
1.5	A semiotic triangle	34
3.1	Syntagmatic and paradigmatic axes	80
3.2	Little Red Riding Hood	96
3.3	Paradigm set for shot size	100
3.4	Markedness of some explicit oppositions in online texts	114
3.5	Saussure's binary priorities	116
3.6	The semiotic square	119
4.1	Substitution in tropes	125
4.2	The four 'master tropes'	137
4.3	Jakobson's axes	139
4.4	Orders of signification	142
6.1	Saussure's speech circuit	176
6.2	Jakobson's model of communication	177

Tables

1.1	Substance and form	54
2.1	Modality cues	62
3.1	Syntagmatic relations	85
3.2	Propp's list of functions	94
3.3	Alignments with the four elements	103
3.4	Contrasting Apple and IBM logos	109
4.1	The ironic, the literal and the lie	135
4.2	The four 'master tropes'	136
4.3	Tropes, genres, worldviews and ideologies	138
5.1	'Bracketed' perception and 'normal' perception	153
6.1	Jakobson's six functions of language	178

Preface

The first version of this text was written in 1994 for my own students. No comparable text on the subject existed at the time so I rashly attempted to create one which suited my own purposes and those of my students. It was partly a way of advancing and clarifying my own understanding of the subject. Like many other readers, my forays into semiotics had been frustrated by many of the existing books on the subject that frequently seemed almost impossible to understand. As an educationalist, I felt that the authors of such books should be thoroughly ashamed of themselves. The subject of meaning-making is of understandable fascination for a very wide readership, but most of the existing books seemed to seek to make it confusing, dull and deeply obscure.

The academic priorities that led me to write this text (teaching a media education class for third-year undergraduates) had consequences for its evolution. However, since I wrote the original text, I have broadened its scope considerably, so that there are now frequent references not only to the mass media but also to other subjects, such as literature, art and mythology. One of the things that attracted me to semiotics was the way in which it supports my own enjoyment of crossing the 'boundaries' of academic disciplines, and of making connections between apparently disparate phenomena. However, I am not a polymath, so there are inevitably many subjects which are neglected here. In this text I have confined myself to *human* semiosis, so that this is not the place to find an introduction to such branches of semiotics as *zoosemiotics* (the study of the behaviour and communication of animals) or *biosemiotics* (the study of the semiotics of biology and of the biological basis of signs). Nor do I discuss computer semiotics or the semiotics of communication between machines. My focus is on the humanities and so there is no mathematical semiotics here either. Even within the humanities, I did not feel competent to cover musical or architectural semiotics. I know that students of some of these subjects are among those who have consulted the online text, which lends me some hope that they will still find the exploration of general principles of some relevance to their own priorities. The exclusion of certain subjects is not, of course, to suggest that they are any less important to the semiotic enterprise. The unavoidable selectivity of the text invites the productivity of the reader in its deconstruction. Driven by their own purposes, readers will no doubt be alert to 'what is conspicuous by its absence'.

Semiotics is a huge field, and no treatment of it can claim to be comprehensive. My attempt to offer a coherent account of some key concepts is in some ways misleading: there are divergent schools of thought in semiotics, and there is remarkably little consensus among contemporary theorists regarding the scope of the subject, core concepts or methodological tools. This particular account betrays its European origins (in a British inflection), focusing on Saussurean and post-Saussurean semiotics (structuralist semiotics and post structuralist critiques) rather than, for instance, on Peircean semiotics (although some key Peircean concepts are mentioned). The focus on structuralist semiotics is intended to be of value to readers who wish to use semiotics as an approach to textual analysis. However, semiotics is far more than a method of analysing texts in a variety of media, and I hope I will also inspire the reader's enthusiasm for exploring some of the fascinating philosophical issues which semiotics raises. In case it is not obvious to readers, I should declare a social constructionist/constructivist bias, which is not shared by all semioticians. For semioticians who are (in contrast) drawn towards philosophical 'realism', reality is wholly external to and independent of how we conceptualize the world. Social constructionism need not involve denying the existence of any external reality but it does assume that our sign-systems (language and other media) play a major part in 'the social construction of reality' and that realities cannot be separated from the sign-systems in which they are experienced. Readers may of course insist on being realists without abandoning semiotics.

This text was not originally written for the medium of print. It was one of the first texts to be originated and developed on the World Wide Web, and I would encourage other academics to disseminate their work more widely using this means. The amount of 'positive feedback' generated by the online version of this publication has amazed and puzzled me (as well as encouraged me), especially since it was originally produced primarily for my own students. One reason may be that exposure to a new medium seems to generate fresh interest in semiotics. Another may be that so much of what is written about semiotics is written as if to keep out those who are not already 'members of the club'. This text is intended to be a 'reader's companion' in approaching more difficult semiotic texts, which so often assume knowledge of much of the jargon. I apologize to any readers who need no such introduction for the occasional oversimplification to which I have sometimes succumbed in the interests of serving my primary audience.

The online version has special advantages: notably, for the writer revisability, for the reader, being able to 'search' the text and, for both, the 'connections' made possible by hypertextual links. However, the main problem for the reader (other than the discomfort of extended reading from the screen) may be that it doesn't stand still long enough to get to know it – one can 'know one's way around' a book precisely because it remains as constant as a map (unlike the terrain it depicts). It is cheaper to buy the book than to print out the online version, and the book is much tidier to shelve and easier to browse! On the other hand, the online text is always more up to date and contains additional materials. Currently, for instance, the online glossary is far more extensive, and there is also further illustrative material online.

In quoting from the text of Saussure's *Course in General Linguistics*, the translation used is that of Roy Harris (Saussure 1983), although, following the practice of John Sturrock in using this translation (Sturrock 1986, 31, 32), I have retained the terms 'signifier' and 'signified' rather than use Harris's translation of *signifiant* as 'signal' and *signifié* as 'signification'. While it is far more recent (1983) than the Wade Baskin translation (1959), Harris's translation is rarely cited in the texts that most students are likely to encounter. Fortunately, however, the page references are seldom more than a page or so different.

Until this text was published as a book by Routledge, there had been only one official printed version. By curious circumstance that book is not in the language in which the text was originated. An authorized Spanish translation of the text as it was in mid-1998 – *Semiótica para Principiantes* – is available in the series *Pluriminor* from Ediciones Abya-Yala, Av. 12 de Octubre 14–30 y Wilson, Casilla 17–12–719, Quito, Ecuador (Chandler 1998). A printed Greek translation is currently in progress. If there is a demand for translations into other languages, I would be pleased to suggest this to my British publishers.

At the time of writing, the online version of this text was at:

http://www.aber.ac.uk/media/Documents/S4B/

URLs change periodically, so, if necessary, you could use a search engine to locate it.

Acknowledgements

I would like to thank Professor Dr Winfried Nöth of the University of Kassel for his useful comments on 'articulation' and 'empty signifiers'. Dr David Mick of the University of Wisconsin-Madison has also been particularly kind in keeping me updated with his own papers on the semiotics of advertising, which have been a very useful source of ideas and observations. Thanks also to Vanessa Hogan Vega and Iván Rodrigo Mendizábal for producing a Spanish translation in association with Escuela de Comunicación Social de la Universidad Politécnica Salesiana in Ecuador, and to Professor Maria Constantopoulou of the Athens University of Economics and Business for the Greek translation online and the adaptation which is in preparation for print. I am also grateful to the University of Wales, Aberystwyth and to colleagues in my former department (Education) for the one-semester sabbatical which I was granted, and without which this book could not have been written. I would particularly like to thank my linguist colleagues Bob Morris Jones and Marilyn Martin-Jones for their continued support and encouragement throughout the evolution of this text and of its author.

Routledge has made every effort to trace copyright holders and to obtain permission to publish extracts. Any omissions brought to our attention will be remedied in future editions.

Introduction

If you go into a bookshop and ask an assistant where to find a book on semiotics you are likely to meet with a blank look. Even worse, you might be asked to define what semiotics is – which would be a bit tricky if you were looking for a beginner's guide. It's worse still if you do know a bit about semiotics, because it can be hard to offer a simple definition which is of much use in the bookshop. If you've ever been in such a situation, you'll probably agree that it's wise not to ask. Semiotics could be anywhere. The shortest definition is that it is *the study of signs*. But that doesn't leave enquirers much wiser. 'What do you mean by a sign?' people usually ask next. The kinds of signs that are likely to spring immediately to mind are those which we routinely refer to as 'signs' in everyday life, such as road signs, pub signs and star signs. If you were to agree with them that semiotics can include the study of all these and more, people will probably assume that semiotics is about 'visual signs'. You would confirm their hunch if you said that signs can also

be drawings, paintings and photographs, and by now they'd be keen to direct you to the art and photography sections. But if you are thick-skinned and tell them that it also includes words, sounds and 'body language' they may reasonably wonder what all these things have in common and how anyone could possibly study such disparate phenomena. If you get this far, they've probably already 'read the signs' which suggest that you are either eccentric or insane and communication may have ceased.

Definitions

Semiotics is *not* widely institutionalized as an academic discipline (although it does have its own associations, conferences and journals, and it exists as a department in a handful of universities). It is a field of study involving many different theoretical stances and methodological tools. Although there are some self-styled 'semioticians', those involved in semiotics include linguists, philosophers, psychologists, sociologists, anthropologists, literary, aesthetic and media theorists, psychoanalysts and educationalists.

One of the broadest definitions is that of Umberto Eco, who states that 'semiotics is concerned with everything that can be taken as a sign' (Eco 1976, 7). Semiotics involves the study not only of what we refer to as 'signs' in everyday speech, but of anything which 'stands for' something else. In a semiotic sense, signs take the form of words, images, sounds, gestures and objects. Contemporary semioticians study signs not in isolation but as part of semiotic 'sign-systems' (such as a medium or genre). They study how meanings are made and how reality is represented.

Semiotics is concerned with meaning-making and representation in many forms, perhaps most obviously in the form of 'texts' and 'media'. Such terms are interpreted very broadly. For the semiotician, a 'text' can exist in any medium and may be verbal, non-verbal, or both, despite the logocentric bias of this distinction. The term *text* usually refers to a message which has been recorded in some way (e.g. writing, audio- and video-recording) so that it is physically independent of its sender or receiver. A text is an assemblage of signs (such as words, images, sounds and/or gestures) constructed (and interpreted) with reference to the conventions associated with a genre and in a particular medium of communication.

The term 'medium' is used in a variety of ways by different theorists, and may include such broad categories as speech and writing or print and broadcasting, or relate to specific technical forms within the mass media (radio, television, newspapers, magazines, books, photographs, films and records) or the media of interpersonal communication (telephone, letter, fax, e-mail, video-conferencing, computer-based chat systems). Some theorists classify media according to the 'channels' involved (visual, auditory, tactile, and so on). Human experience is inherently multisensory, and every representation of experience is subject to the constraints and affordances of the medium involved. Every medium is constrained by the channels that it utilizes. For instance, even in the very flexible medium of language 'words fail us' in attempting to represent some experiences, and we have no way at all of representing smell or touch with conventional media. Different media and genres provide different frameworks for representing experience, facilitating some forms of expression and inhibiting others. The differences between media lead Emile Benveniste to argue that the 'first principle' of semiotic systems is that they are not 'synonymous': 'we are not able to say "the same thing"' in systems based on different units (in Innis 1986, 235) in contrast to Hjelmslev, who asserted that 'in practice, language is a semiotic into which all other semiotics may be translated' (cited in Genosko 1994, 62).

The everyday use of a medium by someone who knows how to use it typically passes unquestioned as unproblematic and 'neutral': this is hardly surprising since media evolve as a means of accomplishing purposes in which they are usually intended to be incidental. And the more frequently and fluently a medium is used, the more 'transparent' or 'invisible' to its users it tends to become. For most routine purposes, awareness of a medium may hamper its effectiveness as a means to an end. Indeed, it is typically when the medium acquires transparency that its potential to fulfil its primary function is greatest. The selectivity of any medium leads to its use having influences of which the user may not always be conscious, and which may not have been part of the purpose in using it. We can be so familiar with the medium that we are 'anaesthetized' to the mediation it involves: we 'don't know what we're missing'. Insofar as we are numbed to the processes involved, we cannot be said to be exercising 'choices' in its use. In this way the means we use may modify our ends. Among the phenomena enhanced or reduced by media selectivity are the ends for which a medium was used. In some cases, our 'purposes' may be subtly (and perhaps invisibly), redefined by our use of a particular medium. This is the opposite of the pragmatic and rationalistic stance, according to which the means are chosen to suit the user's ends, and are entirely under the user's control.

An awareness of this phenomenon of transformation by media has often led media theorists to argue deterministically that our technical means and systems always and inevitably become 'ends in themselves' (a common interpretation of Marshall McLuhan's famous aphorism, 'the medium is the message'), and has even led some to present media as wholly autonomous entities with 'purposes' (as opposed to functions) of their own. However, one need not adopt such extreme stances in acknowledging the transformations involved in processes of mediation. When we use a medium for any purpose, its use becomes part of that purpose. Travelling is an unavoidable part of getting somewhere; it may even become a primary goal. Travelling by one particular method of transport rather than another is part of the experience. So too with writing rather than speaking, or using a word processor rather than a pen. In using any medium, to some extent we serve its 'purposes' as well as it serving ours. When we engage with media we both act and are acted upon, use and are used. Where a medium has a variety of functions it may be impossible to choose to use it for only one of these functions in isolation. The making of meanings with such media must involve some degree of compromise.

While technological determinists emphasize that meaning-making is influenced by the fundamental design features of different media, it is important to recognize the importance of socio-cultural and historical factors in shaping how different media are used and their (ever-shifting) status within particular cultural contexts. For instance, many contemporary cultural theorists have remarked on the growth of the importance of visual media compared with linguistic media in contemporary society and the associated shifts in the communicative functions of such media. Thinking in 'ecological' terms about the interaction of different semiotic structures and languages led the Tartu school cultural semiotician Yuri Lotman to coin the term 'semiosphere' to refer to 'the whole semiotic space of the culture in question' (Lotman 1990, 124–5). This conception of a semiosphere may make semioticians seem territorially imperialistic to their critics, but it offers a more unified and dynamic vision of semiosis than the study of a specific medium as if each existed in a vacuum.

Beyond the most basic definition, there is considerable variation among leading semioticians as to what semiotics involves. It is not only concerned with (intentional) communication but also with our ascription of significance to anything in the world. Semiotics has changed over time, since semioticians have sought to remedy weaknesses in early semiotic approaches. Even with the most basic semiotic terms there are multiple definitions. Consequently, anyone attempting semiotic analysis would be wise to make clear which definitions are being applied and, if a particular semiotician's approach is being adopted, what its source is.

Traditions

Broadly speaking, there are two divergent traditions in semiotics stemming respectively from the Swiss linguist Ferdinand de Saussure (1857–1913) and the American philosopher Charles Sanders Peirce (pronounced 'purse') (1839–1914). Saussure's term *sémiologie* dates from a manuscript of 1894. In his *Course in General Linguistics* (published posthumously in 1916) Saussure (the usual abbreviation), wrote that:

> It is ... possible to conceive of a science *which studies the role of signs as part of social life*. It would form part of social psychology, and hence of general psychology. We shall call it *semiology* (from the Greek *sēmeîon*, 'sign'). It would investigate the nature of signs and the laws governing them. Since it does not yet exist, one cannot say for certain that it will exist.

But it has a right to exist, a place ready for it in advance. Linguistics is only one branch of this general science. The laws which semiology will discover will be laws applicable in linguistics, and linguistics will thus be assigned to a clearly defined place in the field of human knowledge.

(Saussure 1983, 15–16)

While for the linguist Saussure 'semiology' was 'a science which studies the role of signs as part of social life', to the philosopher Charles Peirce the field of study which he called 'semiotic' was the 'formal doctrine of signs', which was closely related to logic (Peirce 1931–58, 2.227). Working quite independently from Saussure across the Atlantic, Peirce borrowed his term from the seventeenth-century British philosopher John Locke. Peirce and Saussure are widely regarded as the co-founders of what is now more generally known as *semiotics*. They established two major theoretical traditions. Sometimes Saussure's term 'semiology' is used to refer to the Saussurean tradition while 'semiotics' (with the added 's') refers to the Peircean tradition. However, nowadays the term 'semiotics' is widely used as an umbrella term to embrace the whole field (Nöth 1990, 14). We will outline and discuss both the Saussurean and Peircean models of the sign in the next chapter.

A rough-and-ready location of key figures within the traditions may be in order here, although further details about the major theorists must await the introduction of some of their key concepts later in the text. The work of Louis Hjelmslev (1899–1966) can be seen as following in the 'semiological' tradition of Saussure. Hjelmslev, who established the 'Copenhagen school', was in turn a major influence on the structuralism of Algirdas Greimas (1917–92), Roland Barthes (1915–80) and Christian Metz (1931–93). Greimas himself established 'the Paris school' of semiotics. As for the Peircean 'semiotic' tradition, this is represented in the writings of Charles William Morris (1901–79), Ivor A. Richards (1893–1979), Charles K. Ogden (1989–1957) and Thomas Sebeok (b. 1920). The Peircean and structuralist traditions are bridged by both the Russian linguist Roman Jakobson (1896–1982) and the celebrated Italian writer Umberto Eco (b. 1932). Jakobson was involved in the establishment of both 'the

Moscow school' (in 1915) and 'the Prague school' (in 1926) and he was also associated with 'the Copenhagen school' from 1939–49. He was much influenced by Peirce and in turn influenced the structuralism of the anthropologist Claude Lévi-Strauss (1908–90) and the psychoanalytical theorist Jacques Lacan (1901–81). Like Hjelmslev, Jakobson was thus influential in his own right within the structuralist tradition. Acting as another bridge between traditions, Umberto Eco in his *Theory of Semiotics* (1976) sought 'to combine the structuralist perspective of Hjelmslev with the cognitive– interpretative semiotics of Peirce' (Eco 1999, 251). Meanwhile, evolving from the structuralist tradition in the late 1960s, *poststructuralism* problematized many of its assumptions. Poststructuralist theorists include the later Barthes and Lacan (already mentioned for their structuralist roots) together with the literary philosopher Jacques Derrida (b. 1930), the historian of ideas Michel Foucault (1926–84) and the feminist theorist Julia Kristeva (b. 1941).

The primary audience for this text is for students of media, communication and cultural studies. Semiotics began to become a major approach to cultural studies in the late 1960s, partly as a result of the work of the French cultural theorist Roland Barthes. The translation into English of his popular essays in a collection entitled *Mythologies* (Barthes 1957), followed in the 1970s and 1980s by many of his other writings, greatly increased scholarly awareness of this approach in the Anglophone world. The adoption of semiotics in Britain was influenced by its prominence in the work of the Centre for Contemporary Cultural Studies (CCCS) at the University of Birmingham while the centre was under the direction of the neo-Marxist sociologist Stuart Hall (director 1969–79).

Methodologies

Some commentators adopt Charles W. Morris's definition of semiotics (a reductive variant of Saussure's) as 'the science of signs' (Morris 1938, 1–2). The term 'science' is misleading. As yet, semiotics involves no widely agreed theoretical assumptions, models or empirical methodologies. Semiotics has tended to be largely theoretical, many of its theorists seeking to establish its scope and general

7

principles. Peirce and Saussure, for instance, were both concerned with the fundamental definition of the sign. Peirce developed elaborate logical taxonomies of types of signs. Subsequent semioticians have sought to identify and categorize the codes or conventions according to which signs are organized. Clearly there is a need to establish a firm theoretical foundation for a subject which is currently characterized by a host of competing theoretical assumptions. As for methodologies, Saussure's theories constituted a starting point for the development of various structuralist methodologies for analysing texts and social practices. These have been very widely employed in the analysis of many cultural phenomena. However, such methods are not universally accepted: socially oriented theorists have criticized their exclusive focus on structure, and no alternative methodologies have as yet been widely adopted. Some semiotic research is empirically oriented, applying and testing semiotic principles. Bob Hodge and David Tripp employed empirical methods in their classic study of *Children and Television* (Hodge and Tripp 1986). But there is at present little sense of semiotics as a unified enterprise building on cumulative research findings.

As an approach to textual analysis, semiotics is one approach among others. Other approaches to this task include rhetorical analysis, discourse analysis and content analysis. In the field of media and communication studies content analysis is a prominent rival to semiotics as a method of textual analysis. Whereas semiotics is now closely associated with cultural studies, content analysis is well established within the mainstream tradition of social science research. While content analysis involves a quantitative approach to the analysis of the manifest 'content' of media texts, semiotics seeks to analyse texts as structured wholes and investigates latent, connotative meanings. Semiotics is rarely quantitative, and often involves a rejection of such approaches. Just because an item occurs frequently in a text does not make it significant. The structuralist semiotician is more concerned with the relation of elements to each other. A social semiotician would also emphasize the importance of the significance which readers attach to the signs within a text. Whereas content analysis focuses on explicit content and tends to suggest that this represents a single, fixed meaning, semiotic studies focus on the system of rules governing the 'discourse' involved in media texts, stressing the role of semiotic context in shaping meaning. However, some researchers have combined semiotic analysis and content analysis (e.g. Glasgow University Media Group 1980; Leiss *et al.* 1990; McQuarrie and Mick 1992).

Relation to linguistics

This book concentrates on structuralist semiotics (and its poststructuralist critiques). It is difficult to disentangle European semiotics from structuralism in its origins. Linguistic structuralism derived primarily from Saussure: Hjelmslev and Jakobson inspired the European structuralists. Structuralism is an analytical method which involves the application of the linguistic model to a much wider range of social phenomena. Structuralists search for 'deep structures' underlying the 'surface features' of sign-systems: Lévi-Strauss in myth, kinship rules and totemism; Lacan in the unconscious; Barthes and Greimas in the 'grammar' of narrative. Julia Kristeva declared that 'what semiotics has discovered . . . is that the *law* governing or, if one prefers, the *major constraint* affecting any social practice lies in the fact that it signifies; i.e. that it is articulated *like* a language' (cited in Hawkes 1977, 125).

Saussure argued that 'nothing is more appropriate than the study of languages to bring out the nature of the semiological problem' (Saussure 1983, 16). Semiotics draws heavily on linguistic concepts, partly because of the influence of Saussure and because linguistics is a more established discipline than the study of other sign-systems. Saussure referred to language (his model being *speech*) as 'the most important' of all of the systems of signs (Saussure 1983, 15). Some theorists insist that language is fundamental: Émile Benveniste observed that 'language is the interpreting system of all other systems, linguistic and non-linguistic' (in Innis 1986, 239), while Claude Lévi-Strauss noted that 'language is the semiotic system *par excellence*; it cannot but signify, and exists only through signification' (Lévi-Strauss 1972, 48). Language is almost invariably regarded as the most powerful communication system by far.

9

One of the most powerful 'design features' of language is called *double articulation* (or 'duality of patterning'). Double articulation enables a semiotic code to form an infinite number of meaningful combinations using a small number of low-level units which in themselves are meaningless (e.g. phonemes in speech or graphemes in writing). The infinite use of finite elements is a feature which in relation to media in general has been referred to as 'semiotic economy'. Traditional definitions ascribe double articulation only to human language, for which this is regarded as a key 'design feature' (Hockett 1958). Louis Hjelmslev regarded it as an essential and defining feature of language (Hjelmslev 1961). Double articulation is seen as being largely responsible for the creative economy of language. The English language, for instance, has only about forty or fifty elements of second articulation (phonemes) but these can generate hundreds of thousands of words. Similarly, from a limited vocabulary we can generate an infinite number of sentences (subject to the constraint of *syntax* which governs structurally valid combinations). It is by *combining* words in multiple ways that we can seek to render the particularity of experience. If we had individual words to represent every particularity we would have to have an infinite number of them, which would exceed our capability of learning, recalling and manipulating them.

Double articulation does not seem to occur in the natural communication systems of animals other than humans. A key semiotic debate is over whether or not semiotic systems such as photography, film or painting have double articulation. The philosopher Susanne Langer argued that while visual media such as photography, painting and drawing have lines, colours, shadings, shapes, proportions and so on which are 'abstractable and combinatory', and which 'are just as capable of *articulation*, i.e. of complex combination, as words', they have no vocabulary of units with independent meanings (Langer 1951, 86–7).

A symbolism with so many elements, such myriad relationships, cannot be broken up into basic units. It is impossible to find the smallest independent symbol, and recognize its identity when the same unit is met in other contexts ... There is, of course, a technique of picturing objects, but the laws governing this technique cannot properly be called a 'syntax', since there are no items that might be called, metaphorically, the 'words' of portraiture.

(Langer 1951, 88)

Rather than dismissing 'non-discursive' media for their limitations, however, Langer argues that they are more complex and subtle than verbal language and are 'peculiarly well-suited to the expression of ideas that defy linguistic "projection"'. She argues that we should not seek to impose linguistic models upon other media since the laws that govern their articulation 'are altogether different from the laws of syntax that govern language'. Treating them in linguistic terms leads us to 'misconceive' them: they resist 'translation' (ibid., 86–9).

Saussure saw linguistics as a branch of 'semiology':

Linguistics is only one branch of this general science [of semiology]. The laws which semiology will discover will be laws applicable in linguistics ... As far as we are concerned ... the linguistic problem is first and foremost semiological ... If one wishes to discover the true nature of language systems, one must first consider what they have in common with all other systems of the same kind ... In this way, light will be thrown not only upon the linguistic problem. By considering rites, customs etc. as signs, it will be possible, we believe, to see them in a new perspective. The need will be felt to consider them as semiological phenomena and to explain them in terms of the laws of semiology.

(Saussure 1983, 16–17)

While Roland Barthes declared that 'perhaps we must invert Saussure's formulation and assert that semiology is a branch of linguistics', most of those who call themselves semioticians at least implicitly accept Saussure's location of linguistics within semiotics (Barthes 1985, xi). However, even if we theoretically locate linguistics within semiotics it is difficult to avoid adopting the linguistic model in exploring other sign-systems. Semioticians commonly refer to films, television and radio programmes, advertising posters and so on as 'texts', and to 'reading television' (Fiske and Hartley 1978). Media such as television and film are regarded by some semioticians as being in some respects like 'languages'. The issue tends to revolve around whether such media are closer to what we treat as 'reality' in the everyday world of our own experience or whether they have more in common with a symbolic system like writing. However, there is a danger of trying to force all media into a linguistic framework. Contemporary *social* semiotics has moved beyond the structuralist focus on signifying systems as languages, seeking to explore the use of signs in specific social situations. Modern semiotic theory is often also allied to a Marxist approach which stresses the role of *ideology*.

Langue and parole

We will shortly examine Saussure's highly influential model of the sign, but before doing so it is important to understand something about the general framework within which he situated it. Saussure made what is now a famous distinction between *langue* (language) and *parole* (speech). *Langue* refers to the system of rules and conventions which is independent of, and pre-exists, individual users; *parole* refers to its use in particular instances. Applying the notion to semiotic systems in general rather than simply to language, the distinction is one between *system* and *usage*, *structure* and *event* or *code* and *message*. According to the Saussurean distinction, in a semiotic system such as cinema, for instance, individual films can be seen as the *parole* of an underlying system of cinema 'language'. Saussure focused on *langue* rather than *parole*. To the traditional, Saussurean semiotician, what matters most are the underlying structures and rules of a semiotic system as a whole rather than specific performances or practices which are merely instances of its use. Saussure's approach was to study the system 'synchronically' as if it were frozen in time (like a photograph) – rather than 'diachronically' – in terms of its evolution over time (like a film). Structuralist cultural theorists subsequently adopted this Saussurean priority, focusing on the functions of social and cultural phenomena within semiotic systems. Theorists differ over whether the system precedes and determines usage (structural determinism) or whether usage precedes and determines the system (social determinism) (although note that most structuralists argue that the system *constrains* rather than completely *determines* usage).

The structuralist dichotomy between usage and system has been criticized for its rigidity, splitting process from product, subject from structure (Coward and Ellis 1977, 4, 14). The prioritization of structure over usage fails to account for changes in structure. Marxist theorists have been particularly critical of this. In the late 1920s, Valentin Voloshinov (1884/5–1936) and Mikhail Bakhtin (1895–1975) criticized Saussure's synchronic approach and his emphasis on internal relations within the system of language (Voloshinov 1973; Morris 1994). Voloshinov reversed the Saussurean priority of *langue* over *parole*: 'The sign is part of organized social intercourse and cannot exist, as such, outside it, reverting to a mere physical artifact' (Voloshinov 1973, 21). The meaning of a sign is not in its relationship to other signs within the language system but rather in the social context of its use. Saussure was criticized for ignoring historicity (ibid., 61). The Russian linguists Roman Jakobson and Yuri Tynyanov declared in 1927 that 'pure synchronism now proves to be an illusion', adding that 'every synchronic system has its past and its future as inseparable structural elements of the system' (cited in Voloshinov 1973, 166). Writing in 1929, Volosinov observed that 'there is no real moment in time when a synchronic system of language could be constructed . . . A synchronic system may be said to exist only from the point of view of the subjective consciousness of an individual speaker belonging to some particular language group at some particular moment of historical time' (Voloshinov 1973, 66). While the French structuralist Claude Lévi-Strauss applied a synchronic approach in the domain of anthropology, most contemporary semioticians have sought to reprioritize historicity and social context. Language is seldom treated as a static, closed and stable system which is inherited from preceding generations but as constantly changing. The sign, as Voloshinov put it, is 'an arena of the class struggle' (ibid., 23). Seeking to establish a wholeheartedly 'social semiotics', Robert Hodge and Gunther Kress declare that 'the social dimensions of semiotic systems are so intrinsic to their nature and function that the systems cannot be studied in isolation' (Hodge and Kress 1988, 1).

Why study semiotics?

While Saussure may be hailed as a founder of semiotics, semiotics has become increasingly less Saussurean since the 1970s. While the current account of semiotics focuses primarily on its 'classical' structuralist form, we will also explore relevant critiques and subsequent developments. But before launching on an exploration of this intriguing subject, let us consider why we should bother: why should we study semiotics? This is a pressing question in part because the writings of semioticians have a reputation for being dense with jargon: one critic wittily remarked that 'semiotics tells us things we already know in a language we will never understand' (Paddy Whannel, cited in Seiter 1992, 1).

The semiotic establishment may seem to be a very exclusive club but its concerns are not confined to members. No one with an interest in how things are represented can afford to ignore an approach which focuses on, and problematizes, the process of representation. While we need not accept the postmodernist stance that there is no external reality beyond sign-systems, studying semiotics can assist us to become more aware of the mediating role of signs and of the roles played by ourselves and others in constructing social realities. It can make us less likely to take reality for granted as something which is wholly independent of human interpretation. Exploring semiotic perspectives, we may come to realize that information or meaning is not 'contained' in the world or in books, computers or audio-visual media. Meaning is not 'transmitted' to us – we actively create it according to a complex interplay of codes or conventions of which we are normally unaware. Becoming aware of such codes is both inherently fascinating and intellectually empowering. We learn from semiotics that we live in a world of signs and we have no way of understanding anything except through signs and the codes into which they are organized. Through the study of semiotics, we become aware that these signs and codes are normally transparent and disguise our task in 'reading' them. Living in a world of increasingly visual signs, we need to learn that even the most realistic signs are not what they appear to be. By making more explicit the codes by which signs are interpreted, we may perform the valuable semiotic function of 'denaturalizing' signs. This is not to suggest that all representations of reality are of equal status – quite the contrary. In defining realities signs serve ideological functions. Deconstructing and contesting the realities of signs can reveal *whose* realities are privileged and whose are suppressed. Such a study involves investigating the construction and maintenance of reality by particular social groups. To decline the study of signs is to leave to others the control of the world of meanings which we inhabit.

Chapter 1

Models of the sign

We seem as a species to be driven by a desire to make meanings: above all, we are surely *homo significans* – meaning-makers. Distinctively, we make meanings through our creation and interpretation of 'signs'. Indeed, according to Peirce, 'we think only in signs' (Peirce 1931–58, 2.302). Signs take the form of words, images, sounds, odours, flavours, acts or objects, but such things have no intrinsic meaning and become signs only when we invest them with meaning. 'Nothing is a sign unless it is interpreted as a sign', declares Peirce (ibid., 2.172). Anything can be a sign as long as someone interprets it as 'signifying' something – referring to or *standing for* something other than itself. We interpret things as signs largely unconsciously by relating them to familiar systems of conventions. It is this meaningful use of signs which is at the heart of the concerns of semiotics.

The two dominant models of what constitutes a sign are those of the Swiss linguist Ferdinand de Saussure and the American philosopher Charles Sanders Peirce. These will be discussed in turn.

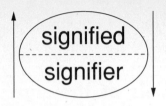

FIGURE 1.1   Saussure's model of the sign

Source: Based on Saussure, 1974

The Saussurean model

Saussure offered a 'dyadic' or two-part model of the sign (see Figure 1.1). Focusing on *linguistic* signs (such as words), he defined a sign as being composed of a 'signifier' (*signifiant*) and a 'signified' (*signifié*). Contemporary commentators tend to describe the signifier as the form that the sign takes and the signified as the concept to which it refers. Saussure makes the distinction in these terms:

> A linguistic sign is not a link between a thing and a name, but between a concept [*signified*] and a sound pattern [*signifier*]. The sound pattern is not actually a sound; for a sound is something physical. A sound pattern is the hearer's psychological impression of a sound, as given to him by the evidence of his senses. This sound pattern may be called a 'material' element only in that it is the representation of our sensory impressions. The sound pattern may thus be distinguished from the other element associated with it in a linguistic sign. This other element is generally of a more abstract kind: the concept.
>
> (Saussure 1983, 66)

For Saussure, both the signifier (the 'sound pattern') and the signified (the concept) were purely 'psychological' (ibid., 12, 14–15, 66). Both were *form* rather than *substance*. Figure 1.2 may help to clarify this aspect of Saussure's own model. Nowadays, while the basic 'Saussurean' model is commonly adopted, it tends to be a more materialistic model than that of Saussure himself. The *signifier* is now

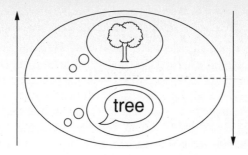

FIGURE 1.2   Concept and sound pattern

commonly interpreted as the *material (or physical) form* of the sign
– it is something which can be seen, heard, touched, smelled or
tasted.

Within the Saussurean model, the *sign* is the whole that results
from the association of the signifier with the signified (ibid., 67).
The relationship between the signifier and the signified is referred
to as 'signification', and this is represented in the Saussurean diagram by the arrows. The horizontal broken line marking the two
elements of the sign is referred to as 'the bar'.

If we take a linguistic example, the word 'open' (when it is
invested with meaning by someone who encounters it on a shop
doorway) is a *sign* consisting of:

- a *signifier*: the word 'open';
- a *signified concept*: that the shop is open for business.

A sign must have both a signifier and a signified. You cannot have a
totally meaningless signifier or a completely formless signified (ibid.,
101). A sign is a recognizable combination of a signifier with a
particular signified. The same signifier (the word 'open') could stand
for a different signified (and thus be a different sign) if it were on a
push-button inside a lift ('push to open door'). Similarly, many signifiers could stand for the concept 'open' (for instance, on top of a
packing carton, a small outline of a box with an open flap for 'open
this end') – again, with each unique pairing constituting a different
sign.

Saussure focused on the linguistic sign and he 'phonocentrically' privileged the *spoken word*. As we have noted, he referred specifically to the signifier as a 'sound pattern' (*image acoustique*). He saw writing as a separate, secondary, dependent but comparable sign-system (ibid., 15, 24–5, 117). Within the ('separate') system of written signs, a signifier such as the written letter 't' signified a sound in the primary sign-system of language (and thus a written word would also signify a sound rather than a concept). Thus for Saussure, writing relates to speech as signifier to signified. Most subsequent theorists who have adopted Saussure's model are content to refer to the form of linguistic signs as either spoken or written. We will return later to the issue of the post-Saussurean 'rematerialization' of the sign.

As for the *signified*, most commentators who adopt Saussure's model still treat this as a mental construct, although they often note that it may nevertheless refer indirectly to things in the world. Saussure's original model of the sign 'brackets the referent': excluding reference to objects existing in the world. His *signified* is not to be identified directly with such a referent but is a *concept* in the mind – not a thing but the notion of a thing. Some people may wonder why Saussure's model of the sign refers only to a concept and not to a thing. An observation from Susanne Langer (who was not referring to Saussure's theories) may be useful here. Note that like most contemporary commentators, Langer uses the term 'symbol' to refer to the linguistic sign (a term which Saussure himself avoided): 'Symbols are not proxy for their objects but are *vehicles for the conception of objects* ... In talking *about* things we have conceptions of them, not the things themselves; and *it is the conceptions, not the things, that symbols directly mean*. Behaviour towards conceptions is what words normally evoke; this is the typical process of thinking'. She adds that 'If I say "Napoleon", you do not bow to the conqueror of Europe as though I had introduced him, but merely think of him' (Langer 1951, 61).

Thus, for Saussure the linguistic sign is wholly immaterial – although he disliked referring to it as 'abstract' (Saussure 1983, 15). The immateriality of the Saussurean sign is a feature which tends to be neglected in many popular commentaries. If the notion seems strange, we need to remind ourselves that words have no value in themselves – that is their value. Saussure noted that it is not the metal in a coin that fixes its value (ibid., 117). Several reasons could be offered for this. For instance, if linguistic signs drew attention to their materiality this would hinder their communicative transparency. Furthermore, being immaterial, language is an extraordinarily economical medium and words are always ready to hand. Nevertheless, a principled argument can be made for the revaluation of the materiality of the sign, as we shall see in due course.

Two sides of a page

Saussure noted that his choice of the terms *signifier* and *signified* helped to indicate 'the distinction which separates each from the other' (Saussure 1983, 67). Despite this, and the horizontal bar in his model of the sign, Saussure stressed that sound and thought (or the signifier and the signified) were as inseparable as the two sides of a piece of paper (ibid., 111). They were 'intimately linked' in the mind 'by an associative link' – 'each triggers the other' (ibid., 66). Saussure presented these elements as wholly interdependent, neither pre-existing the other. Within the context of spoken language, a sign could not consist of sound without sense or of sense without sound. He used the two arrows in the diagram to suggest their interaction. The bar and the opposition nevertheless suggest that the signifier and the signified can be distinguished for analytical purposes. Poststructuralist theorists criticize the clear distinction which the Saussurean bar seems to suggest between the signifier and the signified; they seek to blur or erase it in order to reconfigure the sign. Commonsense tends to insist that the *signifier* takes precedence over, and pre-exists, the signifier: 'look after the sense', quipped Lewis Carroll, 'and the sounds will take care of themselves' (*Alice's Adventures in Wonderland*, chapter 9). However, in dramatic contrast, post-Saussurean theorists have seen the model as implicitly granting primacy to the *signifier*, thus reversing the commonsensical position.

The relational system

Saussure argued that signs only make sense as part of a formal, generalized and abstract system. His conception of meaning was purely *structural* and *relational* rather than *referential*: primacy is given to relationships rather than to things (the meaning of signs was seen as lying in their systematic relation to each other rather than deriving from any inherent features of signifiers or any reference to material things). Saussure did not define signs in terms of some 'essential' or intrinsic nature. For Saussure, signs refer primarily to each other. Within the language system, 'everything depends on relations' (Saussure 1983, 121). No sign makes sense on its own but only in relation to other signs. Both signifier and signified are purely relational entities (ibid., 118). This notion can be hard to understand since we may feel that an individual word such as 'tree' does have some meaning for us, but Saussure's argument is that its meaning depends on its relation to other words within the system (such as 'bush').

Together with the 'vertical' alignment of signifier and signified *within* each individual sign (suggesting two structural 'levels'), the emphasis on the relationship *between* signs defines what are

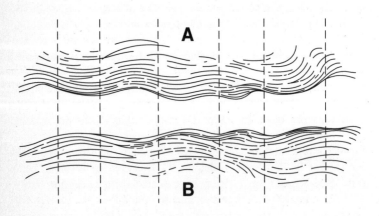

FIGURE 1.3 Planes of thought and sound

Source: Based on Saussure, 1974

in effect two planes – that of the signifier and the signified. Later, Louis Hjelmslev referred to the planes of 'expression' and 'content' (Hjelmslev 1961, 60). Saussure himself referred to *sound* and *thought* as two distinct but correlated planes (see Figure 1.3). 'We can envisage ... the language ... as a series of adjoining subdivisions simultaneously imprinted both on the plane of vague, amorphous thought (A), and on the equally featureless plane of sound (B)' (Saussure 1983, 110–11). The arbitrary division of the two continua into signs is suggested by the dotted lines while the wavy (rather than parallel) edges of the two 'amorphous' masses suggest the lack of any 'natural' fit between them. The gulf and lack of fit between the two planes highlights their relative autonomy. While Saussure is careful not to refer directly to 'reality', the American literary theorist Fredric Jameson reads into this feature of Saussure's system that

> it is not so much the individual word or sentence that 'stands for' or 'reflects' the individual object or event in the real world, but rather that the entire system of signs, the entire field of the *langue*, lies parallel to reality itself; that it is the totality of systematic language, in other words, which is analogous to whatever organized structures exist in the world of reality, and that our understanding proceeds from one whole or Gestalt to the other, rather than on a one-to-one basis.
>
> (Jameson 1972, 32–3)

What Saussure refers to as the 'value' of a sign depends on its relations with other signs within the system (see Figure 1.4). A sign has no 'absolute' value independent of this context (Saussure 1983, 80). Saussure uses an analogy with the game of chess, noting that the

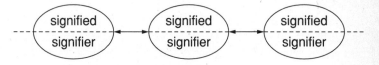

FIGURE 1.4 The relations between signs

Source: Based on Saussure, 1974

value of each piece depends on its position on the chessboard (ibid., 88). The sign is more than the sum of its parts. While *signification* – what is signified – clearly depends on the relationship between the two parts of the sign, the *value* of a sign is determined by the relationships between the sign and other signs within the system as a whole (ibid., 112–13).

> The notion of value . . . shows us that it is a great mistake to consider a sign as nothing more than the combination of a certain sound and a certain concept. To think of a sign as nothing more would be to isolate it from the system to which it belongs. It would be to suppose that a start could be made with individual signs, and a system constructed by putting them together. On the contrary, the system as a united whole is the starting point, from which it becomes possible, by a process of analysis, to identify its constituent elements.
>
> (Saussure 1983, 112)

As an example of the distinction between signification and value, Saussure notes that

> The French word *mouton* may have the same meaning as the English word *sheep*; but it does not have the same value. There are various reasons for this, but in particular the fact that the English word for the meat of this animal, as prepared and served for a meal, is not *sheep* but *mutton*. The difference in value between *sheep* and *mouton* hinges on the fact that in English there is also another word *mutton* for the meat, whereas *mouton* in French covers both.
>
> (ibid., 114)

Saussure's relational conception of meaning was specifically *differential*: he emphasized the differences between signs. Language for him was a system of functional differences and oppositions. 'In a language, as in every other semiological system, what distinguishes a sign is what constitutes it' (ibid., 119). It has been noted that 'a one-term language is an impossibility because its single term could be applied to everything and differentiate nothing; it requires at least one other term to give it definition' (Sturrock 1979, 10). Advertising furnishes a good example of this notion, since what matters in 'positioning' a product is *not* the relationship of advertising signifiers to real-world referents, but the differentiation of each sign from the others to which it is related. Saussure's concept of the relational identity of signs is at the heart of structuralist theory.

Saussure emphasized in particular *negative*, oppositional differences between signs. He argued that 'concepts . . . are defined not positively, in terms of their content, but *negatively* by contrast with other items in the same system. What characterizes each most exactly is *being whatever the others are not*' (Saussure 1983, 115; author's emphasis). This notion may initially seem mystifying if not perverse, but the concept of negative differentiation becomes clearer if we consider how we might teach someone who did not share our language what we mean by the term 'red'. We would be unlikely to make our point by simply showing that person a range of different objects which all happened to be red – we would be probably do better to single out a red object from a sets of objects which were identical in all respects except colour. Although Saussure focuses on speech, he also noted that in writing, 'the values of the letter are purely negative and differential' – all we need to be able to do is to distinguish one letter from another (ibid., 118). As for his emphasis on negative differences, Saussure remarks that although both the signified and the signifier are purely differential and negative when considered separately, the sign in which they are combined is a *positive* term. He adds that 'the moment we compare one sign with another as positive combinations, the term *difference* should be dropped . . . Two signs . . . are not different from each other, but only distinct. They are simply in *opposition* to each other. The entire mechanism of language . . . is based on oppositions of this kind and upon the phonic and conceptual differences they involve' (ibid., 119).

Arbitrariness

Although the signifier is treated by its users as 'standing for' the signified, Saussurean semioticians emphasize that there is no necessary, intrinsic, direct or inevitable relationship between the signifier and the signified. Saussure stressed the *arbitrariness* of the sign (ibid., 67, 78) – more specifically the arbitrariness of the link between the signifier and the signified (ibid., 67). He was focusing on linguistic signs, seeing language as the most important sign-system; for Saussure, the arbitrary nature of the sign was the first principle of language (ibid., 67) – arbitrariness was identified later by Charles Hockett as a key 'design feature' of language (Hockett 1958). The feature of arbitrariness may indeed help to account for the extraordinary versatility of language (Lyons 1977, 71). In the context of natural language, Saussure stressed that there is no inherent, essential, 'transparent', self-evident or 'natural' connection between the signifier and the signified – between the sound or shape of a word and the concept to which it refers (Saussure 1983, 67, 68–9, 76, 111, 117). Note that Saussure himself avoids directly relating the principle of arbitrariness to the relationship between language and an external world, but that subsequent commentators often do, and indeed, lurking behind the purely conceptual 'signified' one can often detect Saussure's allusion to real-world referents (Coward and Ellis 1977, 22). In language, at least, the form of the signifier is not determined by what it signifies: there is nothing 'treeish' about the word 'tree'. Languages differ, of course, in how they refer to the same referent. No specific signifier is 'naturally' more suited to a signified than any other signifier; in principle any signifier could represent any signified. Saussure observed that 'there is nothing at all to prevent the association of any idea whatsoever with any sequence of sounds whatsoever' (Saussure 1983, 76); 'the process which selects one particular sound-sequence to correspond to one particular idea is completely arbitrary' (ibid., 111).

This principle of the arbitrariness of the linguistic sign was not an original conception: Aristotle had noted that 'there can be no natural connection between the sound of any language and the things signified' (cited in Richards 1932, 32). In Plato's *Cratylus* Hermogenes urged Socrates to accept that 'whatever name you give to a thing is its right name; and if you give up that name and change it for another, the later name is no less correct than the earlier, just as we change the name of our servants; for I think no name belongs to a particular thing by nature' (cited in Harris 1987, 67). 'That which we call a rose by any other name would smell as sweet', as Shakespeare put it. While the notion of the arbitrariness of language was not new, the emphasis which Saussure gave it can be seen as an original contribution, particularly in the context of a theory which bracketed the referent. Note that although Saussure prioritized speech, he also stressed that 'the signs used in writing are arbitrary, The letter *t*, for instance, has no connection with the sound it denotes' (Saussure 1983, 117).

Saussure illustrated the principle of arbitrariness at the lexical level – in relation to individual words as signs. He did not, for instance, argue that syntax is arbitrary. However, the arbitrariness principle can be applied not only to the individual sign, but to the whole sign-system. The fundamental arbitrariness of language is apparent from the observation that each language involves different distinctions between one signifier and another (e.g. 'tree' and 'free') and between one signified and another (e.g. 'tree' and 'bush'). The signified is clearly arbitrary if *reality* is perceived as a seamless continuum (which is how Saussure sees the initially undifferentiated realms of both thought and sound): where, for example, does a 'corner' end? Commonsense suggests that the existence of things in the world preceded our apparently simple application of 'labels' to them (a 'nomenclaturist' notion which Saussure rejected and to which we will return in due course). Saussure noted that 'if words had the job of representing concepts fixed in advance, one would be able to find exact equivalents for them as between one language and another. But this is not the case' (ibid., 114–15). Reality is divided up into arbitrary categories by every language and the conceptual world with which each of us is familiar could have been divided up very differently. Indeed, no two languages categorize reality in the same way. As John Passmore puts it, 'Languages differ by differentiating differently' (cited in Sturrock 1986, 17). Linguistic categories are not simply a consequence of some predefined structure in the world. There are no 'natural' concepts or categories which are simply 'reflected' in language. Language plays a crucial role in 'constructing reality'.

If one accepts the arbitrariness of the relationship between signifier and signified then one may argue counter-intuitively that the signified is determined by the signifier rather than vice versa. Indeed, the French psychoanalyst Jacques Lacan, in adapting Saussurean theories, sought to highlight the primacy of the signifier in the psyche by rewriting Saussure's model of the sign in the form of a quasi-algebraic sign in which a capital 'S' (representing the *signifier*) is placed over a lower-case and italicized '*s*' (representing the *signified*), these two signifiers being separated by a horizontal 'bar' (Lacan 1977, 149). This suited Lacan's purpose of emphasizing how the signified inevitably 'slips beneath' the signifier, resisting our attempts to delimit it. Lacan poetically refers to Saussure's illustration of the planes of sound and thought as 'an image resembling the wavy lines of the upper and lower Waters in miniatures from manuscripts of *Genesis*; a double flux marked by streaks of rain', suggesting that this can be seen as illustrating the 'incessant sliding of the signified under the signifier' – although he argues that one should regard the dotted vertical lines not as 'segments of correspondence' but as 'anchoring points' (*points de capiton* – literally, the 'buttons' which anchor upholstery to furniture). However, he notes that this model is too linear, since 'there is in effect no signifying chain that does not have, as if attached to the punctuation of each of its units, a whole articulation of relevant contexts suspended "vertically", as it were, from that point' (ibid., 154). In the spirit of the Lacanian critique of Saussure's model, subsequent theorists have emphasized the temporary nature of the bond between signifier and signified, stressing that the 'fixing' of 'the chain of signifiers' is socially situated (Coward and Ellis 1977, 6, 13, 17, 67). Note that while the intent of Lacan in placing the signifier *over* the signified is clear enough, his representational strategy seems a little curious, since in the modelling of society orthodox Marxists routinely represent the fundamental driving force of 'the [techno-economic] base' as (logically) below 'the [ideological] superstructure'.

The arbitrariness of the sign is a radical concept because it establishes the autonomy of language in relation to reality. The Saussurean model, with its emphasis on internal structures within a sign-system, can be seen as supporting the notion that language does not 'reflect' reality but rather *constructs* it. We can use language 'to say what isn't in the world, as well as what is. And since we come to know the world through whatever language we have been born into the midst of, it is legitimate to argue that our language determines reality, rather than reality our language' (Sturrock 1986, 79). In their book *The Meaning of Meaning*, Charles Ogden and Ivor Richards criticized Saussure for 'neglecting entirely the things for which signs stand' (Ogden and Richards 1923, 8). Later critics have lamented his model's detachment from social context (Gardiner 1992, 11). By 'bracketing the referent', the Saussurean model 'severs text from history' (Stam 2000, 122). We will return to this theme of the relationship between language and reality in Chapter 2.

The arbitrary aspect of signs does help to account for the scope for their interpretation (and the importance of context). There is no one-to-one link between signifier and signified; signs have multiple rather than single meanings. Within a single language, one signifier may refer to many signifieds (e.g. puns) and one signified may be referred to by many signifiers (e.g. synonyms). Some commentators are critical of the stance that the relationship of the signifier to the signified, even in language, is always completely arbitrary (e.g. Lewis 1991, 29). Onomatopoeic words are often mentioned in this context, though some semioticians retort that this hardly accounts for the variability between different languages in their words for the same sounds (notably the sounds made by familiar animals) (Saussure 1983, 69).

Saussure declares that 'the entire linguistic system is founded upon the irrational principle that the sign is arbitrary'. This provocative declaration is followed immediately by the acknowledgement that 'applied without restriction, this principle would lead to utter chaos' (ibid., 131). If linguistic signs were to be *totally* arbitrary in every way language would not be a system and its communicative function would be destroyed. He concedes that 'there exists no language in which nothing at all is motivated' (ibid.). Saussure admits that 'a language is not completely arbitrary, for the system has a certain rationality' (ibid., 73). The principle of arbitrariness does not mean that the form of a word is accidental or random, of course. While the sign is not determined *extralinguistically* it is subject to *intralinguistic* determination. For instance, signifiers must constitute well-formed combinations of sounds which conform with existing patterns within the language in question. Furthermore, we can recognize that a compound noun such as 'screwdriver' is not wholly arbitrary since it is a meaningful combination of two existing signs. Saussure introduces a distinction between *degrees* of arbitrariness:

> The fundamental principle of the arbitrary nature of the linguistic sign does not prevent us from distinguishing in any language between what is intrinsically arbitrary – that is, unmotivated – and what is only relatively arbitrary. Not all signs are absolutely arbitrary. In some cases, there are factors which allow us to recognize different degrees of arbitrariness, although never to discard the notion entirely. *The sign may be motivated to a certain extent.*
>
> (Saussure 1983, 130; *original emphasis*, see following pages)

Here, then, Saussure modifies his stance somewhat and refers to signs as being 'relatively arbitrary'. Some subsequent theorists (echoing Althusserian Marxist terminology) refer to the relationship between the signifier and the signified in terms of 'relative autonomy' (Tagg 1988, 167; Lechte 1994, 150). The *relative* conventionality of relationships between signified and signifier is a point to which we will return shortly.

It should be noted that, while the relationships between signifiers and their signifieds are *ontologically* arbitrary (philosophically, it would not make any difference to the status of these entities in 'the order of things' if what we call 'black' had always been called 'white' and *vice versa*), this is not to suggest that signifying systems are *socially* or *historically* arbitrary. Natural languages are not, of course, arbitrarily established, unlike historical inventions such as Morse Code. Nor does the arbitrary nature of the sign make it socially 'neutral' or materially 'transparent' – for example, in Western culture 'white' has come to be a privileged signifier (Dyer 1997). Even in the case of the 'arbitrary' colours of traffic lights, the original choice of red for 'stop' was not entirely arbitrary, since it already carried relevant associations with danger. As Lévi-Strauss noted, the sign is arbitrary *a priori* but ceases to be arbitrary *a posteriori* – after the sign has come into historical existence it cannot be arbitrarily changed (Lévi-Strauss 1972, 91). As part of its social use within a *code* (a term which became fundamental among post-Saussurean semioticians), every sign acquires a history and connotations of its own which are familiar to members of the sign-users' culture. Saussure remarked that although the signifier 'may seem to be freely chosen', from the point of view of the linguistic community it is 'imposed rather than freely chosen' because 'a language is always an inheritance from the past' which its users have 'no choice but to accept' (Saussure 1983, 71–2). Indeed, 'it is because the linguistic sign is arbitrary that it knows no other law than that of tradition, and [it is] because it is founded upon tradition that it can be arbitrary' (ibid., 74). The arbitrariness principle does *not*, of course mean that an individual can arbitrarily choose any signifier for a given signified. The relation between a signifier and its signified is *not* a matter of individual choice; if it were then communication would become impossible. 'The individual has no power to alter a sign in any respect once it has become established in the linguistic community' (ibid., 68). From the point of view of individual language-users, language is a 'given' – we don't create the system for ourselves. Saussure refers to the language system as a non-negotiable 'contract' into which one is born (ibid., 14) – although he later problematizes the term (ibid., 71). The ontological arbitrariness which it involves becomes invisible to us as we learn to accept it as 'natural'.

The Saussurean legacy of the arbitrariness of signs leads semioticians to stress that the relationship between the signifier and the signified is *conventional* – dependent on social and cultural conventions which have to be learned. This is particularly clear in the case of the linguistic signs with which Saussure was concerned: a word means what it does to us only because we collectively agree to let it do so. Saussure felt that the main concern of semiotics should be 'the whole group of systems grounded in the arbitrariness of the sign'. He argued that: 'signs which are entirely arbitrary convey better than others the ideal semiological process. That is why the most complex and the most widespread of all systems of expression, which is the one we find in human languages, is also the most characteristic of all. In this sense, linguistics serves as a model for the whole of semiology, even though languages represent only one type of semiological system' (ibid., 68). He did not in fact offer many examples of sign-systems other than spoken language and writing, mentioning only: the deaf-and-dumb alphabet; social customs; etiquette; religious and other symbolic rites; legal procedures; military signals and nautical flags (ibid., 15, 17, 68, 74). Saussure added that 'any means of expression accepted in a society rests in principle upon a collective habit, or on convention – which comes to the same thing' (ibid., 68). However, while purely conventional signs such as words are quite independent of their referents, other less conventional forms of signs are often somewhat less independent of them. Nevertheless, since the arbitrary nature of linguistic signs is clear, those who have adopted the Saussurean model have tended to avoid 'the familiar mistake of assuming that signs which appear natural to those who use them have an intrinsic meaning and require no explanation' (Culler 1975, 5).

The Peircean model

At around the same time as Saussure was formulating his model of the sign and of 'semiology' (and laying the foundations of structuralist methodology), across the Atlantic closely related theoretical work was also in progress as the pragmatist philosopher and logician Charles Sanders Peirce formulated his own model of the sign, of 'semiotic' and of the taxonomies of signs. In contrast to Saussure's model of the sign in the form of a 'self-contained dyad', Peirce offered a triadic (three-part) model:

1. The *representamen*: the form which the sign takes (not necessarily material).
2. An *interpretant*: *not* an interpreter but rather the sense made of the sign.
3. An *object*: to which the sign refers.

Thus:

> A sign . . . [in the form of a *representamen*] is something which stands to somebody for something in some respect or capacity.

It addresses somebody, that is, creates in the mind of that person an equivalent sign, or perhaps a more developed sign. That sign which it creates I call the *interpretant* of the first sign. The sign stands for something, its *object*. It stands for that object, not in all respects, but in reference to a sort of idea, which I have sometimes called the *ground* of the representamen.

(Peirce 1931–58, 2.228)

The interaction between the *representamen*, the *object* and the *interpretant* is referred to by Peirce as 'semiosis' (ibid., 5.484). Within Peirce's model of the sign, the traffic light sign for 'stop' would consist of: a red light facing traffic at an intersection (the representamen); vehicles halting (the object) and the idea that a red light indicates that vehicles must stop (the interpretant).

Peirce's model of the sign includes an *object* or referent – which does not, of course, feature directly in Saussure's model. The *representamen* is similar in meaning to Saussure's *signifier* while the *interpretant* is similar in meaning to the *signified*. However, the *interpretant* has a quality unlike that of the *signified*: it is itself a sign in the mind of the interpreter. Peirce noted that 'a sign . . . addresses somebody, that is, creates in the mind of that person an equivalent sign, or perhaps a more developed sign. The sign which it creates I call the *interpretant* of the first sign' (Peirce 1931–58, 2.228). Umberto Eco uses the phrase 'unlimited semiosis' to refer to the way in which this could lead (as Peirce was well aware) to a series of successive interpretants (potentially) *ad infinitum* (Peirce 1931–58, 1.339, 2.303). Elsewhere Peirce added that 'the meaning of a representation can be nothing but a representation' (ibid., 1.339). Any initial interpretation can be reinterpreted. That a signified can itself play the role of a signifier is familiar to anyone who uses a dictionary and finds him- or herself going beyond the original definition to look up yet another word which it employs. This concept can be seen as going beyond Saussure's emphasis on the value of a sign lying in its relation to other signs and it was later to be developed more radically by poststructuralist theorists. Another concept which is alluded to within Peirce's model which has been taken up by later theorists but which was explicitly excluded from Saussure's model

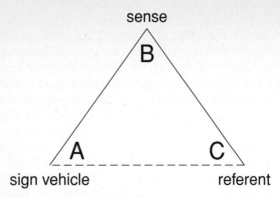

FIGURE 1.5 A semiotic triangle

is the notion of dialogical thought. It stems in part from Peirce's emphasis on 'semiosis' as a *process* which is in distinct contrast to Saussure's synchronic emphasis on *structure* (Peirce 1931–58, 5.484, 5.488). Peirce argued that 'all thinking is dialogic in form. Your self of one instant appeals to your deeper self for his assent' (Peirce 1931–58, 6.338). This notion resurfaced in a more developed form in the 1920s in the theories of Mikhail Bakhtin (Bakhtin 1981). One important aspect of this is its characterization even of internal reflection as fundamentally social.

Variants of Peirce's triad are often presented as '*the* semiotic triangle' (as if there were only one version). Figure 1.5 shows a version which is quite often encountered and which changes only the unfamiliar Peircean terms (Nöth 1990, 89). One fairly well-known semiotic triangle is that of Ogden and Richards, in which the terms used are (a) 'symbol', (b) 'thought or reference' and (c) 'referent' (Ogden and Richards 1923, 14). The broken line at the base of the triangle is intended to indicate that there is not necessarily any observable or direct relationship between the sign vehicle and the referent. Unlike Saussure's abstract *signified* (which is analogous to term **B** rather than to **C**) the *referent* is an 'object'. This need not exclude the reference of signs to abstract concepts and fictional entities as well as to physical things, but Peirce's model allocates a place for an objective reality which Saussure's model did not directly feature (though Peirce was not a naïve realist, and argued that all experience is mediated by signs). Note, however, that Peirce emphasized that 'the dependence of the mode of existence of the thing represented upon the mode of this or that representation of it . . . is contrary to the nature of reality' (Peirce 1931–58, 5.323). The inclusion of a referent in Peirce's model does not automatically make it a better model of the sign than that of Saussure. Indeed, as John Lyons notes:

> There is considerable disagreement about the details of the triadic analysis even among those who accept that all three components, *A*, *B* and *C*, must be taken into account. Should *A* be defined as a physical or a mental entity? What is the psychological or ontological status of *B*? Is *C* something that is referred to on a particular occasion? Or is it the totality of things that might be referred to by uttering the sign . . .? Or, yet a third possibility, is it some typical or ideal representative of this class?
>
> (Lyons 1977, 99)

The notion of the importance of sense-making (which requires an *interpreter* – though Peirce doesn't feature that term in his triad) has had a particular appeal for communication and media theorists who stress the importance of the active process of interpretation, and thus reject the equation of 'content' and meaning. Many of these theorists allude to semiotic triangles in which the interpreter (or 'user') of the sign features explicitly (in place of 'sense' or 'interpretant'). This highlights the *process* of semiosis (which is very much a Peircean concept). The meaning of a sign is not contained within it, but arises in its interpretation. Whether a dyadic or triadic model is adopted, the role of the interpreter must be accounted for – either within the formal model of the sign, or as an essential part of the process of semiosis. The Australian social semiotician Paul Thibault argues that the *interpreter* features implicitly even within Saussure's apparently dyadic model (Thibault 1997, 184).

Note that semioticians make a distinction between a sign and a 'sign vehicle' (the latter being a 'signifier' to Saussureans and a 'representamen' to Peirceans). The sign is more than just a sign vehicle. The term 'sign' is often used loosely, so that this distinction is not always preserved. In the Saussurean framework, some references to 'the sign' should be to the *signifier*, and similarly, Peirce himself frequently mentions 'the sign' when, strictly speaking, he is referring to the *representamen*. It is easy to be found guilty of such a slippage, perhaps because we are so used to 'looking beyond' the form which the sign happens to take. However, to reiterate: the *signifier* or *representamen* is the *form* in which the sign appears (such as the spoken or written form of a word) whereas the *sign* is the whole meaningful ensemble.

Relativity

Whereas Saussure emphasized the arbitrary nature of the (linguistic) sign, most semioticians stress that signs differ in how arbitrary/conventional (or by contrast 'transparent') they are. Symbolism reflects only one form of relationship between signifiers and their signifieds. While Saussure did not offer a typology of signs, Charles Peirce was a compulsive taxonomist and he offered several logical typologies (Peirce 1931–58, 1.291, 2.243). What he himself regarded as 'the most fundamental' division of signs (first outlined in 1867) has been very widely cited in subsequent semiotic studies (ibid., 2.275). Although it is often referred to as a classification of distinct 'types of signs', it is more usefully interpreted in terms of differing 'modes of relationship' between sign vehicles and their referents (Hawkes 1977, 129). Note that in the subsequent account, I have continued to employ the Saussurean terms *signifier* and *signified*, even though Peirce referred to the relation between the 'sign' (*sic*) and the *object*, since the academic applications with which this book is primarily concerned most commonly employ the Peircean distinctions within a broadly Saussurean framework. Such incorporation tends to emphasize (albeit indirectly) the referential potential of the signified within the Saussurean model. Here then are the three modes together with some brief definitions of my own:

1. **Symbol/symbolic**: a mode in which the signifier does *not* resemble the signified but which is fundamentally *arbitrary*

MODELS OF THE SIGN

or purely conventional – so that the relationship must be learned: e.g. language in general (plus specific languages, alphabetical letters, punctuation marks, words, phrases and sentences), numbers, morse code, traffic lights, national flags.

2. **Icon/iconic**: a mode in which the signifier is perceived as *resembling* or imitating the signified (recognizably looking, sounding, feeling, tasting or smelling like it) – being similar in possessing some of its qualities: e.g. a portrait, a cartoon, a scale-model, onomatopoeia, metaphors, 'realistic' sounds in 'programme music', sound effects in radio drama, a dubbed film soundtrack, imitative gestures.

3. **Index/indexical**: a mode in which the signifier is *not arbitrary* but is *directly connected* in some way (physically or causally) to the signified – this link can be observed or inferred: e.g. 'natural signs' (smoke, thunder, footprints, echoes, non-synthetic odours and flavours), medical symptoms (pain, a rash, pulse-rate), measuring instruments (weathercock, thermometer, clock, spirit-level), 'signals' (a knock on a door, a phone ringing), pointers (a pointing 'index' finger, a directional signpost), recordings (a photograph, a film, video or television shot, an audio-recorded voice), personal 'trademarks' (handwriting, catchphrase) and indexical words ('that', 'this', 'here', 'there').

The three forms are listed here in decreasing order of conventionality. Symbolic signs such as language are (at least) highly conventional; iconic signs always involve some degree of conventionality; indexical signs 'direct the attention to their objects by blind compulsion' (Peirce 1931–58, 2.306). *Indexical* and *iconic* signifiers can be seen as more constrained by referential *signifieds* whereas in the more conventional *symbolic* signs the *signified* can be seen as being defined to a greater extent by the *signifier*. Within each form signs also vary in their degree of conventionality. Other criteria might be applied to rank the three forms differently. For instance, Hodge and Kress suggest that indexicality is based on an act of judgement or inference whereas iconicity is closer to 'direct perception', making the highest 'modality' that of iconic signs. Note that the terms 'motivation' (from Saussure) and 'constraint' are sometimes used to describe the extent to which the signified determines the signifier. The more a signifier is constrained by the signified, the more 'motivated' the sign is: iconic signs are highly motivated; symbolic signs are unmotivated. The less motivated the sign, the more learning of an agreed convention is required. Nevertheless, most semioticians emphasize the role of convention in relation to signs. As we shall see, even photographs and films are built on conventions which we must learn to 'read'. Such conventions are an important social dimension of semiotics.

Symbolic mode

Peirce and Saussure used the term 'symbol' differently from each other. While nowadays most theorists would refer to language as a symbolic sign-system, Saussure avoided referring to linguistic signs as 'symbols', since the ordinary everyday use of this term refers to examples such as a pair of scales (signifying *justice*), and he insisted that such signs are 'never wholly arbitrary. They are not empty configurations.' They 'show at least a vestige of natural connection' between the signifier and the signified – a link which he later refers to as 'rational' (Saussure 1983, 68, 73). While Saussure focused on the arbitrary nature of the linguistic sign, a more obvious example of arbitrary symbolism is mathematics. Mathematics does not need to refer to an external world at all: its signifieds are indisputably *concepts* and mathematics is a system of relations (Langer 1951, 28).

For Peirce, a symbol is 'a sign which refers to the object that it denotes by virtue of a law, usually an association of general ideas, which operates to cause the symbol to be interpreted as referring to that object' (Peirce 1931–58, 2.249). We interpret symbols according to 'a rule' or 'a habitual connection' (ibid., 2.292, 2.297, 1.369). 'The symbol is connected with its object by virtue of the idea of the symbol-using mind, without which no such connection would exist' (ibid., 2.299). It 'is constituted a sign merely or mainly by the fact that it is used and understood as such' (ibid., 2.307). A symbol is 'a conventional sign, or one depending upon habit (acquired or

inborn)' (ibid., 2.297). 'All words, sentences, books and other conventional signs are symbols' (ibid., 2.292). Peirce thus characterizes
linguistic signs in terms of their *conventionality* in a similar way to
Saussure. In a rare direct reference to the arbitrariness of symbols
(which he then called 'tokens'), he noted that they 'are, for the most
part, conventional or arbitrary' (ibid., 3.360). A symbol is a sign
'whose special significance or fitness to represent just what it does
represent lies in nothing but the very fact of there being a habit,
disposition, or other effective general rule that it will be so interpreted. Take, for example, the word "*man*". These three letters are
not in the least like a man; nor is the sound with which they are
associated' (ibid., 4.447). He adds elsewhere that 'a *symbol* . . . fulfils
its function regardless of any similarity or analogy with its object
and equally regardless of any *factual* connection therewith' (ibid.,
5.73; original emphasis). It is clear that Peircean symbols are not
limited to words.

Iconic mode

Turning to icons, Peirce declared that an iconic sign represents its
object 'mainly by its similarity' (Peirce 1931–58, 2.276). Note that
despite the name, icons are not necessarily visual. A sign is an icon
'insofar as it is like that thing and used as a sign of it' (ibid., 2.247).
Indeed, Peirce originally termed such modes, 'likenesses' (e.g.
ibid., 1.558). He added that 'every picture (however conventional its
method)' is an icon (ibid., 2.279). Icons have qualities which 'resemble' those of the objects they represent, and they 'excite analogous
sensations in the mind' (ibid., 2.299; cf. 3.362). Unlike the index, 'the
icon has no dynamical connection with the object it represents'
(ibid.). Just because a signifier resembles that which it depicts does
not necessarily make it purely iconic. Susanne Langer argues that 'the
picture is essentially a symbol, not a duplicate, of what it represents'
(Langer 1951, 67). Pictures resemble what they represent only in
some respects. What we tend to recognize in an image are analogous
relations of parts to a whole (ibid., 67–70). For Peirce, icons included
'every diagram, even although there be no sensuous resemblance
between it and its object, but only an analogy between the relations

of the parts of each' (Peirce 1931–58, 2.279). 'Many diagrams resemble their objects not at all in looks; it is only in respect to the relations of their parts that their likeness consists' (ibid., 2.282). Even the most 'realistic' image is not a replica or even a copy of what is depicted. It is not often that we mistake a representation for what it represents.

Semioticians generally maintain that there are no 'pure' icons – there is always an element of cultural convention involved. Peirce stated that although 'any material image' (such as a painting) may be perceived as looking like what it represents, it is 'largely conventional in its mode of representation' (Peirce 1931–58, 2.276).

> We say that the portrait of a person we have not seen is *convincing*. So far as, on the ground merely of what I see in it, I am led to form an idea of the person it represents, it is an icon. But, in fact, it is not a pure icon, because I am greatly influenced by knowing that it is an *effect*, through the artist, caused by the original's appearance . . . Besides, I know that portraits have but the slightest resemblance to their originals, except in certain conventional respects, and after a conventional scale of values, etc.
>
> (ibid., 2.92)

Guy Cook, a British linguist, asks whether the iconic sign on the door of a public lavatory for men actually looks more like a man than like a woman. 'For a sign to be truly iconic, it would have to be transparent to someone who had never seen it before – and it seems unlikely that this is as much the case as is sometimes supposed. We see the resemblance when we already know the meaning' (Cook 1992, 70). Thus, even a 'realistic' picture is *symbolic* as well as iconic.

Iconic and indexical signs are more likely to be read as 'natural' than symbolic signs, when making the connection between signifier and signified, has become habitual. Iconic signifiers can be highly evocative. When we can 'see' the object in an iconic sign, we often feel 'closer' to the truth than if we had seen an index or a symbol (Grayson 1998, 36–41). Such signs do not draw our attention to their mediation, seeming to present reality more directly than symbolic signs.

The linguist John Lyons notes that iconicity is 'always dependent upon properties of the medium in which the form is manifest' (Lyons 1977, 105). He offers the example of the onomatopoeic English word *cuckoo*, noting that it is only iconic in the phonic medium (speech) and not in the graphic medium (writing). While the phonic medium can represent characteristic sounds (albeit in a relatively conventionalized way), the graphic medium can represent characteristic shapes (as in the case of Egyptian hieroglyphs) (Lyons 1977, 103). We will return shortly to the importance of the materiality of the sign.

Indexical mode

Indexicality is perhaps the most unfamiliar concept. Peirce offers various criteria for what constitutes an index. An index 'indicates' something: for example, 'a sundial or clock *indicates* the time of day' (Peirce 1931–58, 2.285). He refers to a 'genuine relation' between the 'sign' and the *object* which does not depend purely on 'the interpreting mind' (ibid., 2.92, 298). The *object* is 'necessarily existent' (ibid., 2.310). The index is connected to its object 'as a matter of fact' (ibid., 4.447). There is 'a real connection' (ibid., 5.75). There may be a 'direct physical connection' (ibid., 1.372, 2.281, 2.299). An indexical sign is like 'a fragment torn away from the object' (ibid., 2.231). Unlike an icon (the object of which may be fictional) an index stands 'unequivocally for this or that existing thing' (ibid., 4.531). While 'it necessarily has some quality in common' with it, the signifier is 'really affected' by the signified; there is an 'actual modification' involved (ibid., 2.248). The relationship is *not* based on 'mere resemblance' (ibid.): 'indices . . . have no significant resemblance to their objects' (ibid., 2.306). 'Similarity or analogy' are not what define the index (ibid., 2.305). 'Anything which focuses the attention is an index. Anything which startles us is an index' (ibid., 2.285; see also 3.434). Indexical signs 'direct the attention to their objects by blind compulsion' (ibid., 2.306; see also 2.191, 2.428). 'Psychologically, the action of indices depends upon association by contiguity, and not upon association by resemblance or upon intellectual operations' (ibid.).

While a photograph is also perceived as resembling that which it depicts, Peirce noted that a photograph is not only iconic but also *indexical*: 'photographs, especially instantaneous photographs, are very instructive, because we know that in certain respects they are exactly like the objects they represent. But this resemblance is due to the photographs having been produced under such circumstances that they were physically forced to correspond point by point to nature. In that aspect, then, they belong to the . . . class of signs . . . by physical connection [the indexical class]' (Peirce 1931–58, 2.281; see also 5.554). So in this sense, since the photographic image is an index of the effect of light on photographic emulsion, all *unedited* photographic and filmic images are indexical (although we should remember that conventional practices are always involved in composition, focusing, developing, and so on). Such images do of course 'resemble' what they depict, and some commentators suggest that the power of the photographic and filmic image derives from the iconic character of the medium. However, while digital imaging techniques are increasingly eroding the indexicality of photographic images, it is arguable that it is the indexicality still routinely attributed to the medium that is primarily responsible for interpreters treating them as 'objective' records of 'reality'. Peirce observed that 'a photograph . . . owing to its optical connection with its object, is evidence that that appearance corresponds to a reality' (Peirce 1931–58, 4.447). In many contexts photographs are indeed regarded as 'evidence', not least in legal contexts. As for the moving image, video-cameras are of course widely used 'in evidence'. Documentary film and location footage in television news programmes depend upon the indexical nature of the sign. Photographic and filmic images may also be *symbolic*: in an empirical study of television news, Davis and Walton found that a relatively small proportion of the total number of shots is iconic or *directly* representative of the people, places and events which are subjects of the news text. A far greater proportion of shots has an oblique relationship to the text; they 'stand for' the subject-matter indexically or symbolically (Davis and Walton 1983b, 45).

Modes not types

It is easy to slip into referring to Peirce's three forms as 'types of signs', but they are not necessarily mutually exclusive: a sign can be an icon, a symbol and an index, or any combination. Peirce was fully aware of this: for instance, he insisted that 'it would be diffi- cult if not impossible to instance an absolutely pure index, or to find any sign absolutely devoid of the indexical quality' (Peirce 1931–58, 2.306). We have already noted that he did not regard a portrait as a pure icon (ibid., 2.92) and he would no doubt have agreed that there are no pure symbols either. A map is indexical in pointing to the locations of things, iconic in representing the directional relations and distances between landmarks, and symbolic in using conven- tional symbols the significance of which must be learned. Film and television use all three modes: icon (sound and image), symbol (speech and writing) and index (as the effect of what is filmed); at first sight the iconic mode seems dominant, but some filmic signs are fairly arbitrary, such as dissolves which signify that a scene from someone's memory is to follow.

Terence Hawkes (a professor of English) notes, following Jakobson, that the three modes 'co-exist in the form of a hierarchy in which one of them will inevitably have dominance over the other two', with dominance determined by context (Hawkes 1977, 129). Whether a sign is symbolic, iconic or indexical depends primar- ily on the way in which the sign is used, so textbook examples chosen to illustrate the various modes can be misleading. The same signi- fier may be used iconically in one context and symbolically in another: a photograph of a woman may stand for some broad cate- gory such as 'women' or may more specifically represent only the particular woman who is depicted. Signs cannot be classified in terms of the three modes without reference to the purposes of their users within particular contexts. A sign may consequently be treated as symbolic by one person, as iconic by another and as indexical by a third. Signs may also shift in mode over time. For instance, a Rolls- Royce is an index of wealth because one must be wealthy to own one, but social usage has led to its becoming a conventional symbol of wealth (Culler 1975, 17).

Changing relations

Despite his emphasis on studying 'the language-state' 'synchronically' (as if it were frozen at one moment in time) rather than 'diachronically' (studying its evolution), Saussure was well aware that the relationship between the signified and the signifier in language was subject to change over time (Saussure 1983, 74ff.). However, this was not the focus of his concern. Critics of structuralist approaches emphasize that the relation between signifier and signified is subject to dynamic change: any 'fixing' of 'the chain of signifiers' is seen as both temporary and socially determined (Coward and Ellis 1977, 6, 8, 13).

In terms of Peirce's three modes, a historical shift from one mode to another tends to occur. Although Peirce made far more allowance for non-linguistic signs than did Saussure, like Saussure, he too granted greater status to *symbolic* signs: 'they are the only general signs; and generality is essential to reasoning' (Peirce 1931–58, 3.363; see also 4.448, 4.531). Saussure's emphasis on the importance of the principle of arbitrariness reflects his prioritizing of symbolic signs while Peirce privileges 'the symbol-using mind' (Peirce 1931–58, 2.299). The idea of the evolution of sign-systems towards the symbolic mode is consistent with such a perspective. Peirce speculates 'whether there be a life in signs, so that – the requisite vehicle being present – they will go through a certain order of development'. Interestingly, he does not present this as *necessarily* a matter of progress towards the 'ideal' of symbolic form since he allows for the theoretical possibility that 'the same round of changes of form is described over and over again' (ibid., 2.111). While granting such a possibility, he nevertheless notes that 'a regular progression . . . may be remarked in the three orders of signs, Icon, Index, Symbol' (ibid., 2.299). Peirce posits iconicity as the original default mode of signification, declaring the icon to be 'an originalian sign' (ibid., 2.92), defining this as 'the most primitive, simple and original of the categories' (ibid., 2.90). Compared to the 'genuine sign . . . or symbol', an index is 'degenerate in the lesser degree' while an icon is 'degenerate in the greater degree'. Peirce noted that signs were 'originally in part iconic, in part indexical' (ibid., 2.92).

He adds that 'in all primitive writing, such as the Egyptian hieroglyphics, there are icons of a non-logical kind, the ideographs' and he speculates that 'in the earliest form of speech there probably was a large element of mimicry' (ibid., 2.280). However, over time, linguistic signs developed a more symbolic and conventional character (ibid., 2.92, 2.280). 'Symbols come into being by development out of other signs, particularly from icons' (ibid., 2.302).

The historical evidence does indicate a tendency of linguistic signs to evolve from indexical and iconic forms towards symbolic forms. Alphabets were not initially based on the substitution of conventional symbols for sounds. Some of the letters in the Greek and Latin alphabets, of course, derive from iconic signs in Egyptian hieroglyphs. The early scripts of the Mediterranean civilizations used pictographs, ideographs and hieroglyphs. Many of these were iconic signs resembling the objects and actions to which they referred either directly or metaphorically. Over time, picture writing became more symbolic and less iconic (Gelb 1963). This shift from the iconic to the symbolic may have been 'dictated by the economy of using a chisel or a reed brush' (Cherry 1966, 33); in general, symbols are semiotically more flexible and efficient (Lyons 1977, 103). The anthropologist Claude Lévi-Strauss identified a similar general movement from motivation to arbitrariness within the conceptual schemes employed by particular cultures (Lévi-Strauss 1974, 156).

Digital and analogue

A distinction is sometimes made between *digital* and *analogical* signs. Indeed, Anthony Wilden, a Canadian communication theorist, declares that 'no two categories, and no two kinds of experience are more fundamental in human life and thought than continuity and discontinuity' (Wilden 1987, 222). While we experience time as a continuum, we may represent it in either analogue or digital form. A watch with an analogue display (with hour, minute and second hands) has the advantage of dividing an hour up like a cake (so that, in a lecture, for instance, we can 'see' how much time is left). A watch with a digital display (displaying the current time as a changing number) has the advantage of precision, so that we can easily see exactly what time it is 'now'. Even an analogue display is now simulated on some digital watches.

We have a deep attachment to analogical modes and we tend to regard digital representations as 'less real' or 'less authentic' – at least initially (as in the case of the audio CD compared to the vinyl LP). The *analogue–digital* distinction is frequently represented as 'natural' versus 'artificial'. The privileging of the analogical may be linked with the defiance of rationality in romantic ideology (which still dominates our conception of ourselves as 'individuals'). The deliberate intention to communicate tends to be dominant in digital codes, while in analogue codes 'it is almost impossible . . . *not* to communicate' (Wilden 1987, 225). Beyond any conscious intention, we communicate through gesture, posture, facial expression, intonation and so on. Analogical codes unavoidably 'give us away', revealing such things as our moods, attitudes, intentions and truthfulness (or otherwise). However, although the appearance of the 'digital watch' in 1971 and the subsequent 'digital revolution' in audio- and video-recording have led us to associate the digital mode with electronic technologies, digital codes have existed since the earliest forms of language – and writing is a 'digital technology'. Signifying systems impose digital order on what we often experience as a dynamic and seamless flux. The very definition of something as a sign involves reducing the continuous to the discrete. As we shall see later, binary (*either/or*) distinctions are a fundamental process in the creation of signifying structures. Digital signs involve discrete units such as words and 'whole numbers' and depend on the categorization of what is signified.

Analogical signs (such as visual images, gestures, textures, tastes and smells) involve graded relationships on a continuum. They can signify infinite subtleties which seem 'beyond words'. Emotions and feelings are analogical signifieds. Unlike symbolic signifiers, motivated signifiers (and their signifieds) blend into one another. There can be no comprehensive catalogue of such dynamic analogue signs as smiles or laughs. Analogue signs can of course be digitally reproduced (as is demonstrated by the digital recording of sounds and of both still and moving images) but they cannot be directly related to a standard 'dictionary' and syntax in the way that linguistic signs can. The North American film theorist Bill Nichols notes that 'the graded quality of analogue codes may make them rich in meaning but it also renders them somewhat impoverished in syntactical complexity or semantic precision. By contrast the discrete units of digital codes may be somewhat impoverished in meaning but capable of much greater complexity or semantic signification' (Nichols 1981, 47; cf. Wilden 1987, 138, 224). The art historian Ernst Gombrich insists that 'statements cannot be translated into images' and that 'pictures cannot assert' – a contention also found in Peirce (Gombrich 1982, 138, 175; Peirce 1931–58, 2.291). Such stances are adopted in relation to images unattached to verbal texts – such commentators would acknowledge that a simple verbal caption may be sufficient to enable an image to be used in the service of an assertion. While images serving such communicative purposes may be more 'open to interpretation', contemporary visual advertisements are a powerful example of how images may be used to make implicit claims which advertisers often prefer not to make more openly in words.

Types and tokens

The Italian semiotician Umberto Eco offers another distinction between sign vehicles; this relates to the concept of *tokens* and *types* which derives from Peirce (Eco 1976, 178ff.; Peirce 1931–58, 4.537). In relation to words in a spoken utterance or written text, a count of the tokens would be a count of the total number of words used (regardless of type), while a count of the types would be a count of the *different* words used, ignoring repetitions. In the language of semantics, tokens *instantiate* (are instances of) their type. Eco notes that 'grouping manifold tokens under a single type is the way in which language . . . works' (Eco 1999, 146). Language and thought depend on categorization: without categories we would be 'slaves to the particular' (Bruner *et al.* 1956, 1).

John Lyons notes that whether something is counted as a token of a type is relative to one's purposes – for instance:

- Are tokens to include words with different meanings which happen to be spelt or pronounced in the same way?

- Does a capital letter instantiate the same type as the corresponding lower-case letter?
- Does a word printed in italics instantiate the same type as a word printed in Roman?
- Is a word handwritten by X ever the same as a word handwritten by Y?

(Lyons 1977, 13–15)

From a semiotic point of view, such questions could only be answered by considering in each case whether the different forms signified something of any consequence to the relevant sign-users in the context of the specific signifying practice being studied.

Eco lists three kinds of sign vehicles, and it is notable that the distinction relates in part at least to material form:

- signs in which there may be any number of tokens (replicas) of the same type (e.g. a printed word, or exactly the same model of car in the same colour);
- 'signs whose tokens, even though produced according to a type, possess a certain quality of material uniqueness' (e.g. a word which someone speaks or which is handwritten);
- 'signs whose token is their type, or signs in which type and token are identical' (e.g. a unique original oil-painting or Princess Diana's wedding dress).

(Eco 1976, 178ff.)

The type–token distinction may influence the way in which a text is interpreted. In his influential essay on 'The work of art in the age of mechanical reproduction', the literary–philosophical theorist Walter Benjamin (1892–1940) noted that technological society is dominated by reproductions of original works – tokens of the original type (Benjamin 1992, 211–44). Indeed, even if we do see, for instance, 'the original' of a famous oil-painting, we are highly likely to have seen it first in the form of innumerable reproductions (books, postcards, posters – sometimes even in the form of pastiches or variations on the theme) and we may only be able to 'see' the original in the light of the judgements shaped by the copies or versions which we have encountered. In the postmodern era, the bulk of our texts are indeed 'copies without originals'.

The type–token distinction in relation to signs is important in social semiotic terms not as an absolute property of the sign vehicle but only insofar as it matters on any given occasion (for particular purposes) to those involved in using the sign. Minute differences in a pattern could be a matter of life and death for gamblers in relation to variations in the pattern on the backs of playing-cards within the same pack, but stylistic differences in the design of each type of card (such as the ace of spades), are much appreciated by collectors as a distinctive feature of different packs of playing cards.

Rematerializing the sign

As already indicated, Saussure saw both the signifier and the signi-fied as non-material 'psychological' forms; the language itself is 'a form, not a substance' (Saussure 1983, 111, 120). He uses several examples to reinforce his point. For instance, in one of several chess analogies, he notes that 'if pieces made of ivory are substituted for pieces made of wood, the change makes no difference to the system' (ibid., 23). Pursuing this functional approach, he notes elsewhere that the 8.25 p.m. Geneva–Paris train is referred to as 'the same train' even though the combinations of locomotive, carriages and person-nel may change. Similarly, he asks why a street which is completely rebuilt can still be 'the same street'. He suggests that this is 'because it is not a purely material structure' (ibid., 107). Saussure insists that this is not to say that such entities are 'abstract' since we cannot con-ceive of a street or train outside of its material realization – 'their physical existence is essential to our understanding of what they are' (ibid., 107; also 15). This can be related to the type–token distinc-tion. Since Saussure sees language in terms of formal function rather than material substance, then whatever performs the same function within the system can be regarded as just another token of the same type. With regard to language, Saussure observes that 'sound, as a material element . . . is merely ancillary, a material the language uses' (ibid., 116). Linguistic signifiers are 'not physical in any way. They are constituted solely by differences which distinguish one such sound pattern from another' (ibid., 117). He admits at one point, with some apparent reluctance, that 'linguistic signs are, so to speak, tangible: writing can fix them in conventional images' (ibid., 15). However, referring to written signs, he comments that 'the actual mode of inscription is irrelevant, because it does not affect the system . . . Whether I write in black or white, in incised characters or in relief, with a pen or a chisel – none of that is of any importance for the meaning' (ibid.). One can understand how a linguist would tend to focus on form and function within language and to regard the material manifestations of language as of peripheral interest. 'The linguist . . . is interested in types, not tokens' (Lyons 1977, 28).

This was not only the attitude of the linguist Saussure, but also of the philosopher Peirce: 'The word "*man*" . . . does not consist of three films of ink. If the word "man" occurs hundreds of times in a book of which myriads of copies are printed, all those millions of triplets of patches of ink are embodiments of one and the same word . . . each of those embodiments a *replica* of the symbol. This shows that the word is not a thing' (Peirce 1931–58, 4.447). Peirce did allude to the materiality of the sign: 'since a sign is not identical with the thing signified, but differs from the latter in some respects, it must plainly have some characters which belong to it in itself . . . These I call the *material* qualities of the sign.' He granted that materiality is a property of the sign which is 'of great importance in the theory of cognition'. However, materiality had 'nothing to do with its representative function' and it did not feature in his classificatory schemes (ibid., 5.287).

While Saussure chose to ignore the materiality of the linguistic sign, most subsequent theorists who have adopted his model have chosen to reclaim the materiality of the sign (or more strictly of the signifier). Semioticians must take seriously any factors to which sign-users ascribe significance, and the material form of a sign does sometimes make a difference. Contemporary theorists tend to acknowledge that the material form of the sign may generate connotations of its own. As early as 1929 Valentin Voloshinov published *Marxism and the Philosophy of Language* which included a materialist critique of Saussure's psychological and implicitly idealist model of the sign. Voloshinov described Saussure's ideas as 'the most striking expression' of 'abstract objectivism' (Voloshinov 1973, 58). He insisted that 'a sign is a phenomenon of the external world' and that 'signs . . . are particular, material things'. Every sign 'has some kind of material embodiment, whether in sound, physical mass, colour, movements of the body, or the like' (ibid., 10–11; cf. 28). For Voloshinov, all signs, including language, have 'concrete material reality' and the physical properties of the sign matter (ibid., 65).

Psychoanalytic theory also contributed to the revaluation of the signifier – in Freudian dream theory the sound of the signifier could be regarded as a better guide to its possible signified than any conventional 'decoding' might have suggested (Freud 1938, 319). For instance, Freud reported that the dream of a young woman engaged to be married featured flowers – including lilies-of-the-valley and violets. Popular symbolism suggested that the lilies were a symbol of chastity and the woman agreed that she associated them with purity. However, Freud was surprised to discover that she associated the word 'violet' phonetically with the English word 'violate', suggesting her fear of the violence of 'defloration' (another word alluding to flowers) (Freud 1938, 382–3). As the psychoanalytical theorist Jacques Lacan emphasized (originally in 1957), the Freudian concepts of *condensation* and *displacement* illustrate the determination of the signified by the signifier in dreams (Lacan 1977, 159ff.). In *condensation*, several thoughts are condensed into one symbol, while in *displacement* unconscious desire is displaced into an apparently trivial symbol (to avoid dream censorship).

Although widely criticized as idealists, poststructuralist theorists have sought to revalorize the signifier. The phonocentrism which was allied with Saussure's suppression of the materiality of the linguistic sign was challenged in 1967, when the French poststructuralist Jacques Derrida, in his book *Of Grammatology*, attacked the privileging of speech over writing which is found in Saussure (as well as in the work of many other previous and subsequent linguists) (Derrida 1976). From Plato to Lévi-Strauss, the spoken word had held a privileged position in the Western worldview, being regarded as intimately involved in our sense of self and constituting a sign of truth and authenticity. Speech had become so thoroughly naturalized that 'not only do the signifier and the signified seem to unite, but also, in this confusion, the signifier seems to erase itself or to become transparent' (Derrida 1981, 22). Writing had traditionally been relegated to a secondary position. The deconstructive enterprise marked 'the return of the repressed' (Derrida 1978, 197). In seeking to establish 'grammatology' or the study of textuality, Derrida championed the primacy of the material word. He noted that the specificity of words is itself a material dimension. 'The materiality of a word cannot be translated or carried over into another language. Materiality is precisely that which translation relinquishes' (ibid., 210). Some readers may note a degree of (characteristically postmodern) irony in such a stance being adopted by a theorist who also attacks Western materialism and whom many critics regard as an extreme idealist (despite his criticisms of idealism). Derrida's ideas have nevertheless informed the perspectives of some theorists who have sought to 'rematerialize' the linguistic sign, stressing that words and texts are *things* (e.g. Coward and Ellis 1977, Silverman and Torode 1980).

Roland Barthes also sought to revalorize the role of the signifier in the act of writing. He argued that in 'classic' literary writing, the writer 'is always supposed to go from signified to signifier, from content to form, from idea to text, from passion to expression' (Barthes 1974, 174). However, this was directly opposite to the way in which Barthes characterized the act of writing. For him, writing was a matter of working with the signifiers and letting the signifieds take care of themselves – a paradoxical phenomenon which other writers have often reported (Chandler 1995, 60ff.).

Jay David Bolter, a North American professor of new media, argues that 'signs are always anchored in a medium. Signs may be more or less dependent upon the characteristics of one medium – they may transfer more or less well to other media – but there is no such thing as a sign without a medium' (Bolter 1991, 195–6). The *sign* as such, of course, is not a material entity, but it has a material dimension – the signifier (or sign vehicle). Robert Hodge and David Tripp insist that, 'fundamental to all semiotic analysis is the fact that any system of signs (semiotic code) is carried by a material medium *which has its own principles of structure*' (Hodge and Tripp 1986, 17; original emphasis). Furthermore, some media draw on several interacting sign-systems: television and film, for example, utilize verbal, visual, auditory and locomotive signs. The medium is not 'neutral'; each medium has its own constraints and, as Umberto Eco notes, each is already 'charged with cultural signification' (Eco 1976, 267). For instance, photographic and audio-visual media are almost invariably regarded as more 'real' than other forms of representation. Gunther Kress and Theo van Leeuwen argue that 'the material expression of the text is always significant; it is a separately variable semiotic feature' (Kress and van Leeuwen 1996, 231). Changing the signifier at the level of the form or medium may thus influence the signified – the sense which readers make of what is ostensibly the same 'content'. Breaking up a relationship by fax is likely to be regarded in a different light from breaking up in a face-to-face situation.

Hjelmslev's framework

The distinction between signifier and signified has sometimes been equated to the familiar dualism of 'form and content'. Within such a framework, the signifier is seen as the *form* of the sign and the signified as the *content*. However, the metaphor of form as a 'container' is problematic, tending to support the equation of content with *meaning*, implying that meaning can be 'extracted' without an active process of interpretation and that form is not in itself meaningful (Chandler 1995, 104–6). The linguist Louis Hjelmslev acknowledged that 'there can be no content without an expression, or expressionless content; neither can there be an expression without a content, or content-less expression' (Hjelmslev 1961, 49). He offered a framework which facilitated analytical distinctions (ibid., 47ff.). While he referred to 'planes' of expression and content (Saussure's *signifier* and *signified*), he enriched this model (ibid., 60). His contribution was to suggest that both *expression* and *content* have *substance* and *form* (see Table 1.1). This strategy thus avoids the dualistic reduction of the sign to form and content.

Within Hjelmslev's framework there are four categories: substance of expression, form of expression, substance of content, form of content. Various theorists such as Christian Metz have built upon this theoretical distinction and they differ somewhat in what they

TABLE 1.1 Substance and form

	Substance	*Form*
Signifiers: plane of **expression**	**Substance of expression:** physical materials of the medium (e.g. photographs, recorded voices, printed words on paper)	**Form of expression:** language, formal syntactic structure, technique and style
Signified: plane of **content**	**Substance of content:** 'human content' (Metz), textual world, subject matter, genre	**Form of content:** 'semantic structure' (Baggaley and Duck), 'thematic structure' (including narrative) (Metz)

Source: Based on Tudor 1974

assign to the four categories (see Tudor 1974, 110; Baggaley and Duck 1976, 149; Metz 1981). Whereas Saussure had insisted that language is 'a form, not a substance', Hjelmslev's framework allows us to analyse texts according to their various dimensions and to grant to each of these the potential for signification. Such a matrix provides a useful framework for the systematic analysis of texts, broadens the notion of what constitutes a sign, and reminds us that the materiality of the sign may in itself signify.

Chapter 2

Signs and things

While semiotics is often encountered in the form of textual analysis, it also involves philosophical theorizing on the role of signs in the construction of reality. Semiotics involves studying representations and the processes involved in representational practices, and to semioticians, 'reality' always involves representation.

Naming things

To semioticians, a defining feature of signs is that they are treated by their users as 'standing for' or representing other things. Jonathan Swift's satirical account of the fictional academicians of Lagado outlined their proposal to abolish words altogether, and to carry around bundles of objects whenever they wanted to communicate. This highlights problems with the simplistic notion of signs being direct substitutes for physical things in the world around us. The academicians adopted the philosophical stance of naïve realism in assuming that words simply mirror objects in

an external world. They believed that 'words are only names for things', a stance involving the assumption that 'things' necessarily exist independently of language prior to them being 'labelled' with words. According to this position (which accords with a still widespread popular misconception of language) there is a one-to-one correspondence between word and referent (sometimes called language–world *isomorphism*), and language is simply a *nomenclature* – an item-by-item naming of things in the world. As Saussure put it, this is 'the superficial view taken by the general public' (Saussure 1983, 16, 65).

Within the lexicon of a language, it is true that most of the words are 'lexical words' (or nouns) which refer to 'things', but most of these things are abstract concepts rather than physical objects in the world. Only 'proper nouns' have specific referents in the everyday world, and only some of these refer to a unique entity (e.g. Llanfairpwllgwyngyllgogerychwyrndrobwllllantysiliogogogoch – the name of a Welsh village). The communicative function of a fully functioning language requires the scope of reference to move beyond the particularity of the individual instance. While each leaf, cloud or smile is different from all others, effective communication requires general categories or 'universals'. Anyone who has attempted to communicate with people who do not share their language will be familiar with the limitations of simply pointing to things. You can't point to 'mind', 'culture' or 'history'; these are not 'things' at all. The vast majority of lexical words in a language exist on a high level of abstraction and refer to classes of things (such as 'buildings') or to concepts (such as 'construction'). Language depends on categorization, but as soon as we group instances into classes (tokens into types), we lose any one-to-one correspondence of word and thing (if by 'things' we mean specific objects). Furthermore, other than lexical words, the remaining elements of the lexicon of a language consist of 'function words' (or grammatical words, such as 'only' and 'under') which do not refer to objects in the world at all. The lexicon of a language consists of many kinds of signs other than nouns. Clearly, language cannot be reduced to the naming of objects.

The less naïve realists might note at this point that words do not necessarily name only physical things which exist in an objective material world but may also label imaginary things and also *concepts*. Peirce's referent, for instance, is not limited to things which exist in the physical world. However, as Saussure noted, the notion of words as labels for concepts 'assumes that ideas exist independently of words' (Saussure 1983, 65), and for him, 'no ideas are established in advance . . . before the introduction of linguistic structure' (ibid., 110; cf. 114–15, 118). It remains a rationalist and 'nomenclaturist' stance on language when words are seen as 'labels' for pre-existing ideas as well as for physical objects. It is reductionist: reducing language to the purely referential function of naming things. When we use language, its various kinds of signs relate to each other in complex ways which make nonsense of the reduction of language to a nomenclature. Referentiality may be a function of language but it is only one of its functions.

A radical response to realists is that things do not exist independently of the sign-systems that we use; reality is created by the media which seem simply to represent it. Language does not simply name pre-existing categories; categories do not exist in 'the world' (where are the boundaries of a cloud? When does a smile begin?). We may acknowledge the cautionary remarks of John Lyons, that such an emphasis on reality as invariably perceptually seamless may be an exaggeration. Lyons speculates that 'most of the phenomenal world, as we perceive it, is *not* an undifferentiated continuum'; and our referential categories do seem to bear some relationship to certain features which seem to be inherently salient (Lyons 1977, 247; my emphasis; cf. ibid., 260). In support of this caveat, we may note that the Gestalt psychologists reported a universal human tendency to separate a salient *figure* from what the viewer relegates to the (back)*ground*. However, such observations clearly do not demonstrate that the lexical structure of language reflects the structure of an external reality. As Saussure noted, if words were simply a nomenclature for a pre-existing set of things in the world, translation from one language to another would be easy (Saussure 1983, 114–15) whereas in fact languages differ in how they categorize the world – the signifieds in one language do not neatly correspond to those in another. Within a language, many words may refer to 'the same thing' but reflect different evaluations of it (one person's 'hovel' is another person's 'home'). Furthermore, what is signified by a word is subject to historical change. In this sense, 'reality' or 'the world' is created by the language we use: this argument insists on *the primacy of the signifier*. Even if we do *not* adopt the radical stance that 'the real world' is a product of our sign-systems, we must still acknowledge that there are many things in the experiential world for which we have no words and that most words do not correspond to objects in the known world at all. Thus, all words are 'abstractions', and there is no direct correspondence between words and 'things' in the world.

Referentiality

Saussure's model of the sign involves no direct reference to reality outside the sign. This was not a 'denial' of extralinguistic reality as such but a reflection of his understanding of his own role as a linguist. Saussure accepted that in most scientific disciplines the 'objects of study' were 'given in advance' and existed independently of the observer's 'point of view'. However, he stressed that in linguistics, by contrast, 'it is the viewpoint adopted which creates the object' (ibid., 8). While such a statement might go without comment in a discipline with an acknowledged self-sufficiency (such as mathe-matics), in the context of human language one can understand how it might be criticized as an idealist model. In the Saussurean model the signified is only a mental concept; concepts are mental constructs, not 'external' objects. A concept may, of course, refer to something in experiential reality but the Saussurean stance is a denial of the 'essentialist' argument that signifieds are distinct, autonomous enti-ties in an objective world which are definable in terms of some kind of unchanging 'essence'. Saussurean semiotics asserts the non-essen-tial nature of objects. Just like signifiers, signifieds are part of the sign-system; signifieds are socially constructed. According to the Whorfian stance, the signified is an arbitrary product of our culture's 'way of seeing'. The Saussurean perspective 'tends to reverse the precedence which a nomenclaturist accords to the world outside language, by proposing that far from the world determining the order of our language, our language determines the order of the world' (Sturrock 1986, 17).

In contrast to the Saussurean model, Peirce's model of the sign explicitly features the *referent* – something beyond the sign to which the sign vehicle refers (though not necessarily a material thing). However, it also features the *interpretant* which leads to an 'infinite series' of signs, so at the same time Peirce's model also seems to suggest the relative independence of signs from any referents (Silverman 1983, 15). For Peirce, reality can only be known via signs. If representations are our only access to reality, determining their accuracy is a critical issue. Peirce adopted from logic the notion of 'modality' to refer to the truth value of a sign, acknowledging three kinds: actuality, (logical) necessity and (hypothetical) possibility (Hodge and Kress 1988, 26). Furthermore, his classification of signs in terms of the mode of relationship of the sign vehicle to its referent reflects their modality – their apparent transparency in relation to reality (the symbolic mode, for instance, having *low* modality). Peirce asserted that, logically, signification could only ever offer a partial truth because if it offered the complete truth it would destroy itself by becoming identical with its object (cited in Grayson 1998, 40).

Theorists who veer towards the extreme position of philosophical *idealism* (for whom reality is purely subjective and is constructed in our use of signs) may see no problem with the Saussurean model. Indeed, the Saussurean model has itself been described as 'idealist' (e.g. Culler 1985, 117). Those drawn towards philosophical *realism* (for whom a single objective reality exists indisputably 'outside' us) would challenge it. According to this stance, reality may be 'distorted' by the media that we use to apprehend it but such media play no part in 'constructing' the world. Even those who adopt an intermediate *constructionist* (or *constructivist*) position – that language and other media play a major part in 'the social construction of reality' – may tend to object to an apparent indifference towards social reality in Saussure's model. Those on the political left in particular would object to its sidelining of the importance of the material conditions of existence. Umberto Eco provocatively asserts that 'semiotics is in principle the discipline studying everything which can be used in order to lie' (Eco 1976, 7).

Modality

From the perspective of *social semiotics* the original Saussurean model is understandably problematic. Whatever our philosophical positions, in our daily behaviour we routinely act on the basis that some representations of reality are more reliable than others. And we do so in part with reference to cues within texts which semioticians (following linguists) call 'modality markers'. Such cues refer to what are variously described as the plausibility, reliability, credibility, truth, accuracy or facticity of texts within a given genre as representations of some recognizable reality. Gunther Kress and Theo van Leeuwen acknowledge that

> A social semiotic theory of truth cannot claim to establish the absolute truth or untruth of representations. It can only show whether a given 'proposition' (visual, verbal or otherwise) is represented as true or not. From the point of view of social semiotics, truth is a construct of semiosis, and as such the truth of a particular social group, arising from the values and beliefs of that group.
>
> (Kress and van Leeuwen 1996, 159)

From such a perspective, reality has authors; thus there are many *realities* rather than the single reality posited by objectivists. This stance is related to Whorfian framings of relationships between language and reality. Constructionists insist that realities are not limitless and unique to the individual as extreme subjectivists would argue; rather, they are the product of social definitions and as such far from equal in status. Realities are contested, and textual representations are thus 'sites of struggle'.

Modality refers to the reality status accorded to or claimed by a sign, text or genre. More formally, Robert Hodge and Gunther Kress declare that 'modality refers to the status, authority and reliability of a message, to its ontological status, or to its value as truth or fact' (Hodge and Kress 1988, 124). In making sense of a text, its interpreters make 'modality judgements' about it, drawing on their knowledge of the world and of the medium. For instance, they assign it to fact or fiction, actuality or acting, live or recorded, and they assess the possibility or plausibility of the events depicted or the claims made in it. Modality judgements involve comparisons of textual representations with models drawn from the everyday world and with models based on the genre; they are therefore obviously dependent on relevant experience of both the world and the medium. Robert Hodge and David Tripp's semiotic study on children and television focuses on the development of children's modality judgements (Hodge and Tripp 1986).

Clearly, the extent to which a text may be perceived as 'real' depends in part on the medium employed. Writing, for instance, generally has a lower modality than film and television. However, no rigid ranking of media modalities is possible. John Kennedy showed children a simple line drawing featuring a group of children sitting in a circle with a gap in their midst (Kennedy 1974). He asked them to add to this gap a drawing of their own, and when they concentrated on the central region of the drawing, many of them tried to pick up the pencil which was depicted in the same style in the top right-hand corner of the drawing! Being absorbed in the task led them to accept unconsciously the terms in which reality was constructed within the medium. This is not likely to be a phenomenon confined to children, since when absorbed in narrative (in many media) we frequently fall into a 'suspension of disbelief' without compromising our ability to distinguish representations from reality. Charles Peirce reflected that 'in contemplating a painting, there is a moment when we lose the consciousness that it is not the thing, the distinction of the real and the copy disappears' (Peirce 1931–58, 3.362).

While in a conscious comparison of a photographic image with a cartoon image of the same thing the photograph is likely to be judged as more realistic, the mental schemata involved in visual recognition may be closer to the stereotypical simplicity of cartoon images than to photographs. People can identify an image as a hand when it is drawn as a cartoon more quickly than when they are shown a photograph of a hand (Ryan and Schwartz 1956). This underlines the importance of perceptual codes in constructing reality. Umberto Eco argues that through familiarity an iconic signifier can acquire

TABLE 2.1 Modality cues

Formal features	Content features
3D–flat	possible–impossible
detailed–abstract	plausible–implausible
colour–monochrome	familiar–unfamiliar
edited–unedited	current–distant in time
moving–still	local–distant in time
audible–silent	

primacy over its signified. Such a sign becomes conventional 'step by step, the more its addressee becomes acquainted with it. At a certain point the iconic representation, however stylized it may be, appears to be more true than the real experience, and people begin to look at things through the glasses of iconic convention' (Eco 1976, 204–5).

Modality cues within texts include both formal features of the medium and content features such as in Table 2.1 (where typical high modality cues are listed as the first in each pair). However, it is their interaction and interpretation, of course, which is most important. The media which are typically judged to be the most 'realistic' are photographic – especially film and television. James Monaco suggests that 'in film, the signifier and the signified are almost identical . . . The power of language systems is that there is a very great difference between the signifier and the signified; the power of film is that there is not' (Monaco 1981, 127–8). This is an important part of what Christian Metz was referring to when he described the cinematic signifier as 'the imaginary signifier'. In being less reliant than writing on symbolic signs, film, television and photography suggest less of an obvious gap between the signifier and its signified, which make them seem to offer 'reflections of reality' (even in that which is imaginary). But photography does not *reproduce* its object: it 'abstracts from, and mediates, the actual' (Burgin 1982b, 61). While we do not mistake one for the other, we do need to remind ourselves that a photograph or a film does not simply record an event, but is only one of an infinite number of possible representations. All media texts, however 'realistic', are representations rather than simply recordings or reproductions of reality.

The film theorist André Bazin describes what he calls the 'reproductive fallacy' according to which the only kind of representation which can show things 'as they really are' would be one which is (or appears to be) exactly like that which it represents in every respect. Texts are almost always constructed from different materials from that which they represent, and representations cannot be replicas. For Bazin, aesthetic realism depended on a broader 'truth to reality' (Bazin 1974, 64; Lovell 1983, 81). Ien Ang (1985) argues that watching television soap operas can involve a kind of *psychological* or *emotional realism* for viewers which exists at the connotative rather than the denotative level. Viewers find some representations emotionally or psychologically 'true-to-life' (even if at the denotative level the treatment may seem 'unrealistic'). I would argue that especially with long-running soaps (which may become more 'real' to their fans over time) what we could call *generic realism* is another factor. Viewers familiar with the characters and conventions of a particular soap opera may often judge the programme largely in its own generic terms rather than with reference to some external 'reality'. For instance, is a character's current behaviour consistent with what we have learned over time about that character? The soap may be accepted to some extent as a world in its own right, in which slightly different rules may sometimes apply. This is of course the basis for what Coleridge called the 'willing suspension of disbelief' on which drama depends.

Robert Hodge and Gunther Kress argue that:

Different genres, whether classified by medium (e.g. comic, cartoon, film, TV, painting) or by content (e.g. Western, Science Fiction, Romance, news) establish sets of modality markers, and an overall value which acts as a baseline for the genre. This baseline can be different for different kinds of viewer/reader, and for different texts or moments within texts.

(Hodge and Kress 1988, 142)

63

What are recognized as 'realistic' styles of representation reflect an aesthetic *code* (a concept which we will explore in detail later). Over time, certain methods of production within a medium and a genre become naturalized. The content comes to be accepted as a 'reflection of reality'. In the case of popular television and film, for instance, the use of 'invisible editing' represents a widespread set of conventions which has come to seem 'natural' to most viewers (as we shall see later). In 'realistic' texts, what is foregrounded is the 'content' rather than the 'form' or style of production. As in the dominant mode of 'scientific' discourse, the medium and codes are discounted as neutral and transparent and the makers of the text retreat to invisibility. Consequently, 'reality' seems to pre-exist its representation and to 'speak for itself'; what is said thus has the aura of 'truth'. In *The Burden of Representation*, John Tagg (a professor of art history) argues that in realist texts,

> The signifier is treated as if it were identical with a pre-existent signified and . . . the reader's role is purely that of a consumer . . . Signifier and signified appear not only to unite, but the signifier seems to become transparent so that the concept seems to present itself, and the arbitrary sign is naturalized by a spurious identity between reference and referents, between the text and the world.
>
> (Tagg 1988, 99)

Tagg adds that such a stance need not involve positing 'a closed world of codes' (ibid., 101) or the denial of the existence of what is represented outside the process which represents it (ibid., 167). However, he stresses 'the crucial relation of meaning to questions of practice and power', arguing that 'the Real is a complex of dominant and dominated discourses which given texts exclude, separate or do not signify' (ibid., 101).

The word is not the thing

The Belgian surrealist René Magritte (1898–1967) painted *La Trahison des Images* (*The Treachery of Images*) in 1936. That it has become one of Magritte's most famous and widely reproduced works suggests the enduring fascination of its theme. At first glance, its subject is banal. We are offered a 'realistic' depiction of an object which we easily recognize: a smoker's pipe (in side-on view). However, the painting also includes the text 'Ceci n'est pas une pipe' ('This is not a pipe'). The inclusion of text *within* the painting is remarkable enough, but the wording gives us cause to pause. If this were part of a language lesson or a child's 'reading book' (the style reminds me of old-fashioned *Ladybird* books for children), we might expect to see the words 'This is a pipe.' To depict a pipe and then provide a 'label' which insists that 'this is not a pipe' initially seems perverse. Is it purely irrational or is there something which we can learn from this apparent paradox? What could it mean? As our minds struggle to find a stable, meaningful interpretation we may not be too happy that there is no single, 'correct' answer to this question – although those of us who are relatively 'tolerant of ambiguity' may accept that it offers a great deal of food for thought about levels (or modes) of reality. The indexical word 'this' can be seen as a key to the interpretation of this painting: what exactly does the word 'this' refer to? Anthony Wilden suggests several alternative interpretations:

- this [pipe] is not a pipe;
- this [image of a pipe] is not a pipe;
- this [painting] is not a pipe;
- this [sentence] is not a pipe;
- [this] this is not a pipe;
- [this] is not a pipe.

(Wilden 1987, 245)

Although we habitually relate the 'meaning' of texts to the stated or inferred purposes of their makers, Magritte's own purposes are not essential to our current concerns. It suits our purposes here to suggest that the painting could be taken as meaning that this representation (or any representation) is not that which it represents. That this image of a pipe is 'only an image' and that we can't smoke it seems obvious – nobody 'in their right mind' would be so foolish as to try to pick it up and use it as a functional pipe (although many readers will have heard by now of the unfortunate, deluded man who 'mistook his wife for a hat'). However, we do habitually refer to such realistic depictions in terms which suggest that they are nothing more nor less than what they depict. Any representation is more than merely a reproduction of that which it represents: it also contributes to the *construction* of reality. Even 'photorealism' does not depict unmediated reality. The most realistic representation may also symbolically or metaphorically 'stand for' something else entirely. Furthermore, the depiction of a pipe is no guarantee of the existence of a specific pipe in the world of which this is an accurate depiction. Indeed, it seems a fairly generalized pipe and could therefore be seen (as is frequently true of language lessons, children's encyclopedia entries and so on) as an illustration of the 'concept' of a pipe rather than of a specific pipe. The label seeks to anchor our interpretation – a concept to which we will return later – and yet at the same time the label is part of the painting itself rather than a title attached to the frame. Magritte's painting could be seen as a kind of defamiliarization: we are so used to seeing things and attaching labels to them that we seldom look deeper and do not see things in their specificity. One function of art (and of surrealistic art in particular) is 'to make the familiar strange' (as the Russian formalists put it).

Alfred Korzybski (1879–1950), the founder of a movement known as 'general semantics', declared that 'the map is not the territory' and that 'the word is not the thing' (Korzybski 1933; cf. Chase 1938 and Hayakawa 1941). The non-identity of sign and thing is, of course, a very basic Saussurean principle. However, while Saussure's model is anti-realist, the general semanticists adopted the realist stance that language comes 'between' us and the objective world and they sought to reform our verbal behaviour to counteract the linguistic distortion of 'reality'. They felt that one reason for the confusion of signifiers and referential signifieds was that we sometimes allow language to take us further up the 'ladder of abstraction' than we think we are. Here is a homely example of levels of verbal abstraction in relation to a cow called 'Bessie':

1. The cow known to science ultimately consists of atoms, electrons etc. according to present-day scientific inference . . .

2. The cow we perceive is not the word but the object of experience, that which our nervous system abstracts (selects) . . .

3. The word 'Bessie' (cow) is the *name* we give to the object of perception of level 2. The name is *not* the object; it merely *stands for* the object and omits reference to many characteristics of the object.

4. The word 'cow' stands for the characteristics we have abstracted as common to cow, cow, cow . . . cow. Characteristics peculiar to particular cows are left out.

5. When Bessie is referred to as 'livestock' only those characteristics she has in common with pigs, chickens, goats, etc. are referred to.

6. When Bessie is included among 'farm assets' reference is made only to what she has in common with all other saleable items on the farm.

7. When Bessie is referred to as an 'asset' still more of her characteristics are left out.

8. The word 'wealth' is an extremely high level of abstraction, omitting *almost* all reference to the characteristics of Bessie.

(McKim 1972, 128; the origins of this example
are in Korzybski, via Hayakawa 1941, 121ff.)

The ladder metaphor is consistent with how we routinely refer to levels of abstraction – we talk of thinkers with 'their heads in the clouds' and of 'realists' with their 'feet on the ground'. As we move up the ladder we move from the particular to the general, from concrete reality to abstract generalization. The general semanticists were of course hard-headed realists and what they wanted was for people to keep their feet firmly planted on the ground. In alerting language-users to levels of abstraction, the general semanticists sought to avoid the confusion of *higher logical types* with *lower logical types*. 'A map' is of a higher (more general) logical type than 'the territory', and linguistic representation in particular lends itself to this process of abstraction. Clearly we can learn more about a place by visiting it than by simply looking at a map of it, and we can tell more about a person by meeting that person than by merely looking at a photograph of that person. Translation from lower levels to higher levels involves an inevitable loss of specificity – like earth being filtered through a series of increasingly fine sieves or like photocopies being repeatedly made of the 'copies' that they produce. Being alert for the consequent losses, absences or exclusions is important to the semiotician as well as the 'general semanticist'. While the logician may be able to keep such levels separate, in most acts of communication some 'slippage' occurs routinely, although we are normally capable of identifying what kind of messages we are dealing with, assigning them to appropriate levels of abstraction. Semioticians observe that some kind of 'translation' is unavoidable in human communication. Claude Lévi-Strauss declared that 'understanding consists in the reduction of one type of reality to another' (Lévi-Strauss 1961, 61). Similarly, Algirdas Greimas observed that 'signification is . . . nothing but . . . transposition from one level of language to another, from one language to a different language, and meaning is nothing but the possibility of such *transcoding*' (cited in Jameson 1972, 215–16).

While it can be useful to consider abstraction in terms of levels and logical typing, the implicit filter metaphor in the general semanticists' 'ladder of abstraction' is too uni-dimensional. Any given 'object' of perception could be categorized in a variety of ways rather than in terms of a single 'objective' hierarchy. The categories applied depend on such factors as experience, roles and purposes. This raises issues of interpretation. For instance, looking at an advertisement featuring a woman's face, some viewers might assume that the image stood for women in general, others that she represented a particular type, role or group, and yet others might recognize her as a particular individual. Knowing the appropriate level of abstraction in relation to interpreting such an image would depend primarily on familiarity with the relevant cultural codes.

The general semanticists set themselves the therapeutic goal of 'purifying' language in order to make its relationship to reality more 'transparent', and from such roots sprang projects such as the development of 'Basic English' (Ogden 1930). Whatever reservations we may have about such goals, Korzybski's popularization of the principle of arbitrariness could be seen as a useful corrective to some of our habits of mind. As a caveat, Korzybski's aphorism seems unnecessary: we all know that the word 'dog' cannot bark or bite, but in some circumstances we do behave as if certain signifiers are inseparable from what they stand for. 'Commonsense' still leads us routinely to identify sign and thing, representation with what it represents.

In his massively influential book *The Interpretation of Dreams* (first published in 1900), Sigmund Freud argued that 'dream-content is, as it were, presented in hieroglyphics, whose symbols must be translated . . . It would of course be incorrect to read these symbols in accordance with their values as pictures, instead of in accordance with their meaning as symbols' (Freud 1938, 319). He also observed that 'words are often treated in dreams as things' (ibid., 330). Magritte played with our habit of identifying the signifier with the signified in a series of drawings and paintings in which objects are depicted with verbal labels which 'don't belong to them'. In an oil-painting entitled *La Clef des Songes* (*The Interpretation of Dreams*, 1930) we are confronted with images of six familiar objects together with verbal labels. Such arrangements are familiar, particularly in the language-learning context suggested by the blackboard-like background. However, we quickly realize that the words do not match the images under which they appear. If we then rearrange them in our minds, we find that the labels do not correspond to *any* of the images. The relation between the image of an object and the verbal label attached to it is thus presented as arbitrary.

The confusion of the representation with the thing represented is a feature of schizophrenia and psychosis (Wilden 1987, 201). 'In order to able to operate with symbols it is necessary first of all to be able to distinguish between the sign and the thing it signifies' (Leach 1970, 43). However, the confusion of 'levels of reality' is also a normal feature of an early phase of cognitive development in childhood. Jerome Bruner observed that for pre-school children thought and the object of thought seem to be the same thing, but that during schooling one comes to separate word and thing (Bruner 1966). The substitution of a sign for its referent (initially in the form of gestures and imitative sounds) constitutes a crucial phase in the infant's acquisition of language. The child quickly discovers the apparently magical power of words for referring to things in their absence – this property of *displacement* being a key 'design feature' of language (Piaget 1971, 64; Hockett 1958). Helen Keller, who became blind and deaf at the age of 18 months, was gradually taught to speak by her nurse (Keller 1945). At the age of 9 while playing with water she felt with her hand the motions of the nurse's throat and mouth vibrating the word 'water'. In a sudden flash of revelation she cried out words to the effect that 'everything has a name!'. It is hardly surprising that, even in mid-childhood, children sometimes appear to have difficulty in separating words from what they represent. Piaget illustrates the 'nominal realism' of young children in an interview with a child aged 9½:

> 'Could the sun have been called "moon" and the moon "sun"?' – *'No.'* 'Why not?' – *'Because the sun shines brighter than the moon . . .'* 'But if everyone had called the sun "moon", and the moon "sun", would we have known it was wrong?' – *'Yes, because the sun is always bigger, it always stays like it is and so does the moon.'* 'Yes, but the sun isn't changed, only its name. Could it have been called . . . etc.?' – *'No . . . Because the moon rises in the evening, and the sun in the day.'*
>
> (Piaget 1929: 81–2)

Thus for the child, words do not seem at all arbitrary. Similarly, Sylvia Scribner and Michael Cole found that unschooled Vai people in Liberia felt that the names of sun and moon could not be changed, one of them expressing the view that these were God-given names (Scribner and Cole 1981, 141).

The anthropologist Lucien Lévy-Bruhl claimed that people in 'primitive' cultures had difficulty in distinguishing between names and the things to which they referred, regarding such signifiers as an intrinsic part of their signifieds (cited in Olson 1994, 28). The fear of 'graven images' within the Judeo-Christian tradition and also magical practices and beliefs such as Voodoo are clearly related to such a phenomenon. Emphasizing the epistemological significance of writing, the Canadian psychologist David Olson argues that the invention (around 4,000 years ago) of 'syntactic scripts' (which superseded the use of tokens) enabled referential words to be distinguished more easily from their referents, language to be seen as more than purely referential, and words to be seen as (linguistic) entities in their own right. He suggests that such scripts marked the end of 'word magic' since referential words came to be seen as representations rather than as intrinsic properties or parts of their referents. However, in the Middle Ages words and images were still seen as having a natural connection to things (which had 'true names' given by Adam at the Creation). Words were seen as the names of things rather than as representations. As Michel Foucault has shown, only in the early modern period did scholars come to see words and other signifiers as representations which were subject to conventions rather than as copies (Foucault 1970). By the seventeenth century, clear distinctions were being made between representations (signifiers), ideas (signifieds) and things (referents). Scholars now regarded signifiers as referring to ideas rather than directly to things. Representations were conventionalized constructions which were relatively independent both of what they represented and of their authors; knowledge involved manipulating such signs. Olson notes that once such distinctions are made, the way is open to making modality judgements about the status of representations – such as their perceived truth or accuracy (Olson 1994, 68–78, 165–8, 279–80). While the seventeenth-century shift in attitudes towards signs was part of a search for 'neutrality', 'objectivity' and 'truth', in more recent times, of course, we have come to recognize that 'there is no representation without intention and interpretation' (ibid., 197).

It is said that someone once asked an astronomer how he had discovered the name of a previously unknown star! Sophisticated literates are able to joke about the notion that names 'belong' to things. In one of Aldous Huxley's novels an old farmworker points out his pigs: 'Look at them, sir,' he said, with a motion of his hand towards the wallowing swine. 'Rightly is they called pigs' (*Chrome Yellow*, Chapter 5). Literate adults may not often seem to be prey to this sort of nominal realism. However, certain signifiers become regarded by some as far from 'arbitrary', acquiring almost magical power – as in relation to 'graphic' swearing and issues of prejudice – highlighting the point that signifiers are not *socially* arbitrary. Children are just as aware of this: many are far from convinced by adult advice that 'sticks and stones may break my bones, but names can never hurt me'. We may all still need some convincing that 'the word is not the thing'.

Terence Hawkes notes the 'anaesthetic function' of language by which we are numbed to the intervention of the medium (Hawkes 1977, 70). Catherine Belsey, another literary theorist, argues that

> Language is *experienced* as a nomenclature because its existence precedes our 'understanding' of the world. Words seem to be symbols for things because things are inconceivable outside the system of differences which constitutes the language. Similarly, these very things seem to be represented in the mind, in an autonomous realm of thought, because thought is in essence symbolic, dependent on the differences brought about by the symbolic order. And so language is 'overlooked', suppressed in favour of a quest for meaning in experience and/or in the mind. The world of things and subjectivity then become the twin guarantors of truth.
>
> (Belsey 1980, 46)

Shakespeare's Hamlet refers to: 'the purpose of playing, whose end, both at the first and now, was and is, to hold, as 'twere, the mirror up to nature' (Shakespeare, *Hamlet*, III, ii), and being 'true to life' is probably still a key criterion in judgements of literary worth. However, Belsey comments:

> The claim that a literary form reflects the world is simply tautological. If by 'the world' we understand the world we experience, the world differentiated by language, then the claim that realism reflects the world means that realism reflects the world constructed in language. This is a tautology. If discourses articulate concepts through a system of signs which signify by means of their relationship to each other rather than to entities in the world, and if literature is a signifying practice, all it can reflect is the order inscribed in particular discourses, not the nature of the world.
>
> (Belsey 1980, 46)

The medium of language comes to acquire the illusion of 'transparency': this feature of the medium tends to blind its users to the part it plays in constructing their experiential worlds. 'Realistic' texts reflect a mimetic purpose in representation – seeking to imitate so closely that which they depict that they may be experienced as virtually identical (and thus unmediated). Obviously, purely verbal signifiers cannot be mistaken for their real-world referents. While it is relatively easy for us to regard words as conventional symbols, it is more difficult to recognize the conventionality of images which resemble their signifieds. Yet even an image is not what it represents – the presence of an image marks the absence of its referent. The difference between signifier and signified is fundamental. Nevertheless, when the signifiers are experienced as highly 'realistic' – as in the case of photography and film – it is particularly easy to slip into regarding them as identical with their signifieds. In contrast even to realistic painting and drawing, photographs seem far less obviously 'authored' by a human being. Just as 'the word is not the thing' and 'the map is not the territory' nor is a photograph or television news footage that which it depicts. Yet in the 'commonsense' attitude of everyday life we routinely treat high modality signifiers in this way. Indeed, many realistic filmic narratives and documentaries seem to invite this confusion of representation with reality (Nichols 1981, 21). Thus television is frequently described as a 'window on the world' and we usually assume that 'the camera never lies'. We know of course that in a film a dog can bark but it cannot bite (though, when 'absorbed', we may 'suspend disbelief' in the context of what we know to be enacted drama). However, we are frequently inclined to accept 'the evidence of our own eyes' even when events are mediated by the cameras of journalists. Highly 'realistic' representations in any medium always involve a point of view. Representations which claim to be 'real' deny the unavoidable difference between map and territory. In the sense that there is always a difference between the represented and its representation, 'the camera always lies'. We do not need to adopt the 'scientific' realism of the so-called general semanticists concerning the 'distortion of reality' by our signifying systems, but may acknowledge instead that reality does not exist independently of signs, turning our critical attention

to the issue of *whose* realities are privileged in particular representations – a perspective which, avoiding a retreat to subjectivism, pays
due tribute to the unequal distribution of power in the social world.

Empty signifiers

While Saussurean semioticians (with language as their model) have
emphasized the arbitrary relationship of the signifier to the signified,
some subsequent theorists have stressed 'the primacy of the signifier' – Jacques Lacan even praised Lewis Carroll's Humpty Dumpty
as 'the master of the signifier' for his declaration that 'when *I* use
a word, it means just what I choose it to mean – neither more nor
less'. Many postmodernist theorists postulate a complete disconnection of the signifier and the signified. An 'empty' or 'floating
signifier' is variously defined as a signifier with a vague, highly variable, unspecifiable or non-existent signified. Such signifiers mean
different things to different people: they may stand for many or even
any signifieds; they may mean whatever their interpreters want them
to mean. In such a state of radical disconnection between signifier
and signified, a sign only means that it means. Such a disconnection
is perhaps clearest in literary and aesthetic texts which foreground
the act and form of expression and undermine any sense of a 'natural'
or 'transparent' connection between a signifier and a referent. However, Jonathan Culler suggests that to refer to an 'empty signifier'
is an implicit acceptance of its status as a signifier and is thus 'to
correlate it with a signified' even if this is not known; 'the most
radical play of the signifier still requires and works through the
positing of signifieds' (Culler 1985, 115). Shakespeare famously
referred to 'a tale told by an idiot, full of sound and fury, signifying
nothing' (*Macbeth* V, iii). As early as 1940 Jakobson referred to the
'zero-sign' in linguistics – the 'unmarked' form of a word (such as
the singular form of words in which the plural involves the addition
of the terminal marker -*s*) (Sebeok 1994, 18). We will return to the
notion of unmarked terms in Chapter 3. The concept of an 'empty
signifier' also has some similarities with other linguistic concepts –
with the notion of an 'empty category' and with Hjelmslev's *figurae*
or non-signifying sign elements (Lechte 1994, 64, 137). The 'floating

signifier' is referred to in the year 1950 in Lévi-Strauss's *Introduction to the Work of Marcel Mauss* (Lévi-Strauss 1987). For Lévi-Strauss such a signifier is like an algebraic symbol which has no immanent symbolic value but which can represent anything. Roland Barthes referred to non-linguistic signs specifically as being so open to interpretation that they constituted a 'floating chain of signifieds' (Barthes 1977, 39). The first explicit reference to an 'empty signifier' of which I am aware is that of Barthes in his essay 'Myth today' (Barthes 1957). Barthes defines an empty signifier as one with no definite signified (see also Barthes 1982, 108).

Whereas Saussure saw the signifier and the signified (however arbitrary their relationship) as being as inseparable as the two sides of a piece of paper, poststructuralists have rejected the apparently stable and predictable relationship embedded in his model. The French psychoanalyst Jacques Lacan wrote of 'the incessant sliding of the signified under the signifier' (Lacan 1977, 154) – he argued that there could be no anchoring of particular signifiers to particular signifieds – although this in itself is hardly contentious in the context of psychoanalysis. Jacques Derrida refers (originally in the 1960s) to the 'play' or 'freeplay' of signifiers: they are not fixed to their signifieds but point beyond themselves to other signifiers in an 'indefinite referral of signifier to signified' (Derrida 1978, 25; 'freeplay' has become the dominant English rendering of Derrida's use of the term *jeu* – see, for instance, Derrida 1976, xix). Derrida championed the 'deconstruction' of Western semiotic systems, denying that there were any ultimate determinable meanings. While for Saussure the meaning of signs derives from how they *differ* from each other, Derrida coined the term *différance* to allude also to the way in which meaning is endlessly *deferred*. There is no 'transcendent signified' (Derrida 1978, 278–80; Derrida 1976, 20). These notions were anticipated by Peirce in his version of 'unlimited semiosis', although Peirce emphasized that in practice this potentially endless process is inevitably cut short by the practical constraints of everyday life (Gallie 1952, 126). Unlike Peirce, postmodernist theories grant no access to any reality outside signification. For Derrida, 'il n'y a rien hors du texte' ('there is nothing outside the text') – although this assertion need not necessarily be taken 'literally'

(Derrida 1976, 158, 163). For materialist Marxists and realists, postmodernist idealism is intolerable: 'signs cannot be permitted to swallow up their referents in a never-ending chain of signification, in which one sign always points on to another, and the circle is never broken by the intrusion of that to which the sign refers' (Lovell 1983, 16). However, an emphasis on the unavoidability of signification need not necessitate denying any external reality. Readers may be tempted to conclude from this brief review of the notion of 'the empty (or free-floating) signifier' that it has become something of an academic 'soundbite' and that the term itself is ironically in danger of being an empty signifier.

The notion of reality as degenerative is found in the Romantic mythology of a primal state of unmediatedness (referring to children before language or human beings before The Fall) (Chandler 1995, 31–2). In his book *The Image*, Daniel Boorstin charted the rise of what he called 'pseudo-events' – events which are staged for the mass media to report (Boorstin 1961). However, any 'event' is a social construction – bounded 'events' have no objective existence, and all news items are 'stories' (Galtung and Ruge 1981).

We might posit three key historical shifts in dominant representational paradigms in relation to Peirce's differential framing of the referential status of signs:

- an *indexical* phase – the signifier and the referent are regarded as directly connected;
- an *iconic* phase – the signifier is not regarded as part of the referent but as depicting it transparently;
- a *symbolic* phase – the signifier is regarded as arbitrary and as referring only to other signs.

Such a schematization bears some similarity to that of the postmodernist Jean Baudrillard. Baudrillard interprets many representations as a means of concealing the absence of reality; he calls such representations 'simulacra' (or copies without originals) (Baudrillard 1984). He sees a degenerative evolution in modes of representation in which signs are increasingly empty of meaning:

These would be the successive phases of the image:

1. It is the reflection of a basic reality.
2. It masks and perverts a basic reality.
3. It masks the absence of a basic reality.
4. It bears no relation to any reality whatever: it is its own pure simulacrum.

(Baudrillard 1988, 170)

Baudrillard argues that when speech and writing were created, signs were invented to point to material or social reality, but the bond between signifier and signified became eroded. As advertising, propaganda and commodification set in, the sign began to hide 'basic reality'. In the postmodern age of 'hyper-reality' in which what are only illusions in the media of communication seem very real, signs hide the absence of reality and only pretend to mean something. For Baudrillard, *simulacra* – the signs that characterize late capitalism – come in three forms: *counterfeit* (imitation) – when there was still a direct link between signifiers and their signifieds; *production* (illusion) – when there was an indirect link between signifier and signified; and *simulation* (fake) – when signifiers came to stand in relation only to other signifiers and not in relation to any fixed external reality. It is hardly surprising that Douglas Kellner has criticized Baudrillard as a 'semiological idealist' who ignores the materiality of sign production (cited in Stam 2000, 306). Baudrillard's claim that the Gulf War never happened is certainly provocative (Baudrillard 1995).

Such perspectives, of course, beg the fundamental question, 'What is "real"?' The semiotic stance which problematizes 'reality' and emphasizes mediation and convention is sometimes criticized as extreme 'cultural relativism' by those who veer towards realism – such critics often object to an apparent sidelining of referential concerns such as 'accuracy' (e.g. Gombrich 1982, 188, 279, 286). However, even philosophical realists would accept that much of our knowledge of the world is indirect; we experience many things primarily (or even solely) as they are represented to us within our media and communication technologies. Since representations cannot be identical copies of what they represent, they can never be neutral and transparent but are instead constitutive of reality. As Judith Butler puts it, we need to ask, 'What does transparency keep obscure?' (Butler 1999, xix). Semiotics helps us to not to take representations for granted as 'reflections of reality', enabling us to take them apart and consider whose realities they represent.

Chapter 3

Analysing structures

Semiotics is probably best known as an approach to textual analysis, and in this form it is characterized by a concern with *structural analysis*. Structuralist analysis focuses on the structural relations which are functional in the signifying system at a particular moment in history. It involves identifying the constituent units in a semiotic system (such as a text or socio-cultural practice) and the structural relationships between them (oppositions, correlations and logical relations). This is not an empty exercise since 'relations are important for what they can explain: meaningful contrasts and permitted or forbidden combinations' (Culler 1975, 14).

Horizontal and vertical axes

Saussure emphasized that meaning arises from the *differences* between signifiers; these differences are of two kinds: *syntagmatic* (concerning positioning) and *paradigmatic* (concerning substitution). Saussure

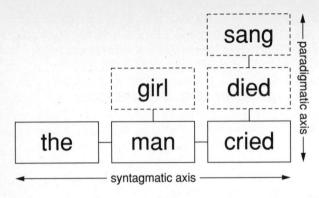

FIGURE 3.1 Syntagmatic and paradigmatic axes

called the latter *associative* relations (Saussure 1983, 121), but Roman Jakobson's term is now used. The distinction is a key one in structuralist semiotic analysis. These two dimensions are often presented as 'axes', where the horizontal axis is the syntagmatic and the vertical axis is the paradigmatic (see Figure 3.1). The plane of the syntagm is that of the *combination* of 'this-*and*-this-*and*-this' (as in the sentence, 'the man cried') while the plane of the paradigm is that of the *selection* of 'this-*or*-this-*or*-this' (e.g. the replacement of the last word in the same sentence with 'died' or 'sang'). While syntagmatic relations are possibilities of combination, paradigmatic relations are functional contrasts – they involve *differentiation*. Temporally, syntagmatic relations refer intratextually to other signifiers *co-present* within the text, while paradigmatic relations refer intertextually to signifiers which are *absent* from the text (ibid., 122). The 'value' of a sign is determined by both its paradigmatic and its syntagmatic relations. Syntagms and paradigms provide a structural context within which signs make sense; they are the structural forms through which signs are organized into codes.

Paradigmatic relationships can operate on the level of the signifier and on the level of the signified (ibid., 121–4; Silverman 1983, 10; Harris 1987, 124). A paradigm is a *set* of associated signifiers or signifieds which are all members of some defining category, but in which each is significantly different. In natural language there are grammatical paradigms such as verbs or nouns. In a given context, one member of the paradigm set is structurally replaceable with another. The choice of one excludes the choice of another. The use of one signifier (e.g. a particular word) rather than another from the same paradigm set (e.g. adjectives) shapes the preferred meaning of a text. Paradigmatic relations can thus be seen as 'contrastive'. Saussure's notion of 'associative' relations was broader and less formal than what is normally meant by 'paradigmatic' relations. He referred to 'mental association' and included perceived similarities in *form* (e.g. homophones) or *meaning* (e.g. synonyms). Such similarities were diverse and ranged from strong to slight, and might refer to only part of a word (such as a shared prefix or suffix). He noted that there was no end (or commonly agreed order) to such associations (Saussure 1983, 121–4).

Paradigms are not confined to the verbal mode. In film and television, paradigms include ways of changing shot (such as cut, fade, dissolve and wipe). The medium or genre are also paradigms, and particular media texts derive meaning from the ways in which the medium and genre used differ from the alternatives. The aphorism of the Canadian media theorist Marshall McLuhan (1911–80) that 'the medium is the message' can thus be seen as reflecting a semiotic concern: to a semiotician the medium is not 'neutral'.

A *syntagm* is an orderly combination of interacting signifiers which forms a meaningful whole within a text – sometimes, following Saussure, called a 'chain'. Such combinations are made within a framework of syntactic rules and conventions (both explicit and inexplicit). In language, a sentence, for instance, is a syntagm of words; so too are paragraphs and chapters. 'there are always larger units, composed of smaller units, with a relation of interdependence holding between both' (ibid., 127): syntagms can contain other syntagms. A printed advertisement is a syntagm of visual signifiers. Syntagmatic relations are the various ways in which elements within the same text may be related to each other. Syntagms are created by the linking of signifiers from paradigm sets which are chosen on the basis of whether they are conventionally regarded as appropriate or may be required by some rule system (e.g. grammar). Syntagmatic relations highlight the importance of part–whole relationships: Saussure stressed that 'the whole depends on the parts, and the parts depend on the whole' (ibid., 126).

Syntagms are often defined as 'sequential' (and thus *temporal* – as in speech and music), but they can represent *spatial relationships*. Saussure himself (who emphasized 'auditory signifiers' which 'are presented one after another' and 'form a chain') noted that visual signifiers (he instanced nautical flags) 'can exploit more than one dimension simultaneously' (ibid., 70). *Spatial* syntagmatic relations are found in drawing, painting and photography. Many semiotic systems – such as drama, cinema, television and the World Wide Web – include both spatial and temporal syntagms.

The structure of any text or cultural practice has both syntagmatic and paradigmatic axes. Roland Barthes (1967) outlined the paradigmatic and syntagmatic elements of the 'garment system'. The paradigmatic elements are the items which cannot be worn at the same time on the same part of the body (such as hats, trousers, shoes). The syntagmatic dimension is the juxtaposition of different elements at the same time in a complete ensemble from hat to shoes. Within a genre, while the syntagmatic dimension is the textual structure, the paradigmatic dimension can be as broad as the *choice of subject-matter* (Thwaites *et al.* 1994, 95). In this framing, *form* is a syntagmatic dimension while *content* is a paradigmatic dimension. However, form is also subject to paradigmatic choices and content to syntagmatic arrangement. In the case of film, our interpretation of an individual shot depends on both paradigmatic analysis (comparing it, not necessarily consciously, with the use of alternative kinds of shot) and syntagmatic analysis (comparing it with preceding and following shots). The same shot used within another sequence of shots could have quite a different preferred reading. Actually, filmic syntagms are not confined to such temporal syntagms (which are manifested in *montage*: the sequencing of shots) but include the spatial syntagms found also in still photography (in *mise-en-scène*: the composition of individual frames).

Both syntagmatic and paradigmatic analysis treat signs as part of a system – exploring their functions within codes and sub-codes – a topic to which we will return. Although we will discuss syntagmatic and paradigmatic relations separately, it should be emphasized that the semiotic analysis of a text or corpus has to tackle the system as a whole, and that the two dimensions cannot be considered in isolation. The description of any semiotic system involves specifying both the membership of all of the relevant paradigmatic sets and also the possible combinations of one set with another in well-formed syntagms. For the analyst, according to Saussure (who was, of course, focusing on the language system as a whole), 'the system as a united whole is the starting point, from which it becomes possible, by a process of analysis, to identify its constituent elements'; one cannot try to construct the system by working upwards from the constituent elements (Saussure 1983, 112). However, Roland Barthes argued that 'an important part of the semiological undertaking' was to divide texts 'into minimal significant units ... then to group these units into paradigmatic classes, and finally to classify the syntagmatic relations which link these units' (Barthes 1967, 48; cf. Leymore 1975, 21 and Lévi-Strauss 1972, 211). In practice, the analyst is likely to need to move back and forth between these two approaches as the analysis proceeds.

The syntagmatic dimension

Saussure, of course, emphasized the theoretical importance of the relationship of signs to each other. He also noted that 'normally we do not express ourselves by using single linguistic signs, but groups of signs, organized in complexes which themselves are signs' (Saussure 1983, 127). However, in practice he treated the individual word as the primary example of the sign. Thinking and communication depend on *discourse* rather than isolated signs. Saussure's focus on the language *system* rather than on its *use* meant that discourse was neglected within his framework. The linking together of signs was conceived solely in terms of the grammatical possibilities which the system offered. This is a key feature of the Saussurean framework which led some theorists to abandon semiotics altogether in favour of a focus on 'discourse' while leading others to seek to reformulate a more socially oriented semiotics (e.g. Hodge and Kress 1988). However, this is not to suggest that structural analysis is worthless. Analysts still engage in formal studies of narrative, film and television editing, and so on which are based on structuralist principles. It remains important for anyone interested in the analysis of texts to be aware of what these principles are. Structuralists study texts as *syntagmatic* structures. The syntagmatic analysis of a text (whether it is verbal or non-verbal) involves studying its structure and the relationships between its parts. Structuralist semioticians seek to identify elementary constituent *segments* within the text – its syntagms. The study of syntagmatic relations reveals the conventions or 'rules of combination' underlying the production and interpretation of texts (such as the grammar of a language). The use of one syntagmatic structure rather than another within a text influences meaning.

Before discussing narrative, perhaps the most obvious form of syntagmatic structure and one which dominates structuralist semiotic studies, it is worth reminding ourselves that there are other forms of syntagmatic relations (Table 3.1). While *narrative* is based on *sequential* (and causal) relationships (e.g. in film and television narrative sequences), there are also syntagmatic forms based on *spatial* relationships (e.g. *montage* in posters and photographs, which works through juxtaposition) and on *conceptual* relationships (such as in exposition or argument). The distinctions between the modes of narrative, description, exposition and argument are not clear-cut (Brooks and Warren 1972, 44). Many texts contain more than one type of syntagmatic structure, though one may be dominant.

Conceptual relations

Exposition relies on the conceptual structure of argument or description but it also has a narrative dimension. The conventions of expository prose in English have been listed as follows: 'A clearly defined topic, introduction, body which explicates all but nothing more than the stated topic, paragraphs which chain from one to the next, and a conclusion which tells the reader what has been discussed . . . no digression . . . is permitted on the grounds that it would violate unity' (R. B. Kaplan and S. Ostler, cited by Swales 1990, 65). Such structural conventions are associated by some theorists with 'masculine' rather than 'feminine' modes of discourse (Goodman 1990;

TABLE 3.1 Syntagmatic relations

Level	Syntagmatic relations	
signified	conceptual	
signifier	sequential	spatial

Easthope 1990). Masculine modes are held to involve clearly observable linear structures with 'tight', orderly and logical arguments leading to 'the main point' without backtracking or sidetracking. They can be seen as 'defensive' structures, which seek to guard the author against academic criticism. As such, these structures tend to support 'masculine' modes of discourse and to exclude 'women's ways of knowing'. Even without tying such conventions to gender bias it is clear that they facilitate certain modes of discourse and frustrate others.

One of the features which Anthony Easthope characterizes as stereotypically 'masculine' is a concern for seamless textual unity (Easthope 1990). Formal writing in general tends to have less obvious 'loose ends' than does casual discourse. While, for the existentialist at least, there are always loose ends in the interpretation of experience, in most expository writing 'loose ends' are considered to be 'out of place': stylistic seamlessness, unity and coherence are expected. A writing teacher asserts that 'in a finished work . . . the flimsy scaffolding is taken away' (Murray 1978, 90–1). Another author, drawing attention to this, remarks: 'the seams do not (I hope) show' (Smith 1982, 2). A cohesive structure reinforces a sense of the argument as 'coherent'. The tidiness of academic texts may also misleadingly suggest the enduring nature of the positions that they represent.

The basic three-part structure of introduction, main body and conclusion is satirized in the sardonic advice: 'First say what you're going to say, then say it, then say what you've already said.' While this formulation masks the inexplicitness of academic writing, it highlights its structural closure. Structural closure suggests that 'the matter is closed' – that the text is 'finished'. Seamlessness and sequential structures reinforce an impression of the ground having been covered, of all the questions having been answered, of nothing important having been left out. Though it is a lie, closure suggests mastery of the material through its control of form. Academic discourse uses univocal textual closure as a way of both controlling the reader and subordinating the topic to the author's purposes. Such closed textual structures can be seen as reflecting authorial attempts to create worlds whose completeness, order and clarity demand our recognition of them as somehow more absolute, more objective, more 'real', than the dynamic flux of everyday experience. Academic authors first fragment that which is experienced as seamless, and then, in conforming to various conventions in the use of the printed word, seek to give an impression of the seamlessness of their creations. The drive towards formal seamlessness suggests an imitation of the existential seamlessness, and hence 'authenticity', of lived experience.

In any expository writing, literary seamlessness may mask weaknesses or 'gaps' in the argument; it also masks the authorial manipulation involved in constructing an apparently 'natural' flow of words and ideas. For instance, the orderliness of the scientific paper offers a misleadingly tidy picture of the process of scientific inquiry. Representation always seems tidier than reality. Seamlessness in writing is a classical and 'realist' convention which may seem to suggest 'objectivity': whereas Romantic craftsmanship typically features the marks of the maker and may even employ 'alienation' – deliberately drawing attention to the making. As the linguist Edward Sapir famously remarked, 'all grammars leak' (Sapir 1971, 38). Those who would learn from semiotics should search for structural leaks, seams and scaffolding as signs of the making of any representation, and also for what has been denied, hidden or excluded so that the text may seem to tell 'the whole truth'.

Spatial relations

Theorists often assert that, unlike verbal language, the visual image is not suited to exposition (e.g. Peirce 1931–58, 2.291; Gombrich 1982, 138, 175). Syntagms are often logocentrically defined purely as sequential or temporal 'chains'. But *spatial* relations are also syntagmatic. While most obviously associated with art and photography, they are no less structurally important alongside temporal syntagms in media such as television, cinema and the World Wide Web. Unlike sequential syntagmatic relations, which are essentially about *before* and *after*, spatial syntagmatic relations include:

- above/below;
- in front/behind;
- close/distant;
- left/right (which can also have sequential significance);
- north/south/east/west; and
- inside/outside (or centre/periphery).

Such structural relationships are not semantically neutral. The 'cognitive semanticists', George Lakoff and Mark Johnson, have shown how fundamental 'orientational metaphors' are routinely linked to key concepts in a culture (Lakoff and Johnson 1980, Chapter 4). Gunther Kress and Theo van Leeuwen identify three key spatial dimensions in visual texts: left/right, top/bottom and centre/margin (Kress and van Leeuwen 1996 and 1998).

The horizontal and vertical axes are not neutral dimensions of pictorial representation. Since writing and reading in European cultures proceed primarily along a horizontal axis from left to right (as in English but unlike, for instance, Arabic, Hebrew and Chinese), the 'default' for reading a picture within such reading/writing cultures (unless attention is diverted by some salient features) is likely to be generally in the same direction. This is especially likely where pictures are embedded in written text, as in the case of magazines and newspapers. There is thus a potential sequential significance in the left-hand and right-hand elements of a visual image – a sense of 'before' and 'after'. Kress and van Leeuwen relate the left-hand and right-hand elements to the linguistic concept of 'the Given' and 'the New'. They argue that on those occasions when pictures make significant use of the horizontal axis, positioning some elements left of centre and others right of centre, then the left-hand side is 'the side of the "already given", something the reader is assumed to know already', a familiar, well-established and agreed-upon point

87

of departure – something which is commonsensical, assumed and self-evident, while the right-hand side is the side of the New. 'For something to be New means that it is presented as something which is not yet known, or perhaps not yet agreed upon by the viewer, hence as something to which the viewer must pay special attention' – something more surprising, problematic or contestable (Kress and van Leeuwen 1996, 186–92; 1998, 189–93).

The vertical compositional axis also carries connotations. Arguing for the fundamental significance of orientational metaphors in framing experience, Lakoff and Johnson observe that (in English usage) *up* has come to be associated with *more* and *down* with *less*. They outline further associations:

- *up* is associated with goodness, virtue, happiness, con-sciousness, health, life, the future, high status, having control or power, and with rationality, while
- *down* is associated with badness, depravity, sickness, death, low status, being subject to control or power, and with emotion.

(Lakoff and Johnson 1980, Chapter 4)

For one signifier to be located 'higher' than another is consequently not simply a spatial relationship but also an evaluative one in relation to the signifieds for which they stand. Erving Goffman's slim volume *Gender Advertisements* (1979) concerned the depictions of male and female figures in magazine advertisements. Although it was unsystematic and only some of his observations have been supported in subsequent empirical studies, it is widely celebrated as a classic of visual sociology. Probably the most relevant of his observations in the context of these notes was that 'men tend to be located higher than women' in these ads, symbolically reflecting the routine subordination of women to men in society (Goffman 1979, 43). Offering their own speculative mapping of the connotations of top and bottom, Kress and van Leeuwen argue that, where an image is structured along a vertical axis, the upper and lower sections represent an opposition between 'the Ideal' and 'the Real' respectively. They suggest that the lower section in pictorial layouts tends to be more 'down-to-earth', concerned with practical or factual details, while the upper part tends to be concerned with abstract or generalized possibilities (a polarization between respectively 'particular/general', 'local/global' etc.). In many Western printed advertisements, for instance, 'the upper section tends to ... show us "what might be"; the lower section tends to be more informative and practical, showing us "what is"' (Kress and van Leeuwen 1996, 193–201; 1998, 193–5).

The third key spatial dimension discussed by Kress and van Leeuwen is that of centre and margin. The composition of some visual images is based primarily not on a left-right or top-bottom structure but on a dominant centre and a periphery. 'For something to be presented as Centre means that it is presented as the nucleus of the information on which all the other elements are in some sense subservient. The Margins are these ancillary, dependent elements' (Kress and van Leeuwen 1996, 206; 1998, 196–8). This is related to the fundamental perceptual distinction between *figure* and *ground*. Selective perception involves 'foregrounding' some features and 'backgrounding' others. We owe the concept of 'figure' and 'ground' in perception to the Gestalt psychologists. Confronted by a visual image, we seem to need to separate a dominant shape (a 'figure' with a definite contour) from what our current concerns relegate to 'background' (or 'ground'). In visual images, the figure tends to be located centrally.

Sequential relations

Turning from spatial to sequential syntagms, brings us to *narrative* (which, as noted, may even underlie left/right spatial structures). Some critics claim that differences between narratives and non-narratives relate to differences among media, instancing individual drawings, paintings and photographs as non-narrative forms; others claim that narrative is a 'deep structure' independent of the medium (Stern 1998, 5). Narrative theory (or narratology) is a major interdisciplinary field in its own right, and is not necessarily framed within a semiotic perspective, although the analysis of narrative is an important branch of semiotics. Semiotic narratology is concerned with narrative in any mode – literary or non-literary, fictional or non-fictional, verbal or visual – but tends to focus on minimal narrative units and the 'grammar of the plot' (some theorists refer to 'story grammars'). It follows in the tradition of the Russian formalist Vladimir Propp and the French anthropologist Claude Lévi-Strauss.

Christian Metz observed that 'a narrative has a beginning and an ending, a fact that simultaneously distinguishes it from the rest of the world' (Metz 1974, 17). There are no 'events' in the world. Reality cannot be reduced objectively to discrete temporal units; what counts as an 'event' is determined by one's purposes. It is narrative form which creates events. Perhaps the most basic narrative syntagm is a linear temporal model composed of three phases – *equilibrium–disruption–equilibrium* – a 'chain' of events corresponding to the beginning, middle and end of a story (or, as Philip Larkin put it, describing the formula of the classic novel: 'a beginning, a *muddle* and an end'; my emphasis). In the orderly Aristotelian narrative form, *causation* and *goals* turn *story* (chronological events) into *plot*: events at the beginning cause those in the middle, and events in the middle cause those at the end. This is the basic formula for classic Hollywood movies in which the storyline is given priority over everything else. The film-maker Jean-Luc Godard declared that he liked a film to have a beginning, a middle and an end, but not necessarily in that order; in 'classical' (realist) narrative, events are always in that order, providing continuity and closure. Roland Barthes argued that narrative is basically translatable – 'international, transhistorical, transcultural' (Barthes 1977, 79). It can be transposed from one medium to another (for instance, from novel to film or radio and vice versa). Some theorists argue that the translatability of narrative makes it unlike other codes and such commentators grant narrative the privileged status of a 'metacode'.

Narratives help to make the strange familiar. They provide structure, predictability and coherence. In this respect they are similar to schemas for familiar events in everyday life. Turning experience into narratives seems to be a fundamental feature of the human drive to make meaning. We are 'storytellers' with 'a readiness or predisposition to organize experience into a narrative form' which is encouraged in our socialization as we learn to adopt our culture's ways of telling (Bruner 1990, 45, 80).

Narrative coherence is no guarantee of referential correspondence. The narrative form itself has a content of its own; the medium has a message. Narrative is such an automatic choice for representing events that it seems unproblematic and 'natural'. Robert Hodge and Gunther Kress argue that the use of a familiar narrative structure serves 'to naturalize the content of the narrative itself' (Hodge and Kress 1988, 230). Where narratives end in a return to predictable equilibrium this is referred to as narrative *closure*. Closure is often effected as the resolution of an opposition. Structural closure is regarded by many theorists as reinforcing a preferred reading, or in Hodge and Kress's terms, reinforcing the status quo. According to theorists applying the principles of Jacques Lacan, conventional narrative (in dominant forms of literature, cinema and so on) also plays a part in the constitution of the subject. While narrative appears to demonstrate unity and coherence within the text, the subject participates in the sense of closure (in part through identification with characters). 'The coherence of narrative reciprocally reinscribes the coherence of the subject', returning the subject to the pre-linguistic realm of the Imaginary where the self had greater fixity and less fluidity than in the Symbolic realm of verbal language (Nichols 1981, 78).

The writing style of professional historians has traditionally involved a variant of the nineteenth-century 'realist' novelist's omniscient narrator and fluent narrative. Historians have only fragmentary 'sources', but this style is characterized by fluent narrative, telling an apparently complete story, leaving no sign of gaps in the evidence. Narrative may imply continuity where there is none. Foucault's poststructuralist history of ideas is radical in insisting instead on 'ruptures', 'discontinuities' and 'disjunctions' (Foucault 1970). Reflecting on his explorations of historiography in his book entitled *The Content of the Form*, Hayden White observes that 'narrative is not merely a neutral discursive form . . . but rather entails ontological and epistemic choices with distinct ideological and even specifically political implications' (White 1987, ix). He adds that 'real life can never be truthfully represented as having the kind of formal coherency met with in the conventional, well-made or fabulistic story' (ibid.).

Structural reduction

The structuralist semiotician's inductive search for underlying structural patterns highlights the similarities between what may initially seem to be very different narratives. As Barthes notes, for the structuralist analyst 'the first task is to divide up narrative and ... define the smallest narrative units ... Meaning must be the criterion of the unit: it is the functional nature of certain segments of the story that makes them units – hence the name "functions" immediately attributed to these first units' (Barthes 1977, 88).

In a highly influential book, *The Morphology of the Folktale* (1928), the Russian narrative theorist Vladimir Propp (1895–1970) reported that a hundred fairy tales which he had analysed were all based on the same basic formula. He reduced them to around thirty 'functions'. 'Function is understood as an act of character defined from the point of view of its significance for the course of the action' (Propp 1928, 21). In other words, such functions are basic units of action. As Barthes notes, structuralists avoid defining human agents in terms of 'psychological essences', and participants are defined by analysts not in terms of 'what they are' as 'characters' but in terms of 'what they do' (Barthes 1977, 106). Propp listed seven *roles*: the *villain*, the *donor*, the *helper*, the *sought-for person (and her father)*, the *dispatcher*, the *hero* and the *false hero* and schematized the various 'functions' within the story (see Table 3.2).

This form of analysis downplays the specificity of individual texts in the interests of establishing *how* texts mean rather than *what* a particular text means. It is by definition, a 'reductive' strategy, and some literary theorists fear that it threatens to make Shakespeare indistinguishable from *Star Wars*. Even Barthes noted that 'the first analysts of narrative were attempting ... to see all the world's stories ... within a single structure' and that this was a task which was 'ultimately undesirable, for the text thereby loses its difference' (Barthes 1974, 3). Difference is, after all, what identifies both the sign and the text. Despite this objection, Fredric

Jameson suggests that the method has redeeming features. For instance, the notion of a grammar of plots allows us to see 'the work of a generation or a period in terms of a given model (or basic plot paradigm), which is then varied and articulated in as many ways possible until it is somehow exhausted and replaced by a new one' (Jameson 1972, 124).

Unlike Propp, both Lévi-Strauss and Greimas based their interpretations of narrative structure on underlying oppositions. Lévi-Strauss saw the myths of a culture as variations on a limited number of basic themes built upon oppositions related to nature versus culture. Any myth could be reduced to a fundamental structure. He wrote that 'a compilation of known tales and myths would fill an imposing number of volumes. But they can be reduced to a small number of simple types if we abstract from among the diversity of characters a few elementary functions' (Lévi-Strauss 1972, 203–4). Myths help people to make sense of the world in which they live. Lévi-Strauss saw myths as a kind of a message from our ancestors about humankind and our relationship to nature, in particular, how we became separated from other animals. However, the meaning was not to be found in any individual narrative but in the patterns underlying the myths of a given culture. Myths make sense only as part of a system. Lévi-Strauss treated the form of myths as a kind of language. He reported that his initial method of analysing the structure of myths into 'gross constituent units' or 'mythemes' involved 'breaking down its story into the shortest possible sentences' (Lévi-Strauss 1972, 211). This approach was based on an analogy with the 'morpheme', which is the smallest meaningful unit in linguistics. In order to explain the structure of a myth, Lévi-Strauss classified each mytheme in terms of its 'function' within the myth and finally related the various kinds of function to each other. He saw the possible combinations of mythemes as being governed by a kind of underlying universal grammar which was part of the deep structure of the mind itself.

A good example of the Lévi-Straussean method is provided by Victor Larrucia in his own analysis of the story of Little Red Riding-Hood (originating in the late seventeenth century in a tale by Perrault) (Larrucia 1975). According to this method the narrative is

TABLE 3.2 Propp's list of functions

	Function	Role
0	**Initial situation**	Members of the family of the hero are introduced.
1	**Absentation**	A family member absents himself from home.
2	**Interdiction**	An interdiction is addressed to the hero.
3	**Violation**	The interdiction is violated.
4	**Reconnaissance**	The villain makes an attempt at reconnaissance.
5	**Delivery**	The villain receives information about his victim.
6	**Trickery**	The villain attempts to deceive the victim.
7	**Complicity**	The victim is deceived.
8	**Villainy**	The villain causes harm or injury to family.
8a	**Lack**	A family member lacks or wants something.
9	**Mediation**	Misfortune or lack is made known. The hero is dispatched.
10	**Counteraction**	The seeker decides upon counter-action.
11	**Departure**	The hero leaves home.
12	**First function of donor**	The hero is tested.
13	**Hero's reaction**	The hero reacts to the actions of the future donor.
14	**Receipt of magic agent**	The hero acquires the use of a magical agent.
15	**Spatial transference**	The hero is led to the object of search.
16	**Struggle**	The hero and villain join in direct combat.
17	**Branding**	The hero is branded.
18	**Victory**	The villain is defeated.
19	**Liquidation**	The initial misfortune or lack is liquidated.
20	**Return**	The hero returns.
21	**Pursuit**	The hero is pursued.

TABLE 3.2 *(continued)*

Function	Role
22 Rescue	Rescue of the hero from pursuit.
23 Unrecognized	The hero, unrecognized, arrives home or in another country.
24 Unfounded claims	A false hero presents unfounded claims.
25 Difficult task	A difficult task is proposed to the hero.
26 Solution	The task is resolved.
27 Recognition	The hero is recognized.
28 Exposure	The false hero or villain is exposed.
29 Transfiguration	The hero is given a new appearance.
30 Punishment	The villain is punished.
31 Wedding	The hero is married and ascends the throne.

Source: Based on Propp 1968, 26–65

summarized in several columns, each corresponding to some unifying function or theme (see Figure 3.2). The original sequence (indicated by numbers) is preserved when the table is read row by row.

Rather than offering any commentators' suggestions as to what themes these columns represent, I will avoid authorial closure and leave it to readers to speculate for themselves. Suggestions can be found in the references (Larrucia 1975; Silverman and Torode 1980, 314ff.).

The structuralist semiotician Algirdas Greimas (who established 'the Paris school' of semiotics) proposed a grammar of narrative which could generate any known narrative structure (Greimas 1983 and 1987). As a result of a 'semiotic reduction' of Propp's seven roles he identified three types of narrative syntagms: *syntagms performanciels* – tasks and struggles; *syntagms contractuels* – the establishment or breaking of contracts; *syntagms disjonctionnels* – departures and arrivals (Greimas 1987; Culler 1975, 213; Hawkes 1977, 94). Greimas claimed that three basic binary oppositions underlie all narrative themes, actions and character types (which he

1 Grandmother s illness causes mother to make grandmother food	2 Little Red Riding Hood (LRRH) obeys mother and goes off to wood	3 LRRH meets (wolf as) friend and talks	
4 Woodcutter s presence causes wolf to speak to LRRH	5 LRRH obeys wolf and takes long road to grandmother s	6 Grandmother admits (wolf as) LRRH	7 Wolf eats grandmother
		8 LRRH meets (wolf as) grandmother	
	9 LRRH obeys grandmother and gets into bed	10 LRRH questions (wolf as) grandmother	11 Wolf eats LRRH

FIGURE 3.2   Little Red Riding Hood

Source: Larrucia 1975, 528

collectively calls 'actants'), namely: *subject–object* (Propp's *hero* and *sought-for person*), *sender–receiver* (Propp's *dispatcher* and *hero* – again) and *helper–opponent* (conflations of Propp's *helper* and *donor*, plus the *villain* and the *false hero*) – note that Greimas argues that the hero is both *subject* and *receiver*. The *subject* is the one who seeks; the *object* is that which is sought. The *sender* sends the object and the *receiver* is its destination. The *helper* assists the action and the *opponent* blocks it. He extrapolates from the *subject–verb–object* sentence structure, proposing a fundamental, underlying 'actantial model' as the basis of story structures. He argues that in traditional syntax, 'functions' are the roles played by words – the *subject* being the one performing the action and the *object* being 'the one who suffers it' (Jameson 1972, 124). For Greimas, stories thus share a common 'grammar'. However, critics such as Jonathan Culler have not always been convinced of the validity of Greimas's methodology or of the workability or usefulness of his model (Culler 1975, 213–14, 223–4).

Syntagmatic analysis can be applied not only to verbal texts but also to audio-visual ones. In film and television, a syntagmatic analysis would involve an analysis of how each *frame*, *shot*, *scene* or *sequence* related to the others (these are the standard levels of analysis in film theory). At the lowest level is the individual *frame*. Since films are projected at a rate of twenty-four frames per second, the viewer is never conscious of individual frames, but significant frames can be isolated by the analyst. At the next level up, a *shot* is a 'single take' – an unedited sequence of frames which may include camera movement. A shot is terminated by a cut (or other transition). A *scene* consists of more than one shot set in a single place and time. A *sequence* spans more than one place and or/time but it is a logical or thematic sequence (having 'dramatic unity'). The linguistic model often leads semioticians to a search for units of analysis in audio-visual media which are analogous to those used in linguistics. In the semiotics of film, crude equivalents with written language are sometimes postulated: such as the frame as morpheme (or word), the shot as sentence, the scene as paragraph, and the sequence as chapter (suggested equivalences vary among commentators). For members of the Glasgow University Media Group the basic unit of analysis was the shot, delimited by cuts and with allowance made for camera movement within the shot and for the accompanying soundtrack (Davis and Walton 1983b, 43). Shots can be broken into smaller meaningful units (above the level of the frame), but theorists disagree about what these might be. Above the level of the sequence, other narrative units can also be posited.

Christian Metz offered elaborate syntagmatic categories for narrative film (Metz 1974, Chapter 5). For Metz, these syntagms were analogous to sentences in verbal language, and he argued that there were eight key filmic syntagms which were based on ways of ordering narrative space and time.

- the *autonomous shot* (e.g. establishing shot, insert);
- the *parallel syntagm* (montage of motifs);
- the *bracketing syntagm* (montage of brief shots);

- the *descriptive syntagm* (sequence describing one moment);
- the *alternating syntagm* (two sequences alternating);
- the *scene* (shots implying temporal continuity);
- the *episodic sequence* (organized discontinuity of shots);
- the *ordinary sequence* (temporal with some compression).

However, Metz's '*grande syntagmatique*' has not proved an easy system to apply to some films. In their study of children's understanding of television, Hodge and Tripp (1986, 20) divide syntagms into four kinds, based on syntagms existing in the same time *(synchronic)*, different times (*diachronic*), same space (*syntopic*), and different space *(diatopic)*.

- *synchronic/synoptic* (one place, one time: one shot);
- *diachronic/synoptic* (same place sequence over time);
- *synchronic/diatopic* (different places at same time);
- *diachronic/diatopic* (shots related only by theme).

They add that, while these are all *continuous syntagms* (single shots or successive shots), there are also *discontinuous syntagms* (related shots separated by others).

Beyond the fourfold distinction between frames, shots, scenes and sequences, the interpretative frameworks of film theorists differ considerably. In this sense at least, there is no cinematic 'language'.

The paradigmatic dimension

Whereas syntagmatic analysis studies the 'surface structure' of a text, *paradigmatic analysis* seeks to identify the various paradigms (or pre-existing sets of signifiers) which underlie the manifest content of texts. This aspect of structural analysis involves a consideration of the positive or negative connotations of each signifier (revealed through the use of one signifier rather than another), and the existence of 'underlying' thematic paradigms (e.g. binary oppositions such as *public–private*).

Semioticians often focus on the issue of why a particular signifier rather than a workable alternative was used in a specific context: on what they often refer to as 'absences'. Saussure noted that a characteristic of what he called 'associative' relations – what would now be called paradigmatic relations – was that (in contrast to syntagmatic relations) such relations held '*in absentia*' – in the absence from a specific text of alternative signifiers from the same paradigm (Saussure 1983, 122). He also argued that signs take their value within the linguistic system from what they are *not* (ibid., 115). We have popular sayings in English concerning two kinds of absences: we refer to 'what goes without saying' and 'what is conspicuous by its absence'. What 'goes without saying' reflects what it is assumed that you 'take for granted' as 'obvious'. In relation to the coverage of an issue (such as in 'factual' genres) this is a profoundly ideological absence which helps to 'position' the text's readers, the implication being that 'people like us already agree what we think about issues like that'. As for the second kind of absence, an item which is present in the text may flout conventional expectations, making the conventional item 'conspicuous by its absence' and the unexpected item 'a statement'. This applies no less to cultural practices. If a man wears a suit at his office it says very little other than that he is conforming to a norm. But if one day he arrives in jeans and a tee-shirt, this will be interpreted as 'making a statement'.

Paradigmatic analysis involves comparing and contrasting each of the signifiers present in the text with absent signifiers which in similar circumstances might have been chosen, and considering the significance of the choices made. It can be applied at any semiotic level, from the choice of a particular word, image or sound to the level of the choice of style, genre or medium. Figure 3.3 shows a basic paradigm set for *shot size* in photography and film. The use of one signifier rather than another from the same paradigm is based on factors such as technical constraints, code (e.g. genre), convention, connotation, style, rhetorical purpose and the limitations of the individual's own repertoire. The analysis of paradigmatic relations helps to define the 'value' of specific items in a text.

The commutation test

Structuralist semioticians refer to the 'commutation test' which can be used in order to identify distinctive signifiers and to define their

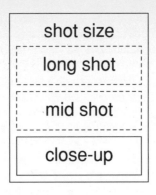

FIGURE 3.3 Paradigm set for shot size

significance – determining whether a change on the level of the signifier leads to a change on the level of the signified. Its origins lie in a linguistic test of substitution applied by the Prague school structuralists (including Roman Jakobson). In order to identity within a language its phonemes and their 'distinctive features', linguists experimented with changes in the phonetic structure of a word in order to see at what point it became a different word. The original commutation test has evolved into a rather more subjective form of textual analysis. Roland Barthes refers to using the commutation test to divide texts into minimal significant units, before grouping these units into paradigmatic classes (Barthes 1967, 48). To apply this test, a particular signifier in a text is selected. Then alternatives to this signifier are considered. The effects of each substitution are evaluated in terms of how this might affect the sense made of the sign. This might involve imagining the use of a close-up rather than a mid-shot, a substitution in age, sex, class or ethnicity, substituting objects, a different caption for a photograph, etc. It could also involve swapping over two of the existing signifiers, changing their original relationship. The influence of the substitution on the meaning can help to suggest the contribution of the original signifier and also to identify syntagmatic units (Barthes 1967, III 2.3; 1985, 19–20). The commutation test can identify the sets (paradigms) and codes to which the signifiers used belong. For instance, if changing the setting used in an advertisement contributes to changing the meaning then 'setting' is one of the paradigms; the paradigm set for the setting would consist of all of those alternative signifiers which could have been used and which would have shifted the meaning.

The commutation test may involve any of four basic transformations, some of which involve the modification of the syntagm. However, the consideration of an alternative syntagm can itself be seen as a paradigmatic substitution.

Paradigmatic transformations
- substitution;
- transposition;

Syntagmatic transformations
- addition;
- deletion.

These four basic tranformational processes were noted as features of perception and recall (Allport and Postman 1945; Newcomb 1952: 88–96). They correspond exactly to the four general categories to which Quintilian (circa 35–100 AD) assigned the rhetorical figures (or tropes) as 'deviations' from 'literal' language (Nöth 1990, 341).

Oppositions

Structuralists emphasize the importance of relations of paradigmatic opposition. Largely through the influence of Jakobson, the primary analytical method employed by many structuralist semioticians involves the identification of binary or polar semantic oppositions (e.g. *us–them*, *public–private*) in texts or signifying practices. Such a quest is based on a form of 'dualism'. Dualism seems to be deeply rooted in the development of human categorization. Jakobson and Halle observe that 'the binary opposition is a child's first logical operation' (Jakobson and Halle 1956, 60). While there are no opposites in 'nature', the binary oppositions which we employ in our cultural practices help to generate order out of the dynamic complexity of experience. At the most basic level of individual survival humans share with other animals the need to distinguish between our own species and others, dominance and submission, sexual availability or non-availability, the edible and the inedible (Leach 1970, 39). The range of human distinctions is far more extensive than those which they share with other animals since it is supported by the elaborate system of categorization which language facilitates. The British anthropologist Sir Edmund Leach reflects that 'a speechless ape presumably has some sort of feelings for the opposition "I"/"Other", perhaps even for its expanded version "We"/"They", but the still more grandiose "Natural"/"Supernatural" ("Man"/"God") could only occur within a linguistic frame . . . The recognition of a distinction Natural/Supernatural (Real/Imaginary) is a basic marker of humanity' (Leach 1982, 108–9).

People have believed in the fundamental character of binary oppositions since at least classical times. For instance, in his *Metaphysics*, Aristotle advanced as primary oppositions: *form–matter*, *natural–unnatural*, *active–passive*, *whole–part*, *unity–variety*, *before –after* and *being–not-being*. But it is not in isolation that the rhetorical power of such oppositions resides, but in their articulation in relation to other oppositions. In Aristotle's *Physics* the four elements of *earth*, *air*, *fire* and *water* were said to be opposed in pairs. For more than two thousand years oppositional patterns based on these four elements were widely accepted as the fundamental structure underlying surface reality (see Table 3.3). The elements of such frameworks appeared in various combinations, their shifting forms driven in part by the tensions inherent within such schemes. The theory of the elements continued to enjoy widespread influence until the time of scientists such as Robert Boyle (1627–91).

The language of opposition

Lyons comments that 'binary opposition is one of the most important principles governing the structure of languages' (Lyons 1977, 271). Saussure, of course, emphasized the *differences* between signs rather than their similarities. Opposites (or antonyms) clearly have a very practical function compared with synonyms: that of *sorting*. Roman Jakobson proposed that linguistic units are bound together

TABLE 3.3 Alignments with the four elements

Element	Quality	Humour	Body fluid	Organ	Season	Cardinal point	Zodiac signs	Planet
air	hot and moist	sanguine (active and enthusiastic)	blood	heart	spring	South	Gemini, Libra, Aquarius	Jupiter
fire	hot and dry	choleric (irritable and changeable)	yellow bile	liver	summer	East	Aries, Leo, Sagittarius	Mars
earth	cold and dry	melancholic (sad and brooding)	black bile	spleen	autumn	North	Taurus, Virgo, Capricorn	Saturn
water	cold and moist	phlegmatic (apathetic and sluggish)	phlegm	brain	winter	West	Cancer, Scorpio, Pisces	Venus

by a system of binary oppositions. Such oppositions are essential to the generation of meaning: the meaning of 'dark' is relative to the meaning of 'light'; 'form' is inconceivable except in relation to 'content'. It is an open question whether our tendency to think in opposites is determined by the prominence of oppositions in language or whether language merely reflects a universal human characteristic.

The various conventionally linked terms with which we are familiar within a culture might more appropriately be described as paired 'contrasts', since they are not always direct 'opposites' (although their use often involves polarization). Distinctions can be made between various types of 'oppositions', perhaps the most important being the following:

- *oppositions* (logical 'contradictories'): mutually exclusive terms (e.g. *alive–dead*, where 'not alive' can only be 'dead');
- *antonyms* (logical 'contraries'): terms which are comparatively graded on the same implicit dimension (e.g. *good–bad*, where 'not good' is not necessarily 'bad').

(Lyons 1977, 270ff.; Langholz Leymore 1975, 7; Barthes 1985, 162ff.)

This is basically a distinction between *digital* and *analogue* oppositions: digital differences are *either/or*; analogue distinctions are '*more-or-less*'. Analogue oppositions clearly allow for intermediate positions. Even the apparently categorical 'black' and 'white' can of course be reconfigured as shades of grey.

Us and them

It is a feature of culture that binary oppositions come to seem 'natural' to members of a culture. Many pairings of concepts (such as *male–female* and *mind–body*) are familiar within a culture and may seem commonsensical distinctions for everyday communicational purposes even if they may be regarded as 'false dichotomies' in critical contexts. Rudyard Kipling satirized the apparently universal tendency to divide the people we know directly or indirectly into 'us' and 'them':

All nice people, like us, are We
And everyone else is They:
But if you cross over the sea,
Instead of over the way,
You may end by (think of it!)
Looking on We
As only a sort of They!
('We and They', Kipling
1977, 289–90)

The opposition of *self–other* (or *subject–object*) is psychologically fundamental. The mind imposes some degree of constancy on the dynamic flux of experience by defining 'the self' in relation to 'the other'. The neo-Freudian psychoanalyst Jacques Lacan argued that initially, in the primal realm of 'the real' (where there is no absence, loss or lack), the infant has no centre of identity and experiences no clear boundaries between itself and the external world. The child emerges from the real and enters 'the Imaginary' at the age of about 6 to 18 months, before the acquisition of speech. This is a private psychic realm in which the construction of the self as subject is initiated. In the realm of visual images, we find our sense of self reflected back by an other with whom we identify. Lacan describes a defining moment in the imaginary which he calls 'the mirror phase', when seeing one's mirror image (and being told by one's mother, 'That's *you*!') induces a strongly defined illusion of a coherent and self-governing personal identity. This marks the child's emergence from a matriarchal state of 'nature' into the patriarchal order of culture. As the child gains mastery within the pre-existing 'symbolic order' (the public domain of verbal language), language (which can be mentally manipulated) helps to foster the individual's sense of a conscious self residing in an 'internal world' which is distinct from 'the world outside'. However, a degree of individuality and autonomy is surrendered to the constraints of linguistic conventions, and the self becomes a more fluid and ambiguous relational signifier rather than a relatively fixed entity. Subjectivity is dynamically constructed through discourse.

105

Alignment

Paired signifiers are seen by structuralist theorists as part of the 'deep [or 'hidden'] structure' of texts, shaping the preferred reading. Such linkages seem to become *aligned* in some texts and codes so that additional 'vertical' relationships (such as *male–mind*, *female–body*) acquire apparent links of their own – as feminists and queer theorists have noted (Silverman 1983, 36; Grosz 1993, 195; Butler 1999, 17). As Kaja Silverman observes, 'a cultural code is a conceptual system which is organized around key oppositions and equations, in which a term like "woman" is defined in opposition to a term like "man", and in which each term is aligned with a cluster of symbolic attributes' (Silverman 1983, 36).

This notion can be traced to Claude Lévi-Strauss's discussion of analogical relationships which generate systems of meaning within cultures. Lévi-Strauss saw certain key binary oppositions as the invariants or universals of the human mind, cutting across cultural distinctions (Lévi-Strauss 1972, 21). His synchronic studies of cultural practices identified underlying semantic oppositions in relation to such phenomena as myths, totemism and kinship rules. Individual myths and cultural practices defy interpretation, making sense only as a part of a system of differences and oppositions expressing fundamental reflections on the relationship of nature and culture. He argued that binary oppositions form the basis of underlying 'classificatory systems', while myths represented a dreamlike working-over of a fundamental dilemma or contradiction within a culture, expressed in the form of paired opposites. Apparently fundamental oppositions such as *male–female* and *left–right* become transformed into 'the prototype symbols of the good and the bad, the permitted and the forbidden' (Leach 1970, 44).

Lévi-Strauss argued that within a culture 'analogical thought' leads to some oppositions (such as *edible–inedible*) being perceived as metaphorically resembling the 'similar differences' of other oppositions (such as *native–foreign*) (Lévi-Strauss 1974). The classification systems of a culture are a way of encoding differences within society by analogy with perceived differences in the natural world (somewhat as in Aesop's *Fables*) (ibid., 90–1, cf. 75–6, 96–7).

They transform what are perceived as natural categories into cultural categories and serve to naturalize cultural practices. 'The mythical system and the modes of representation it employs serve to establish homologies between natural and social conditions or, more accurately, it makes it possible to equate significant contrasts found in different planes: the geographical, meteorological, zoological, botanical, technical, economic, social, ritual, religious and philosophical' (ibid., 93). The aggregation of fourfold distinctions associated with the 'four elements' are of this kind. The alignments which develop within such systems are not without contradictions, and Lévi-Strauss argued that the contradictions within them generate explanatory myths – such codes must 'make sense' (ibid., 228).

Although Lévi-Strauss's analytical approach remains formally synchronic, involving no study of the historical dimension, he does incorporate the possibility of change: oppositions are not fixed and structures are transformable. He notes that we need not regard such frameworks from a purely synchronic perspective. 'Starting from a binary opposition, which affords the simplest possible example of a system, this construction proceeds by the aggregation, at each of the two poles, of new terms, chosen because they stand in relations of opposition, correlation, or analogy to it'. In this way, structures may undergo transformation (Lévi-Strauss 1974,161).

Aesthetic 'movements' can also be interpreted in terms of paradigms of characteristic oppositions. Each movement can be loosely identified in terms of a primary focus of interest: for instance, *realism* tends to be primarily oriented towards the *world*, *neoclassicism* towards the *text* and *romanticism* towards the *author* (which is not to suggest, of course, that such goals have not been shared by *other* movements). Such broad goals generate and reflect associated values. Within a particular movement, various oppositions constitute a palette of possibilities for critical theorists within the movement. For instance, the codes of *romanticism* are built upon various implicit or explicit articulations of such oppositions as: *expressive–instrumental, feeling–thought, emotion–reason, spontaneity–deliberation, passion–calculation, inspiration–effort, genius–method, intensity–reflection, intuition–judgement, impulse– intention, unconsciousness–design, creativity–construction, originality–conventionality, creation–imitation, imagination–learn-ing, dynamism–order, sincerity–facticity, natural–artificial* and *organic–mechanical*. The alignment of some of these pairs generates further associations: for instance, an alignment of *spontaneity–deliberation* with *sincerity–facticity* equates spontaneity with sincer-ity. More indirectly, it may also associate their opposites, so that deliberation reflects insincerity or untruthfulness. Romantic literary theorists often proclaimed spontaneity in expressive writing to be a mark of sincerity, of truth to feeling – even when this ran counter to their own compositional practices (Chandler 1995, 49ff.). Even within 'the same' aesthetic movement, various theorists construct their own frameworks, as is illustrated in Abrams's study of roman-tic literary theory (Abrams 1971). Each opposition (or combination of oppositions) involves an implicit contrast with the priorities and values of another aesthetic movement: thus (in accord with the Saussurean principle of negative differentiation) an aesthetic move-ment is defined by what it is *not*. The evolution of aesthetic movements can be seen as the working-out of tensions between such oppositions. Similarly, within textual analysis, it has been argued that the structure of particular texts (or myths) works to position the reader to privilege one set of values and meanings over the other. Sometimes such oppositions may appear to be resolved in favour of dominant ideologies but poststructuralists argue that tensions between them *always* remain unresolved.

Paradigmatic analysis has also been applied to popular culture. For instance, exploring a basic opposition of *wilderness–civilization*, Jim Kitses analysed the film genre of the *western* in relation to a series of oppositions: *individual–community*; *nature–culture*; *law–gun; sheep/cattle* (Kitses 1970). The cultural theorist John Fiske makes considerable analytical use of such oppositions in relation to mass media texts (Fiske 1987). Binary oppositions can be traced even in company logos. Jean-Marie Floch, a French semiotician, compares and contrasts the logos of the two major computer compa-nies, IBM and Apple, revealing their differences to be based on a series of associated binary oppositions, the most obvious of which are listed in Table 3.4 (Floch 2000, 41). The Apple logo, of course, shows a simplified side-on view of an apple with a semi-circular

TABLE 3.4   Contrasting Apple and IBM logos

	Apple	*IBM*
Structure	non repetition joined lines	repetition disconnected lines
Colour	polychromatic warm	monochromatic cold
Forms	outline curved	substance ('bold') straight

Source: Based on Floch 2000

section removed from the right-hand edge. The apple is only green at the top (including the leaf), with horizontal bands of other colours below it (yellow, orange, red, violet and blue). The IBM logo consists of the letters 'IBM' in a bold serif font, regular stripes of the background colour showing through the letters (the colours vary but typically feature blue). The tonal relationship between the letters and the background may be light on dark or the reverse. The contrast could hardly involve a clearer opposition. Appropriately, Apple's logo seems to be defined purely in opposition to the more established/establishment image of IBM.

A past chairman of the Apple Products division is quoted as saying, 'Our logo is a great mystery: it is a symbol of pleasure and knowledge, partially eaten away and displaying the colours of the rainbow, but not in the proper order. We couldn't wish for a more fitting logo: pleasure, knowledge, hope and anarchy' (Floch 2000, 54). Clearly, the bitten apple refers both to the story of the Tree of Knowledge in the Garden of Eden and to the association of IBM with the east coast and 'the Big Apple' of New York. The psyche-delic mixed-up rainbow signifies the West Coast hippie era of the 1960s, with its associations of idealism and 'doing your own thing'. Thus, despite representing a binary opposition to the IBM logo, the multicoloured Apple logo seeks to signify a rejection of the binarism reflected in the 'black-and-white' (or rather monochrome) linearity of IBM's logo. Competing companies clearly need to establish distinct identities, and such identities are typically reflected in their logos. This example may tempt the reader to compare the visual identities of other competing corporations.

Markedness

Oppositions are rarely equally weighted. The Russian linguist and semiotician Roman Jakobson introduced the theory of *markedness*: 'Every single constituent of any linguistic system is built on an opposition of two logical contradictories: the presence of an attribute ("markedness") in contraposition to its absence ("unmarkedness")' (cited in Lechte 1994, 62). The concept of markedness can be applied to the poles of a paradigmatic opposition: paired signs consist of an 'unmarked' and a 'marked' form. This applies, as we shall see, both at the level of the signifier and at the level of the signified. The 'marked' signifier is distinguished by some special semiotic feature. In relation to linguistic signifiers, two characteristic features of marked forms are commonly identified: these relate to formal features and generic function. The more 'complex' form is marked, which typically involves both of the following features:

- **Formal marking**: in morphologically related oppositions, marking is based on the presence or absence of some particular formal feature. The marked signifier is formed by adding a distinctive feature to the unmarked signifier (for instance, the marked form 'unhappy' is formed by adding the prefix *un-* to the unmarked signifier 'happy') (Greenberg 1966; Clark and Clark, 1977; Lyons 1977, 305ff.).
- **Distributional marking**: formally marked terms show a tendency to be more restricted in the range of contexts in which they occur (Lyons 1977, 306–7).

In English, linguistically *unmarked* forms include the *present tense* of verbs and the *singular* form of nouns (Jakobson's 'zero-sign'). The *active voice* is normally unmarked, although in the restricted genre of traditional academic writing the *passive voice* is still often the unmarked form.

The markedness of linguistic signs includes *semantic* marking: a marked or unmarked status applies not only to *signifiers* but also to *signifieds*. With morphologically related pairings, there is an obvious relation between formal and semantic marking, and John Lyons suggests that distributional marking in oppositions is probably determined by semantic marking (Lyons 1977, 307). One form of semantic marking relates to *specificity*. The unmarked term is often used as a generic term while the marked term is used in a more specific sense. General references to humanity used to use the term 'man' (which in this sense was not intended to be sex specific), and of course the word 'he' has long been used generically. In English, the female category is generally marked in relation to the male, a point not lost on feminist theorists (Clark and Clark 1977, 524).

Where terms are paired, the pairing is rarely symmetrical but rather *hierarchical*. With apologies to George Orwell we might coin the phrase that 'all signifieds are equal, but some are more equal than others'. With many of the familiarly paired terms, the two signifieds are accorded different values. The unmarked term is primary, being given precedence and priority, while the marked term is treated as secondary or even suppressed as an 'absent signifier'. While linguistic markedness may not of itself imply negativity (e.g. the unmarked term *cow* versus the marked term *bull*), morphological markers (such as *un-* or *-in*) can generate negative connotations. When morphological cues are lacking, the 'preferred sequence' or most common order of paired terms usually distinguishes the first as a semantically positive term and the second as a negative one (Lyons 1977, 276; Malkiel 1968).

'Term B' is referred to by some theorists as being produced as an 'effect' of 'Term A'. The unmarked term is presented as fundamental and originative while the marked term 'is conceived in relation to it' as derivative, dependent, subordinate, supplemental or ancillary (Culler 1985, 112). This framing ignores the fact that the unmarked term is logically and structurally dependent on the marked term to lend it substance. Derrida demonstrated that within the oppositional logic of binarism neither of the terms (or concepts) makes sense without the other. This is what he calls 'the logic of supplementarity': the 'secondary' term which is represented as 'marginal' and external is in fact constitutive of the 'primary' term and essential to it (Derrida 1976). The unmarked term is defined by what it seeks to suppress.

In the pairing of oppositions or contraries, Term B is defined *relationally* rather than substantively. The linguistic marking of signifiers in many of these pairings is referred to as 'privative' – consisting of suffixes or prefixes signifying *lack* or *absence* – e.g. *non-*, *un-* or *-less*. In such cases, Term B is defined by *negation* – being everything that Term A is *not*. For example, when we refer to 'non-verbal communication', the very label defines such a mode of communication only in negative relation to 'verbal communication'. Indeed, the unmarked term is not merely neutral but implicitly positive in contrast to the negative connotations of the marked term. For the French psychoanalyst Jacques Lacan the marked term in the pairing of *men–women* is negatively defined within 'the symbolic order' in terms of the *absence* or *lack* of a privileged signifier associated with control and power – the *phallus* (though see feminist critiques of Lacan's *phallocentrism*, e.g. Lovell 1983, 44–5). The association of the marked term with absence and lack is of course problematized by those who have noted the irony that the dependence of Term A on Term B can be seen as reflecting a lack on the part of the *unmarked* term (Fuss 1991, 3).

The unmarked form is typically dominant (e.g. statistically within a text or corpus) and therefore seems to be 'neutral', 'normal' and 'natural'. It is thus 'transparent' – drawing no attention to its invisibly privileged status, while the deviance of the marked form is salient. Where it is not simply subsumed, the marked form is foregrounded – presented as 'different'; it is 'out of the ordinary' – an extraordinary deviational 'special case' which is something other than the standard or default form of the unmarked term. *Unmarked–marked* may thus be read as *norm–deviation*. It is notable that empirical studies have demonstrated that cognitive processing is more difficult with marked terms than with unmarked terms (Clark and Clark 1977). Marked forms take longer to recognize and process and more errors are made with these forms.

On the limited evidence from frequency counts of explicit verbal pairings in written text (online texts retrieved using *Infoseek*, September 2000), while it is very common for one term in such pairings to be marked, in some instances there is not a clearly marked term (see Figure 3.4). For instance, in general usage there seems to be no inbuilt preference for one term in a pairing such as *old–young* (one is just as likely to encounter *young–old*). Furthermore, the extent to which a term is marked is variable. Some terms seem to be far more clearly marked than others: frequency counts based on texts on the World Wide Web suggest that in the pairing *public–private*, for instance, *private* is very clearly the marked term (accorded secondary status). How strongly a term is marked also depends on contextual frameworks such as genres and sociolects, and in some contexts a pairing may be very deliberately and explicitly reversed when an interest group seeks to challenge the ideological priorities which the markedness may be taken to reflect. Not all of the pairs listed will seem to be 'the right way round' to everyone – you may find it interesting to identify which ones seem counter-intuitive to you and to speculate as to why this seems so.

However 'natural' familiar dichotomies and their markedness may seem, their *historical* origins or phases of dominance can often be traced. For instance, perhaps the most influential dualism in the history of Western civilization can be attributed primarily to the philosopher René Descartes (1596–1650) who divided reality into two distinct ontological substances – *mind* and *body*. This distinction insists on the separation of an *external* or 'real' world from an *internal* or 'mental' one, the first being *material* and the second *non-material*. It created the poles of *objectivity* and *subjectivity* and fostered the illusion that 'I' can be distinguished from my body. Furthermore, Descartes's rationalist declaration that 'I think, therefore I am' encouraged the *privileging* of mind over body. He presented the subject as an autonomous individual with an ontological status *prior to* social structures (a notion rejected by poststructural theorists). He established the enduring assumption of the independence of the knower from the known. Cartesian dualism also underpins a host of associated and aligned dichotomies *reason–emotion*, *male–female*, *true–false*, *fact–fiction*, *public–private*, *self–other* and

high				
	90%+*			
	indoor/outdoor			
	up/down			
	yes/no			
	East/West			
	open/closed			
	wet/dry			
	question/answer			
	true/false			
	major/minor	**80%+***		
	hot/cold	on/off		
	reader/writer	public/private		
	before/after	male/female		
	love/hate	high/low		
	top/bottom	parent/child	**70%+***	
I	good/bad	internal/external	black/white	
	cause/effect	gain/loss	mind/body	**60%+***
N	front/back	human/animal	left/right	adult/child
	primary/secondary	past/present	positive/negative	urban/rural
C	birth/death	gay/straight	art/science	product/process
	presence/absence	more/less	active/passive	horizontal/vertical
I	problem/solution	above/below	light/dark	physical/mental
	win/lose	inner/outer	product/system	hard/soft
D	acceptance/rejection	thought/feeling	sex/gender	fast/slow
	inclusion/exclusion	life/death	static/dynamic	quantity/quality
E	success/failure	subject/object	liberal/conservative	foreground/background
	human/machine	producer/consumer	higher/lower	similarity/difference
N	right/wrong	work/play	teacher/learner	temporary/permanent
	nature/nurture	good/evil	war/peace	nature/culture
C	theory/practice	masculine/feminine	body/soul	poetry/prose
	near/far	health/illness	fact/fiction	part/whole	**50%+***
E	self/other	comedy/tragedy	form/content	married/single	new/old
	figure/ground	insider/outsider	form/function	strong/weak	large/small
	rich/poor	happy/sad	simple/complex	subjective/objective	local/global
	fact/opinion	superior/inferior	original/copy	dead/alive	them/us
	system/use	present/absent	means/ends	shallow/deep	system/process
	hero/villain	clean/dirty	appearance/reality	competition/cooperation	young/old
	fact/value	natural/artificial	competence/performance	live/recorded	majority/minority
	text/context	speaker/listener	one/many	head/heart	foreign/domestic
	raw/cooked	classical/romantic	speech/writing	formal/casual	structure/process
	substance/style	type/token	straight/curved	structure/agency	order/chaos
	base/superstructure	nature/technology	signifier/signified	message/medium	concrete/abstract
	knowledge/ignorance	rights/obligations	central/peripheral	form/meaning	words/actions
	fact/fantasy	reason/emotion	wild/domestic	words/deeds	beautiful/ugly
	knower/known	sacred/profane	stability/change	fact/theory	individual/society
low	literal/metaphorical	maker/user	realism/idealism	words/things	strange/familiar

more marked	MARKEDNESS	less marked

*Dominant order as percentage of total occurrences of both forms

FIGURE 3.4 Markedness of some explicit oppositions in online
texts

human–animal. Indeed, many feminist theorists lay a great deal of
blame at Descartes's door for the orchestration of the ontological
framework of patriarchal discourse. One of the most influential of
theorists who have sought to study the ways in which reality is

constructed and maintained within discourse by such dominant frameworks is the French historian of ideas, Michel Foucault, who focused on the analysis of 'discursive formations' in specific historical and socio-cultural contexts (Foucault 1970 and 1974).

Valorizing Term B

The strategy of 'deconstruction' which was adopted by the post-structuralist philosopher Jacques Derrida (1976) sought to challenge the phonocentric privileging of *speech* over *writing* in western culture and to demonstrate the instability of this opposition (Derrida 1976 and 1978). Derrida also challenged the privileging of the signified over the signifier, seeing it as a perpetuation of the traditional opposition of matter and spirit or substance and thought. He noted that within such discourse the *material* form is always subordinated to the *less material* form. Derrida sought to blur the distinction between signifier and signified, insisting that 'the signified always already functions as a signifier' (Derrida 1976, 7). He similarly challenged other loaded oppositions such as presence over absence, nature over culture, masculine over feminine and literal over metaphorical. Other 'critical theorists' have similarly sought to 'valorize term B' in the semiotic analysis of textual representations, though most are content with simply *reversing* the valorization rather than more radically seeking to destabilize the oppositional framework. This strategy is reflected in the way in which some activists in minority groups have hijacked the dominant language of the majority – as in the case of a campaign against homophobia which was launched by the Terrence Higgins Trust in the UK in September 1999 under the slogan 'It's prejudice that's queer.' The posters used neatly inverted heterosexist notions by substituting *homophobia* for *homosexuality*: 'I can't stand homophobes, especially when they flaunt it'; 'My son is homophobic, but I hope it's just a phase'; and 'homophobes shouldn't be left alone with kids'. This strategy of ironic reversal had been foreshadowed in the wittily subversive formulation that 'we don't yet know what causes heterosexuality' (found in gay webpages).

Following on from Derrida's deconstruction of Saussure's *Course in General Linguistics*, Robert Hodge and Gunther Kress

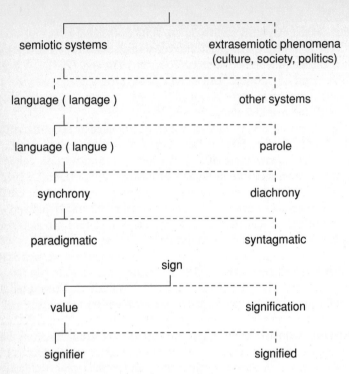

FIGURE 3.5 Saussure's binary priorities

Source: Based on Hodge and Kress 1988

have offered a useful mapping of Saussure's model of semiotics in terms of some of its own explicit oppositions. In Figure 3.5, the leftmost terms represent those which were privileged by Saussure while those on the right represent those which he marginalizes in the *Course*. Seeking to revalorize those terms which Saussure had devalorized, Hodge and Kress build their own more explicitly *social* and *materialist* framework for semiotics on 'the contents of Saussure's rubbish bin'. Their agenda for an 'alternative semiotics' is based on:

1. culture, society and politics as intrinsic to semiotics;
2. other semiotic systems alongside verbal language;

3. *parole*, the act of speaking, and concrete signifying practices in other codes;
4. diachrony, time, history, process and change;
5. the processes of signification, the transactions between signifying systems and structures of reference;
6. structures of the signified;
7. the material nature of signs.

(Hodge and Kress 1988, 17)

The concept of markedness can be applied more broadly than simply to paradigmatic pairings of words or concepts. Whether in textual or social practices, the choice of a marked form 'makes a statement'. Where a text deviates from conventional expectations it is 'marked'. Conventional, or 'over-coded' text (which follows a fairly predictable formula) is unmarked whereas unconventional or 'under-coded' text is marked. Marked or under-coded text requires the interpreter to do more interpretative work.

The existence of marked forms is not simply a structural feature of semiotic systems. The distinction between norm and deviation is fundamental in socialization (Bruner 1990). Social differentiation is constructed and maintained through the marking of differences. Unmarked forms reflect the naturalization of dominant cultural values. Binary oppositions are almost invariably weighted in favour of the male, silently signifying that the norm is to be male and to be female is to be different. Applying the concept of marked forms to mass media genres, Merris Griffiths, then one of my own research students, examined the production and editing styles of television advertisements for toys. Her findings showed that the style of advertisements aimed primarily at boys had far more in common with those aimed at a mixed audience than with those aimed at girls, making 'girls' advertisements' the marked category in commercials for toys. Notably, the girls' ads had significantly longer shots, significantly more dissolves (fade out/fade in of shot over shot), less long shots and more close-ups, less low shots, more level shots and less overhead shots. The gender-differentiated use of production features which characterized these children's commercials reflected a series of binary oppositions – fast vs. slow, abrupt vs. gradual, excited vs. calm, active vs. passive, detached vs. involved. Their close association in such ads led them to line up consistently together as 'masculine' vs. 'feminine' qualities. The 'relative autonomy' of formal features in commercials seems likely to function as a constant symbolic reaffirmation of the broader cultural stereotypes which associate such qualities with gender – especially when accompanied by gender-stereotyped content. Readers may care to reflect on the way in which 'dark goods' and 'light goods' have traditionally been sold in high-street electrical shops. Dark goods such as televisions, video-recorders, camcorders and sound-systems were primarily targeted at men and the sales staff focused on technical specifications. Light goods such as refrigerators, washing-machines and cookers were targeted at women and the sales staff focused on appearance. The extent to which this particular pattern still survives in your own locality may be checked by some investigative 'window-shopping'.

There is a delightfully ironic quip (variously attributed) that 'The world is divided into those who divide people into two types, and those who don't.' The interpretative usefulness of simple dichotomies is often challenged on the basis that life and (perhaps by a misleading 'realist' analogy) texts are 'seamless webs' and thus better described in terms of continua. But it is useful to remind ourselves that any interpretative framework cuts up its material into manageable chunks. The test of its appropriateness can surely only be assessed in terms of whether it advances our understanding of the phenomenon in question.

The semiotic square

Algirdas Greimas introduced the *semiotic square* as a means of analysing paired concepts more fully by mapping the logical conjunctions and disjunctions relating key semantic features in a text (Greimas 1987, xiv, 49). The semiotic square is adapted from the 'logical square' of scholastic philosophy and from Jakobson's distinction between *contradiction* and *contrariety*. Fredric Jameson notes that 'the entire mechanism . . . is capable of generating at least ten conceivable positions out of a rudimentary binary opposition'

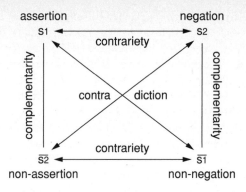

FIGURE 3.6 The semiotic square

(in Greimas 1987, xiv). While this suggests that the possibilities for signification in a semiotic system are richer than the *either/or* of binary logic, they are nevertheless subject to 'semiotic constraints' – 'deep structures' providing basic axes of signification.

In Figure 3.6, the four corners (*S1*, *S2*, *Not S1* and *Not S2*) represent positions within the system which may be occupied by concrete or abstract notions. The double-headed arrows represent bilateral relationships. The upper corners of the Greimasian square represent an opposition between *S1* and *S2* (e.g. white and black). The lower corners represent positions which are not accounted for in simple binary oppositions: *Not S2* and *Not S1* (e.g. non-white and non-black). *Not S1* consists of more than simply *S2* (e.g. that which is not white is not necessarily black). The horizontal relationships represent an opposition between each of the left-hand terms (*S1* and *Not S2*) and its paired right-hand term (*Not S1* and *S2*). The terms at the top (*S1*, *S2*) represent 'presences', while their companion terms (*Not S1* and *Not S2*) represent 'absences'. The vertical relationships of 'implication' offer us an alternative conceptual synthesis of *S1* with *Not S2* and of *S2* with *Not S1* (e.g. of white with not-black or of black with not-white). Greimas refers to the relationships between the four positions as: *contrariety* or opposition (*S1/S2*); *complementarity* or implication (*S1/Not S2* and *S2/Not S1*); and *contradiction* (*S1/Not S1* and *S2/Not S2*). For instance, in the case of the linked terms 'beautiful' and 'ugly', in the semiotic square the four related terms (clockwise) would be 'beautiful', 'ugly', 'not beautiful' and 'not ugly'. The initial pair is not simply a binary opposition because something which is not beautiful is not necessarily ugly and something which is not ugly is not necessarily beautiful (Leymore 1975, 29). The same framework can be productively applied to many other paired terms, such as 'thin' and 'fat'.

Occupying a position within such as framework invests a sign with meanings. The semiotic square can be used to highlight 'hidden' underlying themes in a text or practice. For instance, Fredric Jameson outlines how it might be applied to Charles Dickens's novel, *Hard Times* (Jameson 1972, 167–68). In his foreword to an English translation of a book by Greimas, Jameson reflects on his own use of the technique. He suggests that the analyst should begin by provisionally listing all of the entities to be coordinated and that even apparently marginal entities should be on this initial list. He notes that even the order of the terms in the primary opposition is crucial: we have already seen how the first term in such pairings is typically privileged. He adds that 'the four primary terms . . . need to be conceived polysemically, each one carrying within it its own range of synonyms . . . such that . . . each of the four primary terms threatens to yawn open into its own fourfold system' (in Greimas 1987, xv–xvi). Jameson suggests that *Not S2*, the negation of the negation, 'is always the most critical position and the one that remains open or empty for the longest time, for its identification completes the process and in that sense constitutes the most creative act of the construction' (ibid., xvi). Using the earlier example of aesthetic movements and their dominant focuses, the reader might find it interesting to apply the semiotic square to these. To recap, it was suggested that realism tends to be primarily oriented towards the *world*, neo-classicism towards the *text* and romanticism towards the *author*. We may assign the concepts of world, text and author to three corners of the square – a fourth term is conspicuous by its absence. Jameson's caveats about the order and formulation of terms may be useful here.

Turning to other contexts, in relation to children's toys Dan Fleming offers an accessible application of the semiotic square

(Fleming 1996, 147ff.). Gilles Marion has used the Greimasian square to suggest four purposes in communicating through clothing: wanting to be seen; not wanting to be seen; wanting not to be seen; and not wanting not to be seen (cited in a draft publication by David Mick). Most recently, Jean-Marie Floch has used the grid to illustrate an interesting exploration of the 'consumption values' represented by Habitat and Ikea furniture (Floch 2000, 116–44). However, the Greimasian analysis of texts in terms of the semiotic square has been criticized as easily leading to reductionist and programmatic decodings. Worse still, some theorists seem to use the square as little more than an objective-looking framework which gives the appearance of coherence and grand theory to loose argument and highly subjective opinions.

Critics of structuralist analysis note that binary oppositions need not only to be related to one another and interpreted, but also to be contextualized in terms of the social systems which give rise to texts. Those who use this structuralist approach sometimes claim to be analysing the 'latent meaning' in a text: what it is 'really' about. Unfortunately, such approaches typically understate the subjectivity of the interpreter's framework. Illuminating as they may sometimes be, any inexplicit oppositions which are identified are in the mind of the interpreter rather than contained within the text itself (Culler 1975). Yet another objection is that 'the question of whether categories like sacred/profane and happiness/misery are psychologically real in any meaningful sense is not posed and the internal logic of structuralism would suggest it need not be posed' (Young 1990, 184). None of these criticisms are unanswerable, however, and we would be foolish to forego the insights which may still be gained from exploring the structural analysis of texts and social practices.

Chapter 4

Challenging
the literal

Semiotics represents a challenge to the 'literal' because it rejects the possibility that we can neutrally represent 'the way things are'. In this chapter we will explore the ways in which semioticians have problematized two key distinctions: that at the level of the signifier between the literal and the figurative and that at the level of the signified between denotation and connotation.

Rhetorical tropes

A sea-change in academic discourse, which has been visible in many disciplines, has been dubbed 'the rhetorical turn' or 'the discursive turn'. The central proposition of this contemporary trend is that rhetorical forms are deeply and unavoidably involved in the shaping of realities. Language is not a neutral medium. Our choice of words matters. The North American literary theorist Stanley Fish insists that 'it is

impossible to mean the same thing in two (or more) different ways' (Fish 1980, 32). Form and content are inseparable. In common usage we refer dismissively to 'heated rhetoric', 'empty rhetoric' and 'mere rhetoric', but all discourse is unavoidably rhetorical.

Terence Hawkes tells us that '*figurative language* is language which doesn't mean what it says' – in contrast to *literal language* which is at least intended to be, or taken as, purely denotative (Hawkes 1972, 1; original emphasis). While this is a distinction which goes back to classical times, it has been problematized by poststructuralist theorists (a topic to which we will return shortly). Somewhat less problematically, tropes can be seen as offering us a variety of ways of saying '*this* is (or is *like*) *that*'. Tropes may be essential to understanding if we interpret this as a process of rendering the unfamiliar more familiar. Furthermore, however they are defined, the conventions of figurative language constitute a rhetorical code, and understanding this code is part of what it means to be a member of the culture in which it is employed. Like other codes, figurative language is part of the reality maintenance system of a culture or sub-culture. It is a code which relates ostensibly to *how* things are represented rather than to *what* is represented. Yet such 'form' may have 'content' of its own. Occasionally in everyday life our attention is drawn to an unusual metaphor – such as the critical quip that someone is 'one voucher short of a pop-up toaster'. However, much of the time – outside of 'poetic' contexts – figures of speech retreat to 'transparency'. Such transparency tends to anaesthetize us to the way in which the culturally available stock of tropes acts as an anchor linking us to the dominant ways of thinking within our society (Lakoff and Johnson 1980). Our repeated exposure to, and use of, such figures of speech subtly sustains our tacit agreement with the shared assumptions of our society.

Once we employ a trope, our utterance becomes part of a much larger system of associations which is beyond our control. For instance when we refer metaphorically to 'putting things into words' this involves a further implicit metaphor of language as a 'container' – a particular view of language which has specific implications (Reddy 1979). Yet the use of tropes is unavoidable. We may think of figurative language as most obviously a feature of poetry and

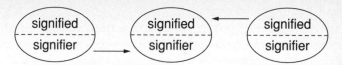

FIGURE 4.1 Substitution in tropes

more generally of 'literary' writing, but there is more metaphor on the street corner than in Shakespeare. According to Roman Jakobson, metaphor and metonymy are the two fundamental modes of communicating meaning, and – according to Lakoff and Johnson – the basis for much of our understanding in everyday life (Jakobson and Halle 1956; Lakoff and Johnson 1980).

Roland Barthes declared that 'no sooner is a form seen than it *must* resemble something: humanity seems doomed to analogy' (cited in Silverman and Torode 1980, 248). The ubiquity of tropes in visual as well as verbal forms can be seen as reflecting our fundamentally *relational* understanding of reality. Reality is framed within systems of analogy. Figures of speech enable us to see one thing in terms of another. A trope such as metaphor can be regarded as a new sign formed from the signifier of one sign and the signified of another (Figure 4.1). The signifier thus stands for a different signified; the new signified replaces the usual one. As I will illustrate, the tropes differ in the nature of these substitutions.

In seventeenth-century England, the scientists of the Royal Society sought 'to separate knowledge of nature from the colours of rhetoric, the devices of the fancy, the delightful deceit of the fables' (Thomas Sprat, 1667: *The History of the Royal Society of London for the Improving of Natural Knowledge*). They saw the 'trick of metaphors' as distorting reality. An attempt to avoid figurative language became closely allied to the realist ideology of objectivism. Language and reality, thought and language, and form and content are regarded by realists as separate, or at least as separable. Realists favour the use of the 'clearest', most 'transparent' language for the accurate and truthful description of 'facts'. However, language isn't 'glass' (as the metaphorical references to clarity and transparency suggest), and it is unavoidably implicated in the construction of the world as we know it. Banishing metaphor is an impossible task since it is central to language. Ironically, the writings of the seventeenth-century critics of rhetoric – such as Sprat, Hobbes and Locke – are themselves richly metaphorical. Those drawn towards philosophical idealism argue that all language is metaphor or even that 'reality' is purely a product of metaphors. Such a stance clearly denies any referential distinction between 'literal' and 'metaphorical'.

Poststructuralists (whose own use of language is typically highly metaphorical) argue that there can be no text which 'means what it says' (which is how 'literal' language is often defined). Constructionists might be content to insist that metaphors are pervasive and largely unrecognized within a culture or sub-culture and that highlighting them is a useful key to identifying whose realities such metaphors privilege. Identifying figurative tropes in texts and practices can help to highlight underlying thematic frameworks; semiotic textual analysis sometimes involves the identification of an 'overarching (or 'root') metaphor' or 'dominant trope'. For instance, Derrida shows how philosophers have traditionally referred to the mind and the intellect in terms of tropes based on the presence or absence of light (Derrida 1974); everyday language is rich in examples of the association of thinking with visual metaphors (bright, brilliant, dull, enlightening, illuminating, vision, clarity, reflection, etc.).

Michel Foucault adopts a stance of linguistic determinism, arguing that the dominant tropes within the discourse of a particular historical period determine what can be known – constituting the basic *episteme* of the age (Foucault 1970). 'Discursive practice' is reduced to 'a body of anonymous, historical rules, always determined by the time and space that have defined a given period, and for a given social, economic, geographical, or linguistic area, the conditions of operation of the enunciative function' (Foucault 1974, 117). Since certain metaphors have become naturalized and we do not tend to notice the ways in which they can channel our thinking about the signifieds to which they refer, deliberately *using* unconventional tropes can sometimes help to denaturalize taken-for-granted ways of looking at phenomena (Stern 1998, 165).

Metaphor

Metaphor is so widespread that it is often used as an 'umbrella' term (another metaphor!) to include other figures of speech (such as metonyms) which can be technically distinguished from it in its narrower usage. Similes can be seen as a form of metaphor in which the figurative status of the comparison is made explicit through the use of the word 'as' or 'like'. Thus 'life is like a box of chocolates' (*Forrest Gump*, 1994). Much of the time we hardly notice that we are using metaphors at all and yet one study found that English speakers produced an average of 3,000 novel metaphors per week (Pollio *et al.* 1977). Lakoff and Johnson argue that 'the essence of metaphor is understanding and experiencing one kind of thing in terms of another' (Lakoff and Johnson 1980, 5). In semiotic terms, a metaphor involves one signified acting as a signifier referring to a different signified. In literary terms, a metaphor consists of a 'literal' primary subject (or 'tenor') expressed in terms of a 'figurative' secondary subject (or 'vehicle') (Richards 1932). For instance: '*Experience* is a good *school*, but the fees are high' (Heinrich Heine). In this case, the primary subject of *experience* is expressed in terms of the secondary subject of *school*. Typically, metaphor expresses an abstraction in terms of a more well-defined model.

The linking of a particular tenor and vehicle is normally unfamiliar: we must make an imaginative leap to recognize the resemblance to which a fresh metaphor alludes. Metaphor is initially unconventional because it apparently disregards 'literal' or denotative resemblance (though some kind of resemblance must become apparent if the metaphor is to make any sense at all to its interpreters). The basis in *resemblance* suggests that metaphor involves the *iconic* mode. However, to the extent that such a resemblance is oblique, we may think of metaphor as *symbolic*. More interpretative effort is required in making sense of metaphors than of more literal signifiers, but this interpretative effort may be experienced as pleasurable. While metaphors may require an imaginative leap in their initial use (such as in aesthetic uses in poetry or the visual arts) many metaphors become so habitually employed that they are no longer perceived as being metaphors at all.

127

Metaphors need not be verbal. In film, a pair of consecutive shots is metaphorical when there is an implied comparison of the two shots. For instance, a shot of an aeroplane followed by a shot of a bird flying would be metaphorical, implying that the aeroplane is (or is like) a bird. So too would a shot of a bird landing accompanied by the sounds of an airport control tower and of a braking plane – as in an airline commercial cited by Charles Forceville (Forceville 1996, 203). In most cases the context would cue us as to which was the primary subject. An ad for an airline is more likely to suggest that an aeroplane is (like) a bird than that a bird is (like) an aeroplane. As with verbal metaphors, we are left to draw our own conclusions as to the points of comparison. Advertisers frequently use visual metaphors. Despite the frequently expressed notion that images cannot assert, metaphorical images often imply that which advertisers would not express in words.

Visual metaphor can also involve a function of 'transference', transferring certain qualities from one sign to another. In relation to advertising this has been explored by Judith Williamson in her book, *Decoding Advertisements* (Williamson 1978). It is of course the role of advertisers to differentiate similar products from each other, and they do this by associating a product with a specific set of social values – in semiotic terms, creating distinct signifieds for it. Indeed, it has been suggested that ads provide 'a kind of dictionary constantly keeping us apprised of new consumer signifieds and signifiers' (McCracken, cited in Stern 1998, 292). One example instanced by Williamson takes the form of a photographic close-up of the head and shoulders of the glamorous French actress Catherine Deneuve (whose name appears in small type). Superimposed on the lower right-hand portion of the advertisement is the image of a bottle of perfume labelled Chanel No. 5. In this advertisement, two key signifiers are juxtaposed. The image of Catherine Deneuve richly signifies French chic, sophistication, elegance, beauty and glamour. The plain image of the bottle simply signifies Chanel No. 5 perfume. This is a rather 'empty' signifier when we cannot actually smell the perfume (contemporary perfume ads in magazines often include a strip of paper impregnated with the scent). At the bottom of the ad, in large letters, the name of the perfume is repeated in its distinctive typographical style, making a link between the two key signifiers. The aim, of course, is for the viewer to transfer the qualities signified by the actress to the perfume, thus substituting one signified for another, and creating a new metaphorical sign which offers us the meaning that Chanel No. 5 **is** beauty and elegance (Williamson 1978, 25).

George Lakoff and Mark Johnson illustrate that underlying most of our fundamental concepts are several kinds of metaphor:

- **orientational** metaphors primarily relating to spatial organization (up/down, in/out, front/back, on/off, near/far, deep/shallow and central/peripheral);
- **ontological** metaphors which associate activities, emotions and ideas with entities and substances (most obviously, metaphors involving personification);
- **structural** metaphors: overarching metaphors (building on the other two types) which allow us to structure one concept in terms of another (e.g. rational argument is war or time is a resource).

Lakoff and Johnson note that metaphors may vary from culture to culture but argue that they are not arbitrary, being derived initially from our physical, social and cultural experience (cf. Vico 1968, 129). They argue that metaphors form systematic clusters such as that *ideas (or meanings) are objects*, *linguistic expressions are containers* and *communication is sending* – an example derived from Michael Reddy's discussion of 'the conduit metaphor' (Reddy 1979). Metaphors not only cluster in this way but extend into myths. Lakoff and Johnson argue that dominant metaphors tend both to reflect and influence values in a culture or subculture: for instance, the pervasive Western metaphors that *knowledge is power* and *science subdues nature* are involved in the maintenance of the ideology of objectivism (Lakoff and Johnson 1980). This is consistent with the Whorfian perspective that different languages impose different systems of spatial and temporal relations on experience through their figures of speech (Whorf 1956).

Metonymy

While metaphor is based on apparent unrelatedness, metonymy is a function which involves using one signified to stand for another signified which is *directly related* to it or *closely associated* with it in some way. Metonyms are based on various *indexical* relationships between signifieds, notably the substitution of *effect* for *cause*. The best definition I have found is that 'metonymy is *the evocation of the whole by a connection*. It consists in using for the name of a thing or a relationship, an attribute, a suggested sense, or something closely related, such as effect for cause . . . the imputed relationship being that of *contiguity*' (Wilden 1987, 198; my emphasis). It can be seen as based on substitution by *adjuncts* (things that are found together) or on *functional relationships*. Many of these forms notably make an abstract referent more concrete, although some theorists also include substitution in the opposite direction (e.g. *cause* for *effect*). *Part–whole* relationships are sometimes distinguished as a special kind of metonymy or as a separate trope, as we will see shortly. Metonymy includes the substitution of:

- *effect* for *cause* ('Don't get hot under the collar!' for 'Don't get angry!');
- *object* for *user* (or associated *institution*) ('the Crown' for the monarchy, 'the stage' for the theatre and 'the press' for journalists);
- *substance* for *form* ('plastic' for 'credit card', 'lead' for 'bullet');
- *place* for *event*: ('Chernobyl changed attitudes to nuclear power');
- *place* for *person* ('No. 10' for the British prime minister);
- *place* for *institution* ('Whitehall isn't saying anything');
- *institution* for *people* ('The government is not backing down').

Lakoff and Johnson comment on several types of metonym, including:

- *producer* for *product* ('She owns a Picasso');
- *object* for *user* ('The ham sandwich wants his check [bill]');
- *controller* for *controlled* ('Nixon bombed Hanoi').

They argue that (as with metaphor) particular kinds of metonymic substitution may influence our thoughts, attitudes and actions by focusing on certain aspects of a concept and suppressing other aspects which are inconsistent with the metonym:

> When we think of a *Picasso*, we are not just thinking of a work of art alone, in and of itself. We think of it in terms of its relation to the artist, this is, his conception of art, his technique, his role in art history, etc. We act with reverence towards a *Picasso*, even a sketch he made as a teenager, because of its relation to the artist. Similarly, when a waitress says, 'The ham sandwich wants his check,' she is not interested in the person as a person but only as a customer, which is why the use of such a sentence is dehumanizing. Nixon may not himself have dropped the bombs on Hanoi, but via the *controller for controlled* metonymy we not only say 'Nixon bombed Hanoi' but also think of him as doing the bombing and hold him responsible for it . . . This is possible because of the nature of the metonymic relationship . . . where responsibility is what is focused on.
>
> (Lakoff and Johnson 1980, 39)

As with metaphors, metonyms may be visual as well as verbal. In film, which Jakobson regarded as a basically metonymic medium, a depicted object which represents a related but non-depicted object is a metonym. An ad for pensions in a women's magazine asked the reader to arrange four images in order of importance: each image was metonymic, standing for related activities (such as shopping bags for material goods). Metonymy is common in cigarette advertising in countries where legislation prohibits depictions of the cigarettes themselves or of people using them. The ads for Benson and Hedges and for Silk Cut are good examples of this.

Jakobson argues that whereas a *metaphorical* term is connected with that for which it is substituted on the basis of *similarity*, *metonymy* is based on *contiguity* or closeness (Jakobson and Halle 1956, 91, 95). The indexicality of metonyms also tends to suggest that they are 'directly connected to' reality in contrast to the mere *iconicity* or *symbolism* of metaphor. Metonyms seem to be more obviously 'grounded in our experience' than metaphors since they usually involve direct associations (Lakoff and Johnson 1980, 39). Metonymy does not require transposition (an imaginative leap) from one domain to another as metaphor does. This difference can lead metonymy to seem more 'natural' than metaphors – which when still 'fresh' are stylistically foregrounded. Metonymic signifiers foreground the signified while metaphoric signifiers foreground the signifier (Lodge 1977, xiv). Jakobson suggested that the metonymic mode tends to be foregrounded in prose whereas the metaphoric mode tends to be foregrounded in poetry (Jakobson and Halle 1956, 95–6). He regarded 'so-called realistic literature' as 'intimately tied with the metonymic principle' (Jakobson 1960, 375; cf. Jakobson and Halle 1956, 92). Such literature represents actions as based on cause and effect and as contiguous in time and space. While metonymy is associated with realism, metaphor is associated with romanticism and surrealism (Jakobson and Halle 1956, 92).

Synecdoche

Some theorists identify synecdoche as a separate trope, some see it as a special form of metonymy and others subsume its functions entirely within metonymy. Jakobson noted that both metonymy and synecdoche are based on *contiguity* (ibid., 95). The definition of synecdoche varies from theorist to theorist (sometimes markedly). The rhetorician Richard Lanham represents the most common tendency to describe synecdoche as 'the substitution of part for whole, genus for species or vice versa' (Lanham 1969, 97). Thus one term is more comprehensive than the other. Some theorists restrict the directionality of application (e.g. part for whole but *not* whole for part). Some limit synecdoche further to cases where one element is *physically* part of the other. Here are some examples:

- *part* for *whole* ('I'm off to the smoke [London]'; 'we need to hire some more hands [workers]'; 'two heads are better than one'; 'I've got a new set of wheels', the American expression 'get your butt over here!');

- *whole* for *part* (e.g. 'I was stopped by the law' – where the law stands for a police officer, 'Wales' for 'the Welsh national rugby team' or 'the market' for customers);
- *species* for *genus* (*hypernymy*) – the use of a *member of a class* (*hyponym*) for the *class* (*superordinate*) which includes it (e.g. *a* 'mother' for 'motherhood', 'bread' for 'food', 'Hoover' for 'vacuum-cleaner');
- *genus* for *species* (*hyponymy*) – the use of a *superordinate* for a *hyponym* (e.g. 'vehicle' for 'car', or 'machine' for 'computer').

Stephen Pepper identified four basic 'worldviews' – formism, mechanism, contextualism and organicism, each with its own distinctive 'root metaphor' – respectively, *similarity, simple machine, historic event* and *organism* (Pepper 1942, 84ff.). The literary theorist Meyer Abrams has identified Pepper's scheme as an application of synecdoche, since each worldview presents the whole of reality in terms of one of its parts (Abrams 1971, 31).

In photographic and filmic media a close-up is a simple synecdoche – a part representing the whole (Jakobson and Halle 1956, 92). Indeed, the formal frame of any visual image (painting, drawing, photograph, film or television frame) functions as a synecdoche in that it suggests that what is being offered is a 'slice-of-life', and that the world outside the frame is carrying on in the same manner as the world depicted within it. This is perhaps particularly so when the frame cuts across some of the objects depicted within it rather than enclosing them as wholly discrete entities. Synecdoche invites or expects the viewer to 'fill in the gaps' and advertisements frequently employ this trope.

Any attempt to represent reality can be seen as involving synecdoche, since it can only involve selection (and yet such selections serve to guide us in envisaging larger frameworks). While indexical relations in general reflect the closest link which a signifier can be seen as having with a signified, the *part–whole* relations of synecdoche reflect the most direct link of all. That which is seen as forming part of a larger whole to which it refers is connected *existentially* to what is signified – as an integral part of its being. Jakobson noted the use of 'synecdochic details' by realist authors (Jakobson and Halle 1956, 92). In 'factual' genres a danger lies in what has been called 'the metonymic fallacy' (more accurately the 'synecdochic fallacy') whereby the represented part is taken as an accurate reflection of the whole of that which it is taken as standing for – for instance, a white, middle-class woman standing for all women (Barthes 1974, 162; Alcoff and Potter 1993, 14). Framing is of course always highly and unavoidably selective. In fictional genres, 'realism' seeks to encourage us to treat that which is missing as 'going without saying' rather than as 'conspicuous by its absence'. In mainstream films and television dramas, for instance, we are not intended to be aware that the stage-set 'rooms' have only three walls.

Whether synecdoche is separable from metonymy in general is disputed by some theorists (e.g. Eco 1984). Others disagree about what constitutes synecdoche. If the distinction is made as outlined above, metonymy in its narrower sense would then be confined to functional connections such as causality. Even if synecdoche is given a separate status, general usage would suggest that metonymy would remain an umbrella term for indexical links as well as having a narrower meaning of its own.

Irony

Irony is the most radical of the four main tropes. As with metaphor, the signifier of the ironic sign seems to signify one thing but we know from another signifier that it actually signifies something very different. Where it means the *opposite* of what it says (as it usually does) it is based on binary opposition. Irony may thus reflect the opposite of the thoughts or feelings of the speaker or writer (as when you say 'I love it' when you hate it) or the opposite of the truth about external reality (as in 'There's a real crowd here' when it's deserted). It can also be seen as being based on substitution by *dissimilarity* or *disjunction*. While typically an ironic statement signifies the opposite of its literal signification, such variations as understatement and overstatement can also be regarded as ironic. At some point, exaggeration may slide into irony.

Unless the ironic sign is a spoken utterance (when a sarcastic intonation may mark the irony) the marker of its ironic status comes

TABLE 4.1 The ironic, the literal and the lie

Modality status	Postcard message	Referential truth status	Perceived intent
literal/factual	'The weather is wonderful'	true (the weather is wonderful)	to inform
ironic	'The weather is wonderful'	false (the weather is dreadful)	to amuse
lie	'The weather is wonderful'	false (the weather is dreadful)	to mislead

from beyond the literal sign. A 'knowing' smile is often offered as a cue. In Britain a fashion for 'air quotes' (gestural inverted commas) in the 1980s was followed in the 1990s by a fashion for some young people to mark spoken irony – after a pause – with the word 'Not!', as in 'he is a real hunk – not!'. However, irony is often more difficult to identify. All of the tropes involve the non-literal substitution of a new signified for the usual one and comprehension requires a distinction between what is *said* and what is *meant*. Thus they are all, in a sense, *double* signs. However, whereas the other tropes involve shifts in what is being referred to, irony involves a shift in *modality* (see Table 4.1). The evaluation of the ironic sign requires the retrospective assessment of its modality status. Re-evaluating an apparently literal sign for ironic cues requires reference to perceived intent and to truth status. An ironic statement is not, of course, the same as a *lie* since it is not intended to be taken as 'true'. Irony thus poses particular difficulties for the literalist stance of structuralists and formalists that meaning is immanent – that it lies *within* a text.

Irony is a marked form which foregrounds the signifier. Adolescents sometimes use it to suggest that they are sophisticated and not naïve. Limited use is usually intended as a form of humour.

Frequent use may be associated with reflexiveness, detachment or scepticism. It sometimes marks a cynical stance which assumes that people never mean or do what they say. Sustained use may even reflect nihilism or relativism (nothing – or everything – is 'true'). While irony has a long pedigree, its use has become one of the most characteristic features of 'postmodern' texts and aesthetic practices. Where irony is used in one-to-one communication it is of course essential that it is understood as being ironic rather than literal. However, with larger audiences it constitutes a form of 'narrow-casting', since not everyone will interpret it as irony. Dramatic irony is a form whereby the reader or viewer knows something that one or more of the depicted people do not know. A British ad for the Nissan Micra published in a women's magazine made effective use of irony. The campaign slogan was 'ask before you borrow it'. In soft focus we see a man absorbed in eating his food at a table; in sharp focus close-up we see a woman facing him, hiding behind her back an open can. As we read the label we realize that she has fed him dog-food.

TABLE 4.2 The four 'master tropes'

Trope	Basis	Linguistic example	Intended meaning
Metaphor	Similarity despite difference (explicit in the case of simile)	I work at the coalface	I do the hard work here
Metonymy	Relatedness through direct association	I'm one of the suits	I'm one of the managers
Synecdoche	Relatedness through categorical hierarchy	I deal with the general public	I deal with customers
Irony	Inexplicit direct opposite (more explicit in sarcasm)	I love working here	I hate working here

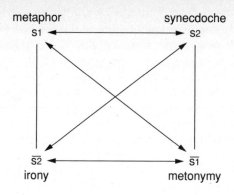

FIGURE 4.2 The four 'master tropes'

Source: Based on Jameson in Greimas 1987

Master tropes

Table 4.2 offers a brief summary of the four tropes with some linguistic examples. Giambattista Vico (1668–1744) is usually credited with being the first to identify metaphor, metonymy, synecdoche and irony as the four basic tropes (to which all others are reducible), although this distinction can be seen as having its roots in the *Rhetorica* of Peter Ramus (1515–72) (Vico 1968, 129–31). This reduction was popularized in the twentieth century by the American rhetorician Kenneth Burke (1897–1993), who referred to the four 'master tropes' (Burke 1969, 503–17). Figure 4.2 shows these tropes as a semiotic square (see Jameson in Greimas 1987, xix). Note that such frameworks depend on a distinction being made between metonymy and synecdoche, but that such terms are often either defined variously or not defined at all. In his book *Metahistory*, White saw the four 'master tropes' as part of the 'deep structure' underlying different historiographical styles (White 1973, ix). Jonathan Culler (following Hans Kellner) even suggests that they may constitute 'a system, indeed *the* system, by which the mind comes to grasp the world conceptually in language' (Culler 1981, 65).

In what is, of course, a rhetorical act of analogy itself, White also linked metaphor, metonymy, synecdoche and irony with four

TABLE 4.3 Tropes, genres, worldviews and ideologies

Trope	Genre ('mode of emplotment')	Worldview ('mode of argument')	Ideology ('mode of ideological implication')
Metaphor	romance	formism	anarchism
Metonymy	comedy	organicism	conservatism
Synecdoche	tragedy	mechanism	radicalism
Irony	satire	contextualism	liberalism

Source: Based on White 1973 and 1978

literary genres, Pepper's worldviews and four basic ideologies (Table 4.3). In Lévi-Straussian rhetoric, he saw these various systems of classification as 'structurally homologous with one another' (White 1978, 70).

Hayden White's four-part tropological system is widely cited and applied beyond the historiographical context in which he originally used it, and the application of such frameworks can often be enlightening. However, some caution is necessary in their use. White himself notes that the 'affinities' suggested by his alignment of tropes with genres, worldviews and ideologies 'are not to be taken as *necessary* combinations of the modes in a given historian. On the contrary, the dialectical tension which characterizes the work of every master historian usually arises from an effort to wed a mode of emplotment with a mode of argument or of ideological implication which is inconsonant with it' (White 1973, 29). There is a danger of over-systematization when threefold or fourfold distinctions are multiplied and correlated by analogy. Taken to relativistic extremes, everything can be taken as resembling everything else. Phenomena are seldom as tidy as our systems of classification. Systems always leak (and it's no good replacing the plumbing with poetry). It is for the individual reader to assess how interpretatively useful the application

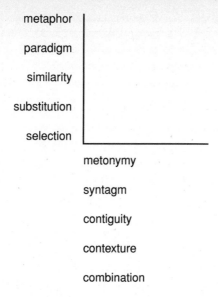

metaphor

paradigm

similarity

substitution

selection

metonymy

syntagm

contiguity

contexture

combination

FIGURE 4.3   Jakobson's axes

of such schemes may be on any particular occasion of use – and what the limitations of such analogies may be. Since they can be extraordinarily compelling, we need to ensure that they do not become 'more real' than what they purport to describe.

White argued that 'the fourfold analysis of figurative language has the added advantage of resisting the fall into an essentially *dualistic* conception of styles'. Roman Jakobson adopted two tropes rather than four as fundamental – metaphor and metonymy (Figure 4.3). White felt that Jakobson's approach, when applied to nineteenth century literature, produced the reductive dichotomy of 'a romantic–poetic–Metaphorical tradition' and 'a realistic–prosaic–Metonymical tradition' (White 1973, 33n.). However, Jakobson's notion of two basic axes has proved massively influential. Jakobson argued that metaphor is a paradigmatic dimension (vertical, based on selection, substitution and similarity) and metonymy a syntagmatic dimension (horizontal, based on combination, contexture and contiguity)

(Jakobson and Halle 1956, 90–6). Many theorists have adopted and adapted Jakobson's framework, such as Lévi-Strauss and Lacan (Lévi-Strauss 1974; Lacan 1977, 160).

Denotation and connotation

While the distinction between literal and figurative language operates at the level of the signifier, that between denotation and connotation operates at the level of the signified. We all know that beyond its 'literal' meaning (its denotation), a particular word may have connotations: for instance, sexual connotations. 'Is there any such thing as a *single entendre*?' quipped the comic actor Kenneth Williams. In semiotics, denotation and connotation are terms describing the relationship between the signifier and its signified, and an analytic distinction is made between two types of signifieds: a *denotative* signified and a *connotative* signified. Meaning includes both denotation and connotation.

'Denotation' tends to be described as the definitional, 'literal', 'obvious' or 'commonsense' meaning of a sign. In the case of linguistic signs, the denotative meaning is what the dictionary attempts to provide. For the art historian Erwin Panofsky, the denotation of a representational visual image is what all viewers from any culture and at any time would recognize the image as depicting (Panofsky 1970, 51–3). Even such a definition raises issues – *all* viewers? One suspects that this excludes very young children and those regarded as insane, for instance. But if it really means 'culturally well-adjusted' then it is already culture specific, which takes us into the territory of connotation. The term 'connotation' is used to refer to the socio-cultural and 'personal' associations (ideological, emotional, etc.) of the sign. These are typically related to the interpreter's class, age, gender, ethnicity and so on. Signs are more 'polysemic' – more open to interpretation – in their connotations than their denotations. Denotation is sometimes regarded as a *digital* code and connotation as an *analogue* code (Wilden 1987, 224).

As Roland Barthes noted, Saussure's model of the sign focused on denotation at the expense of connotation and it was left to subsequent theorists (notably Barthes himself – drawing on Hjelmslev) to offer an account of this important dimension of meaning (Barthes 1967, 89ff.). In 'The photographic message' (1961) and 'The rhetoric of the image' (1964), Barthes argued that in photography connotation can be (analytically) distinguished from denotation (Barthes 1977, 15–31, 32–51). As Fiske puts it 'denotation is *what* is photographed, connotation is *how* it is photographed' (Fiske 1982, 91). However, in photography, denotation is foregrounded at the expense of connotation. The photographic signifier seems to be virtually identical with its signified, and the photograph appears to be a 'natural sign' produced without the intervention of a code (Hall 1980, 132). In analysing the realist literary text Barthes came to the conclusion that connotation produces the illusion of denotation, the illusion of the medium as transparent and of the signifier and the signified as being identical (Barthes 1974, 9). Thus denotation is just another connotation. From such a perspective, denotation can be seen as no more of a 'natural' meaning than is connotation but rather as a process of *naturalization*. Such a process leads to the powerful illusion that denotation is a purely literal and universal meaning which is not at all ideological, and indeed that those connotations which seem most obvious to individual interpreters are just as 'natural'. According to an Althusserian reading, when we first learn denotations, we are also being positioned within ideology by learning dominant connotations at the same time (Silverman 1983, 30). Consequently, while theorists may find it analytically useful to distinguish connotation from denotation, in practice such meanings cannot be neatly separated. Most semioticians argue that no sign is purely denotative – lacking connotation. Valentin Voloshinov insisted that no strict division can be made between denotation and connotation because 'referential meaning is moulded by evaluation . . . meaning is always permeated with value judgement' (Voloshinov 1973, 105). There can be no neutral, 'literal' description which is free of an evaluative element.

For most contemporary semioticians both denotation and connotation involve the use of codes. Structural semioticians who emphasize the relative arbitrariness of signifiers and social semioticians who emphasize diversity of interpretation and the importance of cultural and historical contexts are hardly likely to accept the notion of a 'literal' meaning. Denotation simply involves a broader consensus. The denotational meaning of a sign would be broadly agreed upon by members of the same culture, whereas no inventory of the connotational meanings generated by any sign could ever be complete. However, there is a danger here of stressing the 'individual subjectivity' of connotation: 'intersubjective' responses are shared to some degree by members of a culture; with any individual example only a limited range of connotations would make any sense. Connotations are not purely 'personal' meanings – they are determined by the codes to which the interpreter has access. Cultural codes provide a connotational framework since they are 'organized around key oppositions and equations', each term being 'aligned with a cluster of symbolic attributes' (Silverman 1983, 36). Certain connotations would be widely recognized within a culture. Most adults in Western cultures would know that a car can connote virility or freedom.

Connotation and denotation are often described in terms of *levels of representation* or *levels of meaning*. Roland Barthes adopted from Louis Hjelmslev the notion that there are different *orders of signification* (Barthes 1957; Hjelmslev 1961, 114ff.). The *first order of signification* is that of denotation: at this level there is a sign consisting of a signifier and a signified. Connotation is a *second-order of signification* which uses the denotative sign (signifier and signified) as its signifier and attaches to it an additional signified (Figure 4.4). In this framework, connotation is a sign which derives from the signifier of a denotative sign (so denotation leads to a chain

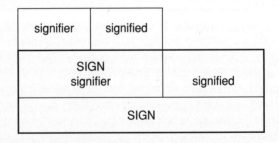

FIGURE 4.4 Orders of signification

of connotations). This tends to suggest that denotation is an underlying and primary meaning – a notion which many other commentators have challenged. As we have noted, Barthes himself later gave priority to connotation, noting in 1971 that it was no longer easy to separate the signifier from the signified, the ideological from the 'literal' (Barthes 1977, 166). In passing, we may note that this formulation underlines the point that 'what is a signifier or a signified depends entirely on the level at which the analysis operates: a signified on one level can become a signifier on another level' (Willemen 1994, 105). This is the mechanism by which signs may seem to signify one thing but are loaded with multiple meanings.

Changing the form of the signifier while keeping the same signified can generate different connotations. Changes of style or tone may involve different connotations, such as when using different typefaces for exactly the same text, or changing from sharp focus to soft focus when taking a photograph. The choice of words often involves connotations, as in references to 'strikes' vs. 'disputes', 'union demands' vs. 'management offers', and so on. Tropes such as metaphor generate connotations.

Connotation is not a purely paradigmatic dimension, as Saussure's characterization of the paradigmatic dimension as 'associative' might suggest. Whilst absent signifiers with which a signifier may be associated are clearly a key factor in generating connotations, so too are syntagmatic associations. The connotations of a signifier relate in part to the other signifiers with which it occurs within a particular text. However, referring to connotation entirely in terms of paradigms and syntagms confines us to the language system, and yet connotation is very much a question of how language is *used*. A purely structuralist account also limits us to a synchronic perspective and yet both connotations and denotations are subject not only to socio-cultural variability but also to historical factors: they change over time. Signs referring to disempowered groups (such as 'woman') can be seen as having had far more negative denotations as well as negative connotations than they do now because of their framing within dominant and authoritative codes of their time – including even supposedly 'objective' scientific codes. Fiske warns that 'it is often easy to read connotative values as denotative facts'

(Fiske 1982, 92). Just as dangerously seductive, however, is the tendency to accept denotation as the 'literal', 'self-evident' 'truth'. Semiotic analysis can help us to counter such habits of mind.

While the dominant methodologies in semiotic analysis are *qualitative*, semiotics is not incompatible with the use of quantitative techniques. In 1957 the psychologist Charles Osgood, together with some of his colleagues, published a book entitled *The Measurement of Meaning* (Osgood *et al.* 1957). In it these communication researchers outlined a technique called the *semantic differential* for the systematic mapping of *connotations* (or 'affective meanings'). The technique involves a pencil-and-paper test in which people are asked to give their impressionistic responses to a particular object, state or event by indicating specific positions in relation to at least nine pairs of bipolar adjectives on a scale of one to seven. The aim is to locate a concept in 'semantic space' in three dimensions: *evaluation* (e.g. good–bad); *potency* (e.g. strong–weak); and activity (e.g. active–passive). The method has proved useful in studying attitudes and emotional reactions. It has been used, for instance, to make comparisons between different cultural groups. While the technique has been used fairly widely in social science, it has not often been used by semioticians (including the self-styled 'scientist of connotations', Roland Barthes), although, as we have seen, binary oppositions have routinely provided theoretical building-blocks for structuralist semioticians.

Myth

Related to connotation is what Roland Barthes refers to as *myth*. We usually associate myths with classical fables about the exploits of gods and heroes. As we have seen, the anthropologist Lévi-Strauss saw myths as mediating between nature and culture. For Barthes, myths were the dominant ideologies of our time. In a departure from Hjelmslev's model, Barthes argues that the orders of signification called denotation and connotation combine to produce ideology – which has been described (though not by Barthes) as a *third order of signification* (Fiske and Hartley 1978, 43; O'Sullivan *et al.* 1994, 287).

Signs and codes are generated by myths and in turn serve to maintain them. Popular usage of the term 'myth' suggests that it refers to beliefs which are demonstrably false, but the semiotic use of the term does not necessarily suggest this. Myths can be seen as extended metaphors. Like metaphors, myths help us to make sense of our experiences within a culture (Lakoff and Johnson 1980, 185–6). They express and serve to organize shared ways of conceptualizing something within a culture. Semioticians in the Saussurean tradition treat the relationship between nature and culture as relatively arbitrary (Lévi-Strauss 1972, 90, 95). For Barthes, myths serve the ideological function of *naturalization* (Barthes 1977, 45–6). Their function is to naturalize the cultural – in other words, to make dominant cultural and historical values, attitudes and beliefs seem entirely 'natural', 'normal', self-evident, timeless, obvious 'commonsense' – and thus objective and 'true' reflections of 'the way things are'. Barthes saw myth as serving the ideological interests of the bourgeoisie. 'Bourgeois ideology ... turns culture into nature,' he declares (Barthes 1974, 206). George Lakoff and Mark Johnson outline key features of the myth of *objectivism* which is dominant and pervasive in Western culture – a myth which allies itself with scientific truth, rationality, accuracy, fairness and impartiality and which is reflected in the discourse of science, law, government, journalism, morality, business, economics and scholarship (Lakoff and Johnson 1980, 188–9). Myths can function to hide the ideological function of signs and codes. The power of such myths is that they 'go without saying' and so appear not to need to be deciphered, interpreted or demystified.

Differences between the three orders of signification are not clear-cut, but for descriptive and analytic purposes some theorists distinguish them along the following lines. The first (denotative) order (or level) of signification is seen as primarily representational and relatively self-contained. The second (connotative) order of signification reflects 'expressive' values which are attached to a sign. In the third (mythological or ideological) order of signification the sign reflects major culturally variable concepts underpinning a particular worldview – such as masculinity, femininity, freedom, individualism, objectivism, Englishness, and so on.

Semiotics demonstrates that deconstructing tropes, connotations and myths can be revealing but that they cannot be reduced to the 'literal'. The task of 'denaturalizing' the cultural assumptions embodied in such forms is problematic when the semiotician is also a product of the same culture, since membership of a culture involves 'taking for granted' many of its dominant ideas. Nevertheless, where we seek to analyse our own cultures in this way it is essential to try to be explicitly reflexive about 'our own' values. Roland Barthes demonstrated that rhetoric, connotation and myths are semiotic *codes*, and it is to the nature of codes that we now turn our attention.

Chapter 5

Codes

The concept of the 'code' is fundamental in semiotics. While Saussure dealt only with the overall code of language, he did of course stress that signs are not meaningful in isolation, but only when they are interpreted in relation to each other. It was another linguistic structuralist, Roman Jakobson, who emphasized that the production and interpretation of texts depends upon the existence of codes or conventions for communication (Jakobson 1971). Since the meaning of a sign depends on the code within which it is situated, codes provide a framework within which signs make sense. Indeed, we cannot grant something the status of a sign if it does not function within a code. Furthermore, if the relationship between a signifier and its signified is relatively arbitrary, then it is clear that interpreting the conventional meaning of signs requires familiarity with appropriate sets of conventions. Codes organize signs into meaningful systems which correlate signifiers and signifieds.

The conventions of codes represent a social dimension in semiotics: a code is a set of practices

familiar to users of the medium operating within a broad cultural framework. Indeed, as Stuart Hall puts it, 'there is no intelligible discourse without the operation of a code' (Hall 1980, 131). Society itself depends on the existence of such signifying systems. When studying cultural practices, semioticians treat as signs any objects or actions which have meaning to members of the cultural group, seeking to identify the rules or conventions of the codes which underlie the production of meanings within that culture. Understanding such codes, their relationships and the contexts in which they are appropriate, is part of what it means to be a member of a particular culture.

Codes are not simply 'conventions' of communication but rather procedural *systems* of related conventions which operate in certain domains.

Types of codes

Semioticians seek to identify codes and the tacit rules and constraints which underlie the production and interpretation of meaning within each code. They have found it convenient to divide codes themselves into groups. Different theorists favour different taxonomies, and while structuralists often follow the 'principle of parsimony' – seeking to find the smallest number of groups deemed necessary – 'necessity' is defined by *purposes*. No taxonomy is innocently 'neutral' and devoid of ideological assumptions. One might start from a fundamental divide between analogue and digital codes, from a division according to sensory channels, from a distinction between 'verbal' and 'non-verbal', and so on. Many semioticians take human language as their starting point. The primary and most pervasive code in any society is its dominant 'natural' language, within which (as with other codes) there are many 'sub-codes'. A fundamental sub-division of language into spoken and written forms – at least insofar as it relates to whether the text is detached from its maker at the point of reception – is often regarded as representing a broad division into different codes rather than merely sub-codes. One theorist's code is another's sub-code and the value of the distinction needs to be demonstrated. Stylistic and personal codes (or *idiolects*) are often described as sub-codes (e.g. Eco 1976, 263, 272). The various kinds of codes overlap, and the semiotic analysis of any text or practice involves considering several codes and the relationships between them. A range of typologies of codes can be found in the literature of semiotics. I refer here only to those which are most widely mentioned in the context of media, communication and cultural studies (this particular tripartite framework is my own).

Social codes

- verbal language (phonological, syntactical, lexical, prosodic and paralinguistic subcodes);
- bodily codes (bodily contact, proximity, physical orientation, appearance, facial expression, gaze, head-nods, gestures and posture);
- commodity codes (fashions, clothing, cars);
- behavioural codes (protocols, rituals, role-playing, games).

Textual codes

- scientific codes, including mathematics;
- aesthetic codes within the various expressive arts (poetry, drama, painting, sculpture, music, etc.) – including classicism, romanticism, realism;
- genre, rhetorical and stylistic codes: exposition, argument, description and narration and so on;
- mass media codes including photographic, televisual, filmic, radio, newspaper and magazine codes, both technical and conventional (including format).

Interpretative codes

- perceptual codes: e.g. of visual perception (Hall 1980, 132; Nichols 1981, 11ff.; Eco 1982) (note that this code does not assume intentional communication);
- ideological codes: more broadly, these include codes for 'encoding' and 'decoding' texts – dominant (or

'hegemonic'), negotiated or oppositional (Hall 1980; Morley 1980). More specifically, we may list the '-isms', such as individualism, liberalism, feminism, racism, materialism, capitalism, progressivism, conservatism, socialism, objectivism and populism; (note, however, that *all* codes can be seen as ideological).

These three types of codes correspond broadly to three key kinds of knowledge required by interpreters of a text, namely knowledge of:

1. the world (social knowledge);
2. the medium and the genre (textual knowledge);
3. the relationship between (1) and (2) (modality judgements).

The 'tightness' of semiotic codes themselves varies from the rule-bound closure of logical codes (such as computer codes) to the interpretative looseness of poetic codes. Some theorists question whether some of the looser systems constitute codes at all (e.g. Guiraud 1975, 24, 41, 43–4, 65).

Perceptual codes

Some theorists argue that even our perception of the everyday world around us involves codes. Fredric Jameson declares that 'all perceptual systems are already languages in their own right' (Jameson 1972, 152). As Derrida would put it, perception is always already representation. 'Perception depends on coding the world into iconic signs that can re-present it within our mind. The force of the apparent identity is enormous, however. We think that it is the world itself we see in our "mind's eye", rather than a coded picture of it' (Nichols 1981, 11–12). According to the Gestalt psychologists there are certain universal features in human visual perception which in semiotic terms can be seen as constituting a perceptual code. We owe the concept of 'figure' and 'ground' in perception to this group of psychologists. Confronted by a visual image, we seem to need to separate a dominant shape (a 'figure' with a definite contour) from what our current concerns relegate to 'background' (or 'ground'). An illustration of this is the famous ambiguous figure which initially seems to be either a white vase on a black background or two human faces in silhouette facing each other against a white background. Images such as this are ambiguous concerning figure and ground. Perceptual set operates in such cases and we tend to favour one interpretation over the other. When we have identified a figure, the contours seem to belong to it, and it appears to be in front of the ground.

In addition to introducing the terms 'figure' and 'ground', the Gestalt psychologists outlined what seemed to be several fundamental and universal principles (sometimes even called 'laws') of perceptual organization. The main ones are as follows (some of the terms vary a little): proximity, similarity, good continuation, closure, smallness, surroundedness, symmetry and prägnanz (Coren *et al.* 1994). The principle of *proximity* is that features which are close together are associated, while the principle of *similarity* is that features which look similar are associated. A third principle of perceptual organization is that of *good continuity*. This principle is that contours based on smooth continuity are preferred to abrupt changes of direction. *Closure* is a fourth principle of perceptual organization: interpretations which produce 'closed' rather than 'open' figures are favoured. A fifth principle of perceptual organization is that of *smallness*. Smaller areas tend to be seen as figures against a larger background. The principle of symmetry is that symmetrical areas tend to be seen as figures against asymmetrical backgrounds. Then there is the principle of *surroundedness*, according to which areas which can be seen as surrounded by others tend to be perceived as figures. All of these principles of perceptual organization serve the overarching principle of *prägnanz*, which is that the simplest and most stable interpretations are favoured.

What the Gestalt principles of perceptual organization suggest is that we may be predisposed towards interpreting ambiguous images in one way rather than another by universal principles. We may accept such a proposition at the same time as accepting that such predispositions may also be generated by other factors. Similarly, we may accept the Gestalt principles while at the same time regarding other aspects of perception as being *learned* and culturally variable rather than innate. The Gestalt principles can be seen as reinforcing the notion that the world is not simply and objectively

151

'out there' but is constructed in the process of perception. As Bill Nichols comments, 'a useful habit formed by our brains must not be mistaken for an essential attribute of reality. Just as we must learn to read an image, we must learn to read the physical world. Once we have developed this skill (which we do very early in life), it is very easy to mistake it for an automatic or unlearned process, just as we may mistake our particular way of reading, or seeing, for a natural, ahistorical and noncultural given' (Nichols 1981, 12).

We are rarely aware of our own habitual ways of seeing the world. It takes deliberate effort to become more aware of everyday visual perception as a code. Its habitual application obscures the traces of its intervention. However, a simple experiment allows us to 'bracket' visual perception at least briefly. For this to be possible, you need to sit facing the same direction without moving your body for a few minutes, registering a visual impression of what is before your eyes without trying to separate it out into objects and spaces. For the duration of your success in this, 'depth' will disappear.

This process of bracketing perception will be more familiar to those who draw or paint who are used to converting three dimensions into two. For those who do not, this little experiment may be quite surprising. We are routinely anaesthetized to a psychological mechanism called 'perceptual constancy' which stabilizes the relative shifts in the apparent shapes and sizes of people and objects in the world around us as we change our visual viewpoints in relation to them. Without mechanisms such as categorization and perceptual constancy the world would be no more than what William James called a 'great blooming and buzzing confusion' (James 1890, 488). Perceptual constancy ensures that 'the variability of the everyday world becomes translated by reference to less variable codes. The environment becomes a text to be read like any other text' (Nichols 1981, 26).

Key differences between 'bracketed' perception and everyday perception may be summarized as in Table 5.1 (Nichols 1981, 13, 20).

TABLE 5.1 'Bracketed' perception and normal perception

Bracketed perception	Normal perception
A bounded visual space, oval, approximately 180° laterally, 150° vertically	Unbounded visual space
Clarity of focus at only one point with a gradient of increasing vagueness toward the margin (clarity of focus corresponds to the space whose light falls upon the fovea)	Clarity of focus throughout
Parallel lines appear to converge: the lateral sides of a rectangular surface extending away from the viewer appear to converge	Parallel lines extend without converging: the sides of a rectangular surface extending away from the viewer remain parallel
If the head is moved, the shapes of objects appear to be deformed	If the head is moved, shapes remain constant
The visual space appears to lack depth	Visual space is never wholly depthless
A world of patterns and sensation, of surfaces, edges and gradients	A world of familiar objects and meaning

Source: Nichols 1981, 13, 20

Social codes

Constructionist theorists argue that linguistic codes play a key role in the construction and maintenance of social realities. We learn not the world but the codes into which it has been structured. The Whorfian hypothesis, or Sapir–Whorf theory, is named after the American linguists Edward Sapir and Benjamin Lee Whorf. In its most extreme version the Sapir–Whorf hypothesis can be described as relating two associated principles: *linguistic determinism* and *linguistic relativism*. Applying these two principles, the Whorfian thesis is that people who speak languages with very different phonological, grammatical and semantic distinctions perceive and think about the world quite differently, their worldviews being shaped or determined by their language (Sapir 1958, 69; Whorf 1956, 213–14). The extreme determinist form of the Sapir–Whorf hypothesis is rejected by most contemporary linguists. Critics note that we cannot make inferences about differences in worldview solely on the basis of differences in linguistic structure. While few linguists would accept the Whorfian hypothesis in its 'strong', extreme or deterministic form, many now accept a 'weak', more moderate, or limited Whorfianism, namely that the ways in which we see the world may be *influenced* by the kind of language we use.

Within a culture, social differentiation is 'over-determined' by a multitude of social codes. We communicate our social identities through the work we do, the way we talk, the clothes we wear, our hairstyles, our eating habits, our domestic environments and possessions, our use of leisure time, our modes of travelling and so on. Language use acts as a key marker of social identity. A controversial distinction regarding British linguistic usage was introduced in the 1960s by the sociologist Basil Bernstein between so-called 'restricted code' and 'elaborated code' (Bernstein 1971). Restricted code was used in informal situations and was characterized by a reliance on situational context, a lack of stylistic variety, an emphasis on the speaker's membership of the group, simple syntax and the frequent use of gestures and tag questions (such as 'Isn't it?'). Elaborated code was used in formal situations and was characterized by less dependence on context, wide stylistic range (including the passive voice), more adjectives, relatively complex syntax and the use of the pronoun 'I'. Bernstein's argument was that middle-class children had access to both of these codes while working-class children had access only to restricted codes. Such clear-cut distinctions and correlations with social class are now widely challenged by linguists (Crystal 1987, 40). However, we still routinely use such linguistic cues as a basis for making inferences about people's social backgrounds.

Social differentiation is observable not only from linguistic codes, but from a host of non-verbal codes. A survey of non-verbal codes is not manageable here, and the interested reader should consult some of the classic texts and specialist guides to the literature (e.g. Hall 1959 and 1966; Argyle 1969, 1983 and 1988, Birdwhistell 1971). In the context of the present text a few examples must suffice to illustrate the importance of non-verbal codes. Non-verbal codes which regulate a 'sensory regime' are of particular interest. Within particular cultural contexts there are, for instance, largely inexplicit 'codes of looking' which regulate how people may look at other people (including taboos on certain kinds of looking). Such codes tend to retreat to transparency when the cultural context is one's own. 'Children are instructed to "look at me", not to stare at strangers, and not to look at certain parts of the body . . . People have to look in order to be polite, but not to look at the wrong people or in the wrong place, e.g. at deformed people' (Argyle 1988, 158). In Luo in Kenya one should not look at one's mother-in-law; in Nigeria one should not look at a high-status person; among some South American Indians during conversation one should not look at the other person; in Japan one should look at the neck, not the face; and so on (Argyle 1983, 95).

The duration of the gaze is also culturally variable: in 'contact cultures' such as those of the Arabs, Latin Americans and southern Europeans, people look more than the British or white Americans, while black Americans look less (Argyle 1988, 158). In contact cultures too little gaze is seen as insincere, dishonest or impolite while in non-contact cultures too much gaze ('staring') is seen as threatening, disrespectful and insulting (Argyle 1988, 165 and 1983, 95). Within the bounds of the cultural conventions, people who avoid one's gaze may be seen as nervous, tense, evasive and lacking in confidence, while people who look a lot may tend to be seen as friendly and self-confident (Argyle 1983, 93). Such codes may sometimes be deliberately violated. In the USA in the 1960s, bigoted white Americans employed a sustained 'hate stare' directed against blacks, which was designed to depersonalize the victims (Goffman 1969).

Codes of looking are particularly important in relation to gender differentiation. One woman reported to a male friend: 'One of the things I really envy about men is the right to look.' She pointed out that in public places, 'men could look freely at women, but women could only glance back surreptitiously' (Dyer 1992, 103). Brian Pranger (1990) reports on his investigation of 'the gay gaze':

> Gay men are able to subtly communicate their shared world-view by a special gaze that seems to be unique to them ... Most gay men develop a canny ability to instantly discern from the returned look of another man whether or not he is gay. The gay gaze is not only lingering, but also a visual probing ... Almost everyone I interviewed said that they could tell who was gay by the presence or absence of this look.
>
> (in Higgins 1993, 235–6)

We learn to read the world in terms of the codes and conventions which are dominant within the specific socio-cultural contexts and roles within which we are socialized. In the process of adopting a way of seeing, we also adopt an 'identity'. The most important constancy in our understanding of reality is our sense of who we are as an individual. Our sense of self as a constancy is a social construction which is 'over-determined' by a host of interacting codes within our culture (Berger and Luckmann 1967; Burr 1995). 'Roles, conventions, attitudes, language – to varying degrees these are internalized in order to be repeated, and through the constancies of repetition a consistent locus gradually emerges: the self. Although never fully determined by these internalizations, the self would be entirely undetermined without them' (Nichols 1981, 30). When we first encounter the notion that the self is a social construction we are likely to find it counter-intuitive. We usually take for granted our status as autonomous individuals with unique 'personalities'. We will return later to the notion of our 'positioning' as 'subjects'. For the moment, we will note simply that 'society depends upon the fact that its members grant its founding fictions, myths or codes a taken-for-granted status' (ibid.). Culturally variable perceptual codes are typically inexplicit, and we are not normally conscious of the roles which they play. To users of the dominant, most widespread codes, meanings generated within such codes tend to appear 'obvious' and 'natural'. Stuart Hall comments:

> Certain codes may . . . be so widely distributed in a specific language community or culture, and be learned at so early an age, that they appear not to be constructed – the effect of an articulation between sign and referent – but to be 'naturally' given. Simple visual signs appear to have achieved a 'near-universality' in this sense: though evidence remains that even apparently 'natural' visual codes are culture-specific. However, this does not mean that no codes have intervened; rather, that the codes have been profoundly *naturalized*.
>
> (Hall 1980, 132)

Learning these codes involves adopting the values, assumptions and 'worldviews' which are built into them without normally being aware of their intervention in the construction of reality.

Textual codes

Every text is a system of signs organized according to codes and subcodes which reflect certain values, attitudes, beliefs, assumptions and practices. Codes transcend single texts, linking them together in an interpretative framework which is used by their producers and interpreters. In creating texts we select and combine signs in relation to the codes with which we are familiar. Codes help to simplify phenomena in order to make it easier to communicate experiences. In reading texts, we interpret signs with reference to what seem to be appropriate codes. This helps to limit their possible meanings.

Usually the appropriate codes are obvious, 'overdetermined' by all sorts of contextual cues. The medium employed clearly influences the choice of codes. In this sense we routinely 'judge a book by its cover'. We can typically identify a text as a poem simply by the way in which it is set out on the page. The use of what is sometimes called 'scholarly apparatus' (such as introductions, acknowledgements, section headings, tables, diagrams, notes, references, bibliographies, appendices and indexes) – is what makes academic texts immediately identifiable as such to readers. Such cueing is part of the *metalingual* function of signs. With familiar codes we are rarely conscious of our acts of interpretation, but occasionally a text requires us to work a little harder – for instance, by pinning down the most appropriate signified for a key signifier (as in jokes based on word play) – before we can identify the relevant codes for making sense of the text as a whole. Textual codes do not *determine* the meanings of texts but dominant codes do tend to *constrain* them. Social conventions ensure that signs cannot mean whatever an individual wants them to mean. The use of codes helps to guide us towards what Stuart Hall calls 'a preferred reading' and away from what Umberto Eco calls 'aberrant decoding', though media texts do vary in the extent to which they are open to interpretation (Hall 1980, 134).

One of the most fundamental kinds of textual code relates to *genre*. Traditional definitions of genres tend to be based on the notion that they constitute particular conventions of content (such as themes or settings) and/or form (including structure and style) which are shared by the texts which are regarded as belonging to them. This mode of defining a genre is deeply problematic. For instance, genres overlap and texts often exhibit the conventions of more than one genre. It is seldom hard to find texts which are exceptions to any given definition of a particular genre. Furthermore, the structuralist concern with synchronic analysis ignores the way in which genres are involved in a constant process of change.

An overview of genre taxonomies in various media is beyond the scope of the current text, but it is appropriate here to allude to a few key cross-media genre distinctions. The organization of public libraries suggests that one of the most fundamental contemporary genre distinctions is between *fiction* and *non-fiction* – a categorization which highlights the importance of modality judgements. Even such an apparently basic distinction is revealed to be far from straightforward as soon as one tries to apply it to the books on one's own shelves or to an evening's television viewing. Another binary distinction is based on the *kinds of language* used: *poetry* and *prose* – the 'norm' being the latter, as Molière's Monsieur Jourdain famously discovered: 'Good Heavens! For more than forty years I have been speaking prose without knowing it!' Even here there are grey areas, with literary prose often being regarded as 'poetic'. This is related to the issue of how librarians, critics and academics decide what is 'literature' as opposed to mere 'fiction'. As with the typology of codes in general, no genre taxonomy can be ideologically neutral. Traditional rhetoric distinguishes between four kinds of discourse: *exposition*, *argument*, *description* and *narration* (Brooks and Warren 1972, 44). These four forms, which relate to *primary purposes*, are often referred to as different genres (e.g. Fairclough 1995, 88). However, texts frequently involve any combination of these forms and they are perhaps best thought of as 'modes'. More widely described as genres are the four 'modes of emplotment' which Hayden White adopted from Northrop Frye in his study of historiography: *romance*, *tragedy*, *comedy* and *satire* (White 1973). Useful as such interpretative frameworks can be, however, no taxonomy of textual genres adequately represents the diversity of texts.

Despite such theoretical problems, various interpretative communities (at particular periods in time) do operate on the basis of a negotiated (if somewhat loose and fluid) consensus concerning what they regard as the primary genres relevant to their purposes. While there is far more to a genre code than that which may seem to relate to specifically textual features it can still be useful to consider the distinctive properties attributed to a genre by its users. For instance, if we take the case of film, the textual features typically listed by theorists include:

- **narrative** – similar (sometimes formulaic) plots and structures, predictable situations, sequences, episodes, obstacles, conflicts and resolutions;

- **characterization** – similar types of characters (sometimes stereotypes), roles, personal qualities, motivations, goals, behaviour;
- basic **themes**, topics, subject-matter (social, cultural, psychological, professional, political, sexual, moral) and values;
- **setting** – geographical and historical;
- **iconography** (echoing the narrative, characterization, themes and setting) – a familiar stock of images or motifs, the connotations of which have become fixed; primarily but not necessarily visual, including décor, costume and objects, certain 'typecast' performers (some of whom may have become 'icons'), familiar patterns of dialogue, characteristic music and sounds, and appropriate physical topography; and
- **filmic techniques** – stylistic or formal conventions of camerawork, lighting, sound-recording, use of colour, editing, etc. (viewers are often less conscious of such conventions than of those relating to content).

Some film genres tend to be defined primarily by their *subject-matter* (e.g. detective films), some by their *setting* (e.g. the western) and others by their *narrative* form (e.g. the musical). Less easy to place in one of the traditional categories are *mood* and *tone* (which are key features of the *film noir*). In addition to *textual* features, different genres (in any medium) also involve different purposes, pleasures, audiences, modes of involvement, styles of interpretation and text–reader relationships. A particularly important feature which tends not to figure in traditional accounts and which is often assigned to *text–reader relationships* rather than to textual features in contemporary accounts is *mode of address*, which involves inbuilt assumptions about the audience, such as that the 'ideal' viewer is male (the usual categories here are class, age, gender and ethnicity). We will return to this important issue shortly.

Codes of realism

All representations are systems of signs: they signify rather than 'represent', and they do so with primary reference to codes rather than to 'reality'. Adopting such a stance need not, of course, entail a denial of the existence of an external reality but it does involve the recognition that textual codes which are 'realistic' are nonetheless (to some degree) conventional. From the Renaissance until the nineteenth century, Western art was dominated by a mimetic or representational purpose which still prevails in popular culture. Such art denies its status as a signifying system, seeking to represent a world which is assumed to exist before, and independently of, the act of representation. Realism involves an instrumental view of the medium as a neutral means of representing reality. The signified is foregrounded at the expense of the signifier. Realist representational practices tend to mask the processes involved in producing texts, as if they were slices of life 'untouched by human hand'. As Catherine Belsey notes, 'realism is plausible not because it reflects the world, but because it is constructed out of what is (discursively) familiar' (Belsey 1980, 47). Ironically, the 'naturalness' of realist texts comes not from their 'reflection of reality' but from their uses of codes which are derived from other texts. The familiarity of particular semiotic practices renders their mediation invisible. Our recognition of the familiar in realist texts repeatedly confirms the 'objectivity' of our habitual ways of seeing.

However, the codes of the various realisms are not always initially familiar. In the context of painting, the art historian Ernst Gombrich has illustrated (for instance, in relation to John Constable) how aesthetic codes which now seem 'almost photographic' to many viewers were regarded at the time of their emergence as strange and radical (Gombrich 1977). Eco adds that early viewers of Impressionist art could not recognize the subjects represented and declared that real life was not like this (Eco 1976, 254; Gombrich 1982, 279). Most people had not previously noticed coloured shadows in nature (Gombrich 1982, 27, 30, 34). Even photography involves a translation from three dimensions into two, and anthropologists have often reported the initial difficulties experienced by people in primal tribes

161

in making sense of photographs and films (Deregowski 1980), while historians note that even in recent times the first instant snapshots confounded Western viewers because they were not accustomed to arrested images of transient movements and needed to go through a process of cultural habituation or training (Gombrich 1982, 100, 273). Photography involved a new 'way of seeing' (to use John Berger's phrase) which had to be learned before it could become 'transparent'. What human beings see does not resemble a sequence of rectangular frames, and camerawork and editing conventions are not direct replications of the way in which we see the everyday world. When we look at things around us in everyday life we gain a sense of depth from our binocular vision, by rotating our head or by moving in relation to what we are looking at. To get a clearer view we can adjust the focus of our eyes. But for making sense of depth when we look at a photograph none of this helps. We have to decode the cues. Semioticians argue that, although exposure over time leads 'visual language' to seem 'natural', we need to learn how to 'read' even visual and audio-visual texts (though see Messaris 1982 and 1994 for a critique of this stance).

In the cinema, 'the gestural codes and the bodily and facial expressions of actors in silent films belonged to conventions which connoted realism when they were made and watched' (Bignell 1997, 193), whereas now such codes stand out as 'unrealistic'. When the pioneering American film-maker D. W. Griffith initially proposed the use of close-ups, his producers warned him that the audience would be disconcerted since the rest of the actor was missing (Rosenblum and Karen 1979, 37–8). What count as 'realistic' modes of representation are both culturally and historically variable. To most contemporary western audiences the conventions of American cinema seem more 'realistic' than the conventions of modern Indian cinema, for instance, because the latter are so much less familiar. Even within a culture, over historical time particular codes become increasingly less familiar, and as we look back at texts produced centuries ago we are struck by the strangeness of their codes – their maintenance systems having long since been superseded. In his influential book, *Languages of Art*, the North American philosopher Nelson

Goodman (1906–98) insisted that 'realism is relative, determined by the system of representation standard for a given culture or person at a given time' (Goodman 1968, 37).

As noted earlier, Peirce referred to signs in (unedited) photographic media as being *indexical* as well as *iconic* – meaning that the signifiers did not simply 'resemble' their signifieds but were mechanical recordings and reproductions of them (within the limitations of the medium). John Berger also argued in 1968 that photographs are 'automatic' 'records of things seen' and that 'photography has no language of its own' (cited in Tagg 1988, 187). In 'The photographic message' (1961), Roland Barthes famously declared that 'the photographic image ... is a *message without a code*' (Barthes 1977, 17). Since this phrase is frequently misunderstood, it may be worth clarifying its context with reference to this essay together with an essay published three years later – 'The rhetoric of the image' (ibid., 32–51). Barthes was referring to the 'absolutely analogical, which is to say, *continuous*' character of the medium (ibid., 20). 'Is it possible', he asks, 'to conceive of an analogical code (as opposed to a digital one)?' (ibid., 32). The relation between the signifier and the thing signified is not arbitrary as in language (ibid., 35). He grants that photography involves both mechanical *reduction* (flattening, perspective, proportion and colour) and human *intervention* (choice of subject, framing, composition, optical point of view, distance, angle, lighting, focus, speed, exposure, printing and 'trick effects'). However, photography does not involve rule-governed *transformation* as codes can (ibid., 17, 20–5, 36, 43, 44). 'In the photograph – at least at the level of the literal message – the relationship of signifieds to signifiers is not one of "transformation" but of "recording".' Alluding to the indexical nature of the medium, he notes that the image is 'captured mechanically' and that this reinforces the myth of its 'objectivity' (ibid., 44). Unlike a drawing or a painting, a photograph reproduces 'everything': it 'cannot intervene *within* the object (except by trick effects)' (ibid., 43). 'In order to move from the reality to the photograph it is in no way necessary to divide up this reality into units and to constitute these units as signs, substantially different from the object they communicate; there is no necessity to set up . . . a code, between the object and its image' (ibid., 17). In consequence, he noted, photographs cannot be reduced to words.

However, 'every sign supposes a code' and at a level higher than the 'literal' level of denotation, a *connotative* code can be identified. He noted that at the 'level of production', 'the press photograph is an object that has been worked on, chosen, composed, constructed, treated according to professional or ideological norms' and, at the 'level of reception', the photograph 'is not only perceived, received, it is *read*, connected by the public that consumes it to a traditional stock of signs' (ibid., 19). Reading a photograph involved relating it to a 'rhetoric' (ibid., 18, 19). In addition to the photographic techniques already noted, he refers for instance to the signifying functions of: postures, expressions and gestures; the associations evoked by depicted objects and settings; sequences of photographs, e.g. in magazines (which he refers to as 'syntax'); and relationships with accompanying text (ibid., 21–5). He added that 'thanks to the code of connotation the reading of the photograph is . . . always historical; it depends on the reader's "knowledge" just as though it were a matter of a real language, intelligible only if one has learned the signs' (ibid., 28).

Clearly, therefore, it would be a misinterpretation of Barthes' declaration that 'the photographic image . . . is a *message without a code*' to suggest that he meant that no codes are involved in producing or 'reading' photographs. His main point was that it did not (at least yet) seem possible to reduce the photographic image itself to elementary 'signifying units'. Far from suggesting that photographs are purely denotative, he declared that the 'purely "denotative" status of the photograph . . . has every chance of being mythical (these are the characteristics that commonsense attributes to the photograph)'. At the level of the analogue image itself, while the connotative code was implicit and could only be inferred, he was convinced that it was nonetheless 'active' (ibid., 19). Citing Bruner and Piaget, he notes the possibility that 'there is no perception without immediate categorization' (ibid., 28). Reading a photograph also depends closely on the reader's culture, knowledge of the world, and ethical and ideological stances (ibid., 29). Barthes adds that 'the viewer receives *at one and the same time* the perceptual message and the cultural message' (ibid., 36).

In *Writing Degree Zero*, Roland Barthes sought to demonstrate that the classical textual codes of French writing (from the mid-seventeenth century until the mid-nineteenth century) had been used to suggest that such codes were natural, neutral and transparent conduits for an innocent and objective reflection of reality (i.e. the operation of the codes was masked). Barthes argues that while generating the illusion of a 'zero-degree' of style, these codes served the purpose of fabricating reality in accord with the bourgeois view of the world and covertly propagating bourgeois values as self-evident (Barthes 1953; Hawkes 1977, 107–8). In 'The Rhetoric of the image' Barthes developed this line of argument in relation to the medium of photography, arguing that because it appears to record rather than to transform or signify, it serves an ideological function. Photography 'seems to found in nature the signs of culture . . . masking the constructed meaning under the appearance of the given meaning' (Barthes 1977, 45–6).

Most semioticians emphasize that photography involves visual codes, and that film and television involve both visual and aural codes. John Tagg argues that 'the camera is never neutral. The representations it produces are highly coded' (Tagg 1988, 63–4; cf. 187). Cinematic and televisual codes include: genre; camerawork (shot size, focus, lens movement, camera movement, angle, lens choice, composition); editing (cuts and fades, cutting rate and rhythm); manipulation of time (compression, flashbacks, flashforwards, slow motion); lighting; colour; sound (soundtrack, music); graphics; and narrative style. Christian Metz added authorial style, and distinguished codes from sub-codes, where a sub-code was a particular choice from within a code (e.g. western within genre, or naturalistic or expressionist lighting subcodes within the lighting code). The syntagmatic dimension was a relation of combination between different codes and sub-codes; the paradigmatic dimension was that of the film-maker's choice of particular sub-codes within a code. Since, as Metz noted, 'a film is not "cinema" from one end to another' (cited in Nöth 1990, 468), film and television involve many codes which are not specific to these media.

While some photographic and filmic codes are relatively arbitrary, many of the codes employed in 'realistic' photographic images or films simulate many of the perceptual cues used in encountering the physical world (Nichols 1981, 35; see also Messaris 1982 and 1994). This is a key reason for their perceived 'realism'. The depiction of 'reality' even in iconic signs involves variable codes which have to be learned, yet which, with experience, come to be taken for granted as transparent and obvious. Eco argues that it is misleading to regard such signs as less 'conventional' than other kinds of signs (Eco 1976, 190ff.): even photography and film involve conventional codes. Paul Messaris, however, stresses that the formal conventions of representational visual codes (including paintings and drawings) are not 'arbitrary' (Messaris 1994), and Ernst Gombrich offers a critique of what he sees as the 'extreme conventionalism' of Nelson Goodman's stance (Gombrich 1982, 278–97), stressing that 'the so-called conventions of the visual image [vary] according to the relative ease or difficulty with which they can be learned' (Gombrich 1982, 283) – a notion familiar from the Peircean ranking of signifier-signified relationships in terms of relative conventionality.

Invisible editing

Semioticians often refer to 'reading' film or television – a notion which may seem strange since the meaning of filmic images appears not to need decoding at all. When we encounter a shot in which someone is looking offscreen we usually interpret the next shot as what they are looking at. Consider the following example offered by Ralph Rosenblum, a major professional film editor. In an initial shot, 'a man awakens suddenly in the middle of the night, bolts up in bed, stares ahead intensely, and twitches his nose'. If we then cut to 'a room where two people are desperately fighting a billowing blaze, the viewers realize that through clairvoyance, a warning dream, or the smell of smoke, the man in bed has become aware of danger'. Alternatively, if we cut from the first shot to 'a distraught wife defending her decision to commit her husband to a mental institution, they will understand that the man in bed is her husband and that the dramatic tension will surround the couple'. If it's a Hitchcock movie 'the juxtaposition of the man and the wife will immediately raise questions in the viewers' minds about foul play on the part of the woman'. This form of editing may alert us not only to a link between the two consecutive shots but in some cases to a genre. If we cut to an image of clouds drifting before the full moon, we know that we can expect a 'wolf-man' adventure (Rosenblum and Karen 1979, 2).

Such interpretations are not 'self-evident': they are a feature of a filmic editing code. Having internalized such codes at a very young age we then cease to be conscious of their existence. Once we know the code, decoding it is almost automatic and the code retreats to invisibility. The convention just described is known as an *eyeline match* and it is part of the dominant editing code in film and television narrative which is referred to as 'the continuity system' or as 'invisible editing' (Reisz and Millar 1972; Bordwell *et al.* 1988, Chapter 16; Bordwell and Thompson 1993, 261ff.). While minor elements within the code have been modified over time, most of the main elements are still much the same now as when they were developed many decades ago. This code was originally developed in Hollywood feature films but most narrative films and television dramas now routinely employ it. Editing supports rather than dominates the narrative: the story and the behaviour of its characters are the centre of attention. While nowadays there may be cuts every few seconds, these are intended to be unobtrusive. The technique gives the impression that the edits are always required and are motivated by the events in the 'reality' that the camera is recording rather than the result of a desire to tell a story in a particular way. The 'seamlessness' convinces us of its 'realism', but the code consists of an integrated system of technical conventions. These conventions serve to assist viewers in transforming the two-dimensional screen into a plausible three-dimensional world in which they can become absorbed.

A major cinematic convention is the use of the *establishing shot*: soon after a cut to a new scene we are given a long shot of it, allowing us to survey the overall space – followed by closer 'cut-in' shots focusing on details of the scene. Re-establishing shots are used when needed, as in the case of the entry of a new character. Another key convention involved in helping the viewer to make sense of the spatial organization of a scene is the so-called *180° rule*. Successive shots are not shown from both sides of the 'axis of action' since this would produce apparent changes of direction on screen. For instance, a character moving right to left across the screen in one shot is not shown moving left to right in the next shot. This helps to establish where the viewer is in relation to the action. In separate shots of speakers in a dialogue, one speaker always looks left while the other looks right. Even in telephone conversations the characters are oriented as if facing each other.

In *point-of-view (POV) shots*, the camera is placed (usually briefly) in the spatial position of a character to provide a subjective point of view. This is often in the form of alternating shots between two characters – a technique known as *shot/reverse-shot*. Once the 'axis of action' has been established, the alternation of shots with reverse-shots allows the viewer to glance back and forth at the participants in a dialogue (*matched shots* are used in which the shot-size and framing of the subject is similar). In such sequences, some of these shots are *reaction shots*. All of the techniques described so far reflect the goal of ensuring that the same characters are always in the same parts of the screen.

Because this code foregrounds the narrative, it employs what are called *motivated cuts*: changes of view or scene occur only when the action requires it and the viewer expects it. When cuts from one distance and/or angle to another are made, they are normally *matches on action*: cuts are usually made when the subject is *moving*, so that viewers are sufficiently distracted by the action to be unaware of the cut. There is a studious avoidance of *jump-cuts*: the so-called *30° rule* is that a shot of the same subject as the previous shot must differ in camera angle by at least 30° (otherwise it will feel to the viewer like an apparently pointless shift in position).

This cinematic editing code has become so familiar to us that we no longer consciously notice its conventions until they are broken. Indeed, it seems so 'natural' that some will feel that it closely reflects phenomenal reality and thus find it hard to accept it as a code at all. Do we not mentally 'cut' from one image to another all of the time in everyday visual perception? This case seems strongest when all that is involved is a shift corresponding to a turn of our head or a refocusing of our eyes (Reisz and Millar 1972, 213–16). But of course many cuts would require us to change our viewing position. A common response to this – at least if we limit ourselves to moderate changes of angle or distance and ignore changes of scene – is to say that the editing technique represents a reasonable analogy with the normal mental processes involved in everyday perception. A cut to close-up can thus be seen to reflect as well as direct a purposive shift in attention. Of course, when the shot shifts so radically that it would be a physical impossibility to imitate this in everyday life, then the argument by perceptual analogy breaks down. And cuts reflect such shifts more often than not; only fleetingly does film *editing* closely reflect the perceptual experience of 'being there' in person. But of course a gripping narrative will already have led to our 'suspension of disbelief'. We thus routinely and unconsciously grant the film-maker the same 'dramatic licence' with which we are familiar not only from the majority of films which we watch but also from analogous codes employed in other media – such as theatre, the novel or the comic-strip.

For an argument questioning the interpretative importance of a cinematic editing code and emphasizing real-life analogies, see the lively and interesting book by Paul Messaris entitled *Visual Literacy* (Messaris 1994, 71ff.). However, his main focus of attack is on the stance that the cinematic editing code is *totally arbitrary* – a position which few would defend. Clearly these techniques were designed where possible to be analogous to familiar codes so that they would quickly become invisible to viewers once they were habituated to them. Messaris argues that context is more important than code; it likely that where the viewer is in doubt about the meaning of a specific cut, interpretation may be aided by applying knowledge either from other textual codes (such as the logic of the narrative) or from relevant social codes (such as behavioural expectations in analogous situations in everyday life). The interpretation of film draws on knowledge of multiple codes. Adopting a semiotic approach to cinematic editing is not simply to acknowledge the importance of conventions and conventionality but to highlight the process of naturalization involved in the 'editing out' of what 'goes without saying'.

The emphasis given to *visual* codes by most theorists is perhaps partly due to their use of printed media for their commentaries – media which are inherently biased towards the visual, and may also derive from a Western tendency to privilege the visual over other channels. We need to remind ourselves that it is not only the visual image which is mediated, constructed and codified in the various media – in film, television and radio, this also applies to *sound*. Film and television are not simply visual media but *audio-visual* media. Even where the mediated character of the visual is acknowledged, there is a tendency for sound to be regarded as largely unmediated. But codes are involved in the choice and positioning of microphones, the use of particular equipment for recording, editing and reproduction, the use of diegetic sound (ostensibly emanating from the action in the story) versus non-diegetic sound, direct versus post-synchronous (dubbed) recording, simulated sounds (such as the highly conventionalized signifier for a punch) and so on (Stam 2000, 212–23; Altman 1992). In the dominant Hollywood tradition, conventional sound codes included features such as:

- *diegesis*: sounds should be relevant to the story;
- *hierarchy*: dialogue should override background sound;
- *seamlessness*: no gaps or abrupt changes in sound;
- *integration*: no sounds without images or vice versa;
- *readability*: all sounds should be identifiable;
- *motivation*: unusual sounds should be what characters are supposed to be hearing.

(Stam 2000, 216–17)

Sound can also assist in making visual editing 'invisible': within the same scene a 'sound-bridge' (carrying the same unbroken sound sequence) is used across a cut from one shot to another, as if there had been no cut at all.

Broadcast and narrowcast codes

Some codes are more widespread and accessible than others. Those which are widely distributed and which are learned at an early age may seem 'natural' rather than constructed (Hall 1980, 132). John Fiske distinguishes between *broadcast* codes, which are shared by member of a mass audience, and *narrowcast* codes which are aimed at a more limited audience; pop music is a broadcast code; ballet is a narrowcast code (Fiske 1982, 78ff.). Broadcast codes are learned through experience; narrowcast codes often involve more deliberate learning (Fiske 1989, 315). Following the controversial sociolinguistic theories of Basil Bernstein, what Fiske refers to as broadcast codes are described by some media theorists as 'restricted codes', with Fiske's narrowcast codes being described as 'elaborated codes' (Bernstein 1971). 'Restricted' codes are described as structurally simpler and more repetitive ('overcoded'), having what information theorists call a high degree of *redundancy*. In such codes several elements serve to emphasize and reinforce preferred meanings. Umberto Eco describes as 'closed' those texts (such as many mass media texts) which show a strong tendency to encourage a particular interpretation (Eco 1981). In contrast, literary writing – in particular poetry – has a minimum of redundancy (Lotman 1976). The distinction between 'restricted' and 'elaborated' codes serves to stress the difference between an élite ('highbrows') and the majority ('lowbrows'). Art for the élite is held to be more 'original' and unpredictable. Fiske suggests that narrowcast (elaborated) codes have the potential to be more subtle; broadcast (restricted) codes can lead to cliché. Terry Eagleton argues that 'literary texts are "code-productive" and "code-transgressive"' rather than merely 'code-confirming' (Eagleton 1983, 125). Insofar as such positions suggest that broadcast codes restrict expressive possibilities this arguments has affinities with Whorfianism. The dangers of élitism inherent in such stances make it particularly important that the evidence is closely examined in the context of the particular code under study.

Interaction of textual codes

Any text uses not one code, but many. Theorists vary in their classification of such codes. In his book *S/Z*, Roland Barthes itemized five codes employed in literary texts: *hermeneutic* (narrative turning-points); *proairetic* (basic narrative actions); *cultural* (prior social knowledge); *semic* (medium-related codes) and *symbolic* (themes) (Barthes 1974). Yuri Lotman argued that a poem is a 'system of systems' – lexical, syntactical, metrical, morphological, phonological, and so on – and that the relations between such systems generated powerful literary effects. Each code sets up expectations which other codes violate (Lotman 1976). The same signifier may play its part in several different codes. The meaning of literary texts may thus be 'overdetermined' by several codes. Just as signs need to be analysed in their relation to other signs, so codes need to be analysed in relation to other codes. Becoming aware of the interplay of such codes requires a potentially recursive process of rereading. Nor can such readings be confined to the internal structure of a text, since the codes utilized within it extend beyond any specific text – an issue of 'intertextuality' to which we will return.

Codification

The synchronic perspective of structuralist semioticians tends to give the impression that codes are static. But codes have origins and they do evolve, and studying their evolution is a legitimate semiotic endeavour. Guiraud argues that there is a gradual process of 'codification' whereby systems of implicit interpretation acquire the status of codes (Guiraud 1975, 41). Codes are dynamic systems which change over time, and are thus historically as well as socioculturally situated. Codification is a *process* whereby conventions are established. For instance, Metz shows how in Hollywood cinema the white hat became codified as the signifier of a 'good' cowboy; eventually this convention became over-used and was abandoned (Metz 1974).

In historical perspective, many of the codes of a new medium evolve from those of related existing media (for instance, many televisual techniques owe their origins to their use in film and photography). New conventions also develop to match the technical potential of the medium and the uses to which it is put. Some codes are unique to (or at least characteristic of) a specific medium or to closely related media (e.g. 'fade to black' in film and television);

others are shared by (or similar in) several media (e.g. scene breaks); and some are drawn from cultural practices which are not tied to a medium (e.g. body language) (Monaco 1981, 146ff.). Some are more specific to particular genres within a medium. Some are more broadly linked either to the domain of science ('logical codes', suppressing connotation and diversity of interpretation) or to that of the arts ('aesthetic codes', celebrating connotation and diversity of interpretation), though such differences are differences of degree rather than of kind.

Whatever the nature of any embedded ideology, it has been claimed that as a consequence of their internalization of the codes of the medium, 'those born in the age of radio perceive the world differently from those born into the age of television' (Gumpert and Cathcart 1985). Critics have objected to the degree of technological determinism which is sometimes involved in such stances, but this is not to suggest that our use of such tools and techniques is without influence on our habits of mind. If this is so, the subtle phenomenology of new media is worthy of closer attention than is typically accorded to it. Whatever the medium, learning to notice the operation of codes when representations and meanings seem natural, obvious and transparent is clearly not an easy task. Understanding what semioticians have observed about the operation of codes can help us to *denaturalize* such codes by making their implicit conventions explicit and amenable to analysis. Semiotics offers us some conceptual crowbars with which to deconstruct the codes at work in particular texts and practices, providing that we can find some gaps or fissures which offer us the chance to exert some leverage.

Chapter 6

Textual
interactions

In this chapter we will consider semiotic approaches
to the interactions between makers, texts and users.
First, we will explore the issue of the encoding and
decoding of texts and the ways in which readers are
'positioned' in this process. Then we will consider
intertextuality – or the interactions between texts.

Models of communication

Contemporary semioticians refer to the creation and
interpretation of texts as 'encoding' and 'decoding'
respectively. This unfortunately tends to make these
processes sound too programmatic: the use of these
terms is of course intended to emphasize the importance of the semiotic *codes* involved, and thus to
highlight social factors. In the context of semiotics,
'decoding' involves not simply basic recognition and
comprehension of what a text 'says' but also the *interpretation* and *evaluation* of its meaning with reference to relevant codes. Where a distinction is made
between comprehension and interpretation this tends

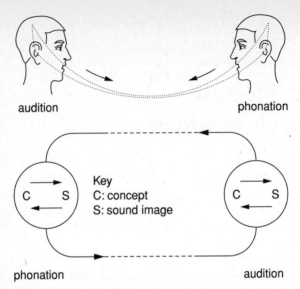

FIGURE 6.1 Saussure's speech circuit

Source: Based on Saussure 1974

to be primarily with reference to purely *verbal* text, but even in this context such a distinction is untenable; what is 'meant' is invariably more than what is 'said' (Smith 1988; Olson 1994). Everyday references to communication are based on a 'transmission' model in which a sender transmits a message to a receiver – a formula which reduces meaning to 'content' which is delivered like a parcel (Reddy 1979). This is the basis of Shannon and Weaver's well-known model of communication, which makes no allowance for the importance of social contexts and codes (Shannon and Weaver 1949).

Figure 6.1 shows Saussure's model of oral communication. While (for its time) it is innovatingly labelled as a 'speech circuit' and includes directional arrows indicating the involvement of both participants (thus at least implying 'feedback'), it too was nevertheless a linear transmission model (albeit a 'two-track' one). It was based on the notion that comprehension on the part of the listener is a kind of mirror of the speaker's initial process of expressing a

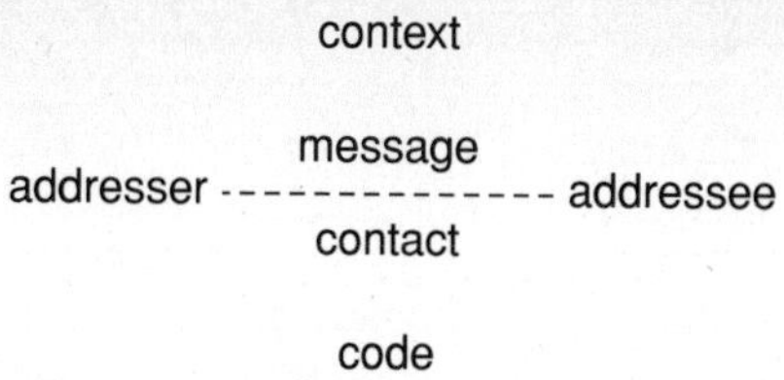

context

message
addresser --------------- addressee
contact

code

FIGURE 6.2 Jakobson's model of communication

Source: Jakobson 1960

thought (Saussure 1983, 11–13; Harris 1987, 22–5, 204–18). In this model there is only the briefest of allusions to the speaker's use of 'the code provided by the language', together with the implicit assumption that a fixed code is shared (Saussure 1983, 14; Harris 1987, 216, 230).

In 1960 another structural linguist – Roman Jakobson (drawing on work by Bühler dating from the 1930s) – proposed a model of interpersonal verbal communication which moved beyond the basic transmission model of communication and highlighted the importance of the codes and social contexts involved (Jakobson 1960; see Figure 6.2). Jakobson noted elsewhere that 'the efficiency of a speech event demands the use of a common code by its participants' (Jakobson and Halle 1956, 72). He outlines what he regards as the six 'constitutive factors . . . in any act of verbal communication' thus:

> The *addresser* sends a message to the *addressee*. To be operative the message requires a *context* referred to ('referent' in another, somewhat ambivalent, nomenclature), seizable by the addressee, and either verbal or capable of being verbalized, a *code* fully, or at least partially, common to the addresser and addressee (or in other words, to the encoder and decoder of the message); and finally, a *contact*, a physical channel and psychological connection between the addresser and the addressee, enabling both of them to stay in communication.
>
> (Jakobson 1960, 353)

TABLE 6.1 Jakobson's six functions of language

Type	Oriented towards	Function	Example
referential	context	imparting information	It's raining.
expressive	addresser	expressing feelings or attitudes	It's bloody pissing down again!
conative	addressee	influencing behaviour	Wait here till it stops raining!
phatic	contact	establishing or maintaining social relationships	Nasty weather again, isn't it?
metalingual	code	referring to the nature of the interaction (e.g. genre)	This is the weather forecast.
poetic	message	foregrounding textual features	It droppeth as the gentle rain from heaven.

Jakobson proposed that 'each of these six factors determines a different function of language' (ibid.; see Table 6.1).

This model avoids the reduction of language to 'communication'. Referential content is not always foregrounded. Jakobson argued that in any given situation one of these factors is 'dominant', and that this dominant function influences the general character of the 'message'. For instance, the *poetic* function (which is intended to refer to any creative use of language rather than simply to poetry) highlights 'the palpability of signs', undermining any sense of a 'natural' or 'transparent' connection between a signifier and a referent. Jakobson's model demonstrates that messages and meanings cannot be isolated from such constitutive contextual factors. In its acknowledgement of social functions this is a model which is consonant with the structuralist theory that the subject (here in the form of the 'addresser' and the 'addressee') is constructed through discourse.

While these earlier models had been concerned with *interpersonal communication*, in an essay entitled 'Encoding/decoding' (Hall 1980, originally published as 'Encoding and decoding in television discourse' in 1973), the British sociologist Stuart Hall proposed a model of *mass communication* which highlighted the importance of signifying practices within relevant codes. A televisual text emerged as 'meaningful' discourse from processes of encoding and decoding. Each of these processes involved 'meaning structures' which consisted of 'frameworks of knowledge', 'relations of production' and 'technical infrastructure'. Despite the apparent symmetry, Hall rejected textual determinism, noting that 'decodings do not follow inevitably from encodings' (Hall 1980, 136). In contrast to the earlier models, Hall thus gave a significant role to the 'decoder' as well as to the 'encoder' and presented communication as a socially contingent practice.

Mass media codes offer their readers social identities which some may adopt as their own. But readers do not necessarily accept such codes. Where those involved in communicating do not share common codes and social positions, decodings are likely to be different from the encoder's intended meaning. Umberto Eco uses the term 'aberrant decoding' to refer to a text which has been decoded by means of a different code from that used to encode it (Eco 1965).

The positioning of the subject

'A sign ... addresses somebody,' Charles Peirce declared (Peirce 1931–58, 2.228). Signs 'address' us within particular codes. A genre is a semiotic code within which we are 'positioned' as 'ideal readers' through the use of particular 'modes of address'. Modes of address can be defined as the ways in which relations between addresser and addressee are constructed in a text. In order to communicate, a producer of any text must make some assumptions about an intended audience; reflections of such assumptions may be discerned in the text (advertisements offer particularly clear examples of this).

Rather than a specifically semiotic concept, 'the positioning of the subject' is a structuralist notion – although Stuart Hall notes its absence in early structuralist discourse (Hall 1996, 46); Saussure did not discuss it. It is a concept which has been widely adopted by semioticians and so it needs to be explored in this context. The term 'subject' needs some initial explanation. In 'theories of subjectivity' a distinction is made between 'the subject' and 'the individual'. While the *individual* is an actual person, the *subject* is a set of *roles* constructed by dominant cultural and ideological values (e.g. in terms of class, age, gender and ethnicity). Ideology turns individuals into subjects. Subjects are not actual people but exist only in relation to interpretative practices and are constructed through the use of signs. The psychoanalytical theorist Jacques Lacan undermined the humanist notion of a unified and consistent subject. The individual can occupy multiple subject positions, some of them contradictory, and 'identity' can be seen as the interaction of subject-positions.

According to theorists of textual positioning, understanding the meaning of a text involves taking on an appropriate ideological identity. In order to make sense of the signs in a text the reader is obliged to adopt a 'subject-position' in relation to it. For instance, to understand an advertisement we would have to adopt the identity of a consumer who desired the advertised product. Some theorists argue that this position already exists within the structure and codes of the text. 'Narratives or images always imply or construct a position or positions from which they are to be read or viewed' (Johnson 1996, 101). What Colin MacCabe famously called the 'classic realist text' is orchestrated to effect closure: contradictions are suppressed and the reader is encouraged to adopt a position from which everything seems 'obvious' (MacCabe 1974). This stance assumes both that a text is homogeneous and that it has only one meaning – that which was intended by its makers – whereas contemporary theorists contend that there may be several alternative (even contradictory) subject-positions from which a text may make sense. While these may sometimes be anticipated by the author, they are not necessarily built into the text itself. Not every reader is the 'ideal reader' envisaged by the producer(s) of the text. The phrase, 'the positioning of the subject' implies a 'necessary "subjection" to the text' (Johnson 1996, 101) and is thus problematic since there is always some freedom of interpretation. We may for instance choose to regard a poorly translated set of instructions for assembling flat-pack furniture as a text constructed purely for our amusement.

The notion that the human subject is 'constituted' (constructed) by pre-given structures (such as texts) is a general feature of structuralism. It constitutes a radical opposition to the liberal humanist (or 'bourgeois') stance which presents society as 'consisting of "free" individuals whose social determination results from their pre-given essences like "talented", "efficient", "lazy", "profligate", etc.' (Coward and Ellis 1977, 2). The French neo-Marxist philosopher Louis Althusser (1918–90) was the first ideological theorist to give prominence to the notion of the subject. For him, ideology was a system of representations of reality offering individuals certain subject positions which they could occupy. He famously declared that 'what is represented in ideology is . . . not the system of real relations which govern the existence of individuals, but the imaginary relation of these individuals to the real relations in which they live' (Althusser 1971, 155). Individuals are transformed into subjects through the ideological mechanism which he called *interpellation* (Althusser 1971, 174).

The Althusserian concept of interpellation is used by Marxist media theorists to explain the political function of mass media texts. According to this view, the subject (viewer, listener, reader) is constituted by the text, and the power of the mass media resides in their ability to position the subject in such a way that their representations are taken to be reflections of everyday reality. Such structuralist framings of positioning reflect a stance of *textual determinism* which has been challenged by contemporary social semioticians who tend to emphasize the 'polysemic' nature of texts (their plurality of meanings) together with the diversity of their use and interpretation by different audiences ('multiaccentuality'). However, a distinction may be appropriate here between *message* and *code*. While resistance at the level of the message is always possible, resistance at the level of the code is generally much more difficult when the code is a dominant one. The familiarity of the codes in 'realist' texts (especially photographic and filmic texts) leads us to routinely 'suspend our disbelief' in the form (even if not necessarily in the manifest content). Recognition of the familiar (in the guise of the 'natural') repeatedly confirms our conventional ways of seeing and thus reinforces our sense of self while at the same time invisibly contributing to its *construction*. 'When we say "I see (what the image means)" this act simultaneously installs us in a place of knowledge and slips us into place as subject to this meaning . . . All the viewer need do is fall into place as subject' (Nichols 1981, 38). Falling into place in a realist text is a pleasurable experience which few would wish to disrupt with reflective analysis (which would throw the security of our sense of self into question). Thus we freely submit to the ideological processes which construct our sense of ourselves as free-thinking individuals.

A primary textual code involved in the construction of the subject is that of *genre*. Genres are ostensibly 'neutral', functioning to make *form* (the conventions of the genre) more 'transparent' to those familiar with the genre, foregrounding the distinctive *content* of individual texts. Certainly genre provides an important frame of reference which helps readers to identify, select and interpret texts (as well as helping writers to compose economically within the medium). However, a genre can also be seen as embodying certain values and ideological assumptions and as seeking to establish a particular worldview. Changes in genre conventions may both reflect and help to shape the dominant ideological climate of the time. Some Marxist commentators see genre as an instrument of social control which reproduces the dominant ideology. Within this perspective, the genre is seen as positioning the audience in order to naturalize the reassuringly conservative ideologies which are typically embedded in the text. Certainly, genres are far from being ideologically neutral. Different genres produce different positionings of the subject which are reflected in their modes of address. Tony Thwaites and his colleagues in Australia note that in many television crime dramas in the tradition of *The Saint*, *Hart to Hart*, and *Murder, She Wrote*,

> Genteel or well-to-do private investigators work for the wealthy, solving crimes committed by characters whose social traits and behaviour patterns often type them as members of a 'criminal class' ... The villains receive their just rewards not so much because they break the law, but because they are entirely distinct from the law-abiding bourgeoisie. This TV genre thus reproduces a hegemonic ideology about the individual in a class society.
>
> (Thwaites *et al.* 1994, 158)

Thus, over and above the specific 'content' of the individual text, generic frameworks can be seen as involved in the construction of their readers.

Adopting a perspective

The mathematically based technique of *linear perspective* was invented in 1425 by Filippo Brunelleschi and codified as *perspectiva artificialis* (artificial perspective) by Leon Battista Alberti in his treatise, *Della pittura* (*On Painting*), published in 1435–6 (Alberti 1966). For the artist it is a rational geometrical technique for the systematic representation of objects in space which mimics the everyday visual illusion that the parallel edges of rectilinear objects converge at what we now call a 'vanishing point' on the horizon (which is set at the eye level of an observer who is imagined to be staring straight ahead). We need reminding that this 'style of vision' is a historical invention: 'nothing like it appears earlier in medieval painting, suggesting that men and women of earlier ages simply did not see in this fashion' (Romanyshyn 1989, 40). Linear perspective thus constituted a new way of seeing which Samuel Edgerton characterizes as 'the most *appropriate* convention for the pictorial representation of "truth"' within 'the Renaissance paradigm' (a view of the world which reflected our understanding until the advent of Einstein's theory of relativity) (Edgerton 1975, 162). We have become so accustomed to reading pictures in terms of this illusionistic pictorial code that it now appears 'natural' to us to do so: we are rarely conscious of it as a code at all. Indeed, to be fair, there are still some semioticians who would dispute its status as a code.

In an essay entitled 'Perspective as symbolic form' published in German in the 1920s, the great art historian Erwin Panofsky generated considerable controversy by making the claim that linear perspective was a 'symbolic form' – a historically situated system of conventions for representing pictorial space which reflected the dominant cultural worldview of the Italian Renaissance (Edgerton 1975, 153ff.). Similarly, Herbert Read noted that 'we do not always realize that the theory of perspective developed in the fifteenth century is a scientific convention; it is merely one way of describing space and has no absolute validity' (cited in Wright 1983, 2–3). Critics retorted that strict geometrical perspective is scientifically 'accurate' and accused Panofsky and other heretics of 'relativism' (see Kubovy 1986, 162ff.). Certainly, if we discount phenomenal reality, what William Ivins calls 'the grammar of perspective' can be seen as having an indexical character related to human visual physiology (Ivins 1975, 10). However, it can hardly be doubted that 'to close one eye and hold the head still at a single predetermined point in space is not the normal way of looking at things' (White 1967, 274).

Strict linear perspective does not reflect phenomenal reality, since we are habituated to the stabilizing psychological mechanism of 'perceptual constancy' which we encountered earlier. If you are not an artist, try holding a vertical pencil at arm's length in front of you as a measuring-stick for objects within your field of view. If you have not tried this before you may be shocked to discover that some of the things which are close to you seem implausibly large. This is perhaps most noticeable in relation to the foreshortening of the human form – protruding feet can seem comically massive. In tackling the task of depicting the foreshortened body of the dead Christ, even the great Renaissance artist Andrea Mantegna (1431–1506) clearly felt that he needed to compensate for the sacrilege of the distortion introduced by linear perspective, since he both reduced the size of the feet and enlarged the head, showing a 'sense of proportion' appropriate to his subject. Alberti had written that veri-similitude should be tempered by appropriate respect for dignity and decorum (Alberti 1966, 72–7).

Artificial perspective, in short, distorts the familiar size and shape of things. In this sense, Mantegna's representational code is closer to phenomenal reality than a photograph is. It was not easy even for Alberti to see things in terms of this code: he found it necessary to place a thin 'veil' or net marked out in parallels 'between the eye and the thing seen' (ibid., 68). Marshall McLuhan asserted that 'far from being a normal mode of human vision, three-dimensional perspective is a conventionally acquired mode of seeing, as much acquired as is the means of recognizing the letters of the alphabet, or of following chronological narrative' (McLuhan 1970, 16). *Artificial perspective* is a code which everyone with sufficient exposure to it can easily learn to read, although employing it effec-tively as an artist or architect requires far more deliberate learn-ing. The introduction of 'artificial perspective' both reflected and promoted a preoccupation with verisimilitude; its use became an essential condition of 'realistic' pictorial representation. There is of course no doubt that this technique generates a powerful impres-sion of depth, 'approximating the cues relating to normal perception better than any other strategy until the emergence of photography' (Nichols 1981, 52). But its revolutionary implications were not simply representational.

The Renaissance code of central, one-point linear perspec-tive is not simply a technique for indicating depth and relative dis-tance in a two-dimensional medium. It is a pictorial code reflecting the growing humanism of the period, presenting images from a single, subjective, individual and unique visual point of view. Mirror-ing the 'vanishing point' within the picture is the projected 'point of origin' in front of the canvas which was adopted by the artist and left vacant for the 'subject' whose position we adopt when we look at the picture. From this position, the represented world is framed as if by a window on a wall. Alberti himself wrote that 'I inscribe a quadrangle of right angles, as large as I wish, which is considered to be an open window through which I see what I want to paint' (Alberti 1966, 56). Painters should 'seek to present the forms of things seen on this plane as if it were of transparent glass' (ibid., 51).

At the same time as simulating a view of the world through a window, this clearly bounded, static and two-dimensional representation separates the viewer from the represented world. Reflecting on the phenomenology of technology, Robert Romanyshyn comments that this mode of representation 'establishes as a condition for perception a formal *separation* between a subject who sees the world and the world that is seen; and in doing so it sets the stage, as it were, for that retreat or withdrawal of the self from the world which characterizes the dawn of the modern age. Ensconced behind the window the self becomes an observing *subject*, a *spectator*, as against a world which becomes a *spectacle*, an *object* of vision' (Romanyshyn 1989, 40). Thus 'seeing things in perspective' is implicated in the development of the subject in its distancing of the knower from the known. William Ivins, an influential historian of visual communication, considered linear perspective to be part of 'the rationalization of sight' which he declared was 'the most important event of the Renaissance' (Ivins 1975, 13).

Where linear perspective is very dominant in a work of art it undoubtedly gives it 'a cold effect' (White 1967, 274). Marshall McLuhan regarded 'the detached observer' as 'the Renaissance legacy', declaring that 'the viewer of Renaissance art is systematically placed outside the frame of experience' (McLuhan and Fiore 1967, 53). 'The arbitrary selection of a single static position' for the artist and for viewers of the work requires 'a fixed point of view', which McLuhan associates with the 'private stance' of 'separate individuals' and not just with a viewing location (McLuhan 1962, 16, 56; McLuhan and Fiore 1967, 68). Looking at the represented world as through a window confirms us in our sense of ourselves as individuals with our own unique 'outlook on the world'. 'Gaining perspective' reflected 'our deeply embedded habit of regarding all phenomena from a fixed point of view' (McLuhan and Fiore 1967, 68). McLuhan attributed this not only to linear perspective but also to 'the effect of typography': 'inner direction toward remote goals is inseparable from print culture and the perspective and vanishing point organization of space that are part of it' (McLuhan 1962, 125,

214). This apparently purely technical innovation thus had subtle but profound ideological implications. The focus on the subject in Renaissance painting has been seen as reflecting 'a growing emphasis upon the individual rather than a chain of being, an emphasis that flourished with the emergence of entrepreneurial capitalism' (Nichols 1981, 53). The Renaissance code of *artificial perspective* constitutes visible testimony to the constitution of the self as subject.

Learning to read the pictorial code of linear perspective prepared us for the camera. McLuhan observed that 'photography is the mechanization of the perspective painting and of the arrested eye' (McLuhan 1970, 11). Photography offers a powerful illusion of a medium as a transparent 'window on the world'; as with paintings, photographic images are framed (even if only by their edges). In the early nineteenth century the camera obscura was fitted with a rectangular ground glass which showed only a rectangular section of the circular image from the lens (which is blurred at the edges) (Snyder and Allen 1982, 68–9). This made the camera image conform to the dominant form of framing used for paintings. While sharing the single, central viewing point of painterly *artificial perspective*, photography involves the most remorseless application of this code. Photographs sometimes exhibit even more 'distortion' of phenomenal realism than paintings do: snapshots of tall buildings exhibit a disturbingly pronounced convergence of the vertical lines (we are less accustomed to *vertical* convergence because even Renaissance artists avoided it). In 35mm photography, the illusion of depth is most striking when 'normal' lenses of about 50mm are used: we become more aware of 'distortion' when a telephoto or wide-angle lens is used (Nichols 1981, 19). 'Photorealism' has nevertheless become the standard by which 'realistic' representations in visual art are subjectively judged (Kress and van Leeuwen 1996, 163–4).

Just as illusionism of Renaissance linear perspective performed the ideological function of 'positioning the subject', so too did the photographic image. French theorists associated with the journals *Tel Quel* and *Cinéthique* argued that since the code of linear perspective is *built into* the camera, photography and film, while appearing to involve simply a neutral recording of reality, serve to reinforce bourgeois individualism. Film and television add a narrative dimension to the positioning of the subject, incorporating not only linear perspective but also dominant narrative devices specific to filmic media. Film theorists refer to the use of 'suture' (surgical stitching) – the 'invisible editing' of shot relationships which seeks to foreground the narrative and mask the ideological processes which shape the subjectivity of viewers. Some Lacanian theorists argue that in the context of conventional narrative (with its possibilities of identification and opposition), the unique character of the cinema (e.g. watching a large bright screen in the dark) offers us the seductive sense of a 'return' to the pre-linguistic 'mirror-phase' of the 'imaginary' in which the self was constructed (ibid., 300).

Modes of address

The *modes of address* employed by texts within a code are influenced primarily by three interrelated factors:

- **textual context**: the conventions of the genre and of a specific syntagmatic structure;
- **social context** (e.g. the presence or absence of the producer of the text, the scale and social composition of the audience, institutional and economic factors); and
- **technological constraints** (features of the medium employed).

Modes of address differ in their directness, their formality and their narrative point of view. The various narrative points of view in literature are as follows:

- *third-person* narration
  - *omniscient* narrator
    - intrusive (e.g. Dickens)
    - self-effacing (e.g. Flaubert)
  - *selective* point of view of character(s) presented by self-effacing narrator (e.g. Henry James)
- *first-person* narration: narrated directly by a character (e.g. Salinger's *Catcher in the Rye*)

In television and film drama the camera typically offers the viewer a relatively detached perspective on a scene which is independent of any single character in the narrative. This can be seen as resembling the 'third-person' narrative style of an omniscient and self-effacing narrator – which of course does not necessarily entail such a narrator 'revealing all' to the viewer. Camera treatment is called 'subjective' when the camera shows us events as if from a particular participant's visual point of view (encouraging viewers to identify with that person's way of seeing events or even to feel like an eye-witness to the events themselves). This first-person style in filmic media is rarely sustained, however (or we would never see that character). The point of view is *selective* when we are mainly concerned with a single character but the camerawork is not subjective. Voice-overs are sometimes used for first-person narration by a character in a drama; they are also common as a third-person narrative mode in genres such as documentary. Where first-person commentary shifts from person to person within a text, this produces 'polyvocality' (multiple voices) – contrasting strongly with the interpretative omni-science of 'univocal' narrative which offers a single reading of an event. Where the agency of a narrator is backgrounded, events or facts deceptively seem to 'speak for themselves'.

Modes of address also differ in their *directness*. In linguistic codes, this is related to whether 'you' are explicitly addressed, which in literary modes is quite rare. In Laurence Sterne's highly 'uncon-ventional' novel *Tristram Shandy* (1760), one chapter begins thus: 'How could you, Madam, be so inattentive in reading the last chapter?' (vol. 1, ch. 20). 'Realist' fiction avoids such 'alienatory' strategies. In representational visual codes directness is related to whether or not a depicted person appears to look directly at the viewer (in the case of television, film and photography, via the camera lens). A direct gaze simulates interaction with each individual viewer (an impossibility, of course, outside one-to-one communicative media, but a feature of 'cam-to-cam' communication on the Internet or in video-conferences). In film and television, directness of address is reflected in linguistic codes as well as camerawork. Films and (especially) television programmes within the documentary genre frequently employ a disembodied voice-over which directly addresses the audience, as do television commercials. On television, directness of address is also a matter of the extent to which participants look directly into the camera lens. In this way too, commercials frequently include direct address. As for programmes, in a book entitled *The Grammar of Television*, an industry professional warned: 'Never let a performer look straight into the lens of a camera unless it is necessary to give the impression that he is speaking directly to the viewer personally' (Davis 1960, 54). In television programmes, a direct mode of address is largely confined to newsreaders, weather forecasters, presenters and interviewers – which is why it seems so strange on the rare occasions when we notice an interviewee glancing at the camera lens. In short, people from outside the television industry are seldom allowed to talk to us directly on television. The head of state or the leader of a political party are among the few outsiders allowed to look directly at the viewer, and then typically only within special genres such as a party political broadcast or an 'address to the nation'. Direct address reflects the power of the addresser and the use of this signifier typically signifies 'authority'. Direct address is rare in the cinema, and when it is used it tends to be for comic effect. *Indirect address* is the principal mode employed in conventional narrative, masking authorial agency in the interests of foregrounding the story. Conventional film and television drama, of course, depends on the illusion that the participants do not know they are being watched.

Additionally, the mode of address varies in its *formality* or *social distance*. Kress and van Leeuwen distinguish between 'intimate', 'personal', 'social' and 'public' (or 'impersonal') modes of address (Kress and van Leeuwen 1996, 130–5). In relation to language, formality is quite closely tied to explicitness, so that intimate language tends to be minimally explicit and maximally dependent on non-verbal cues, while public language tends to reverse these features (especially in print). In usage related also to directness of address, social distance can also established through the use of loaded quasi-synonyms to reflect ideological distinctions of 'us' from 'them', as in '*I* am a patriot; *you* are a nationalist; *they* are xenophobes.'

In visual representation, social distance is related in part to *apparent proximity*. In camerawork, degrees of formality are reflected in *shot sizes* – close-ups signifying intimate or personal modes, medium shots a social mode and long shots an impersonal mode (Kress and van Leeuwen 1996, 130–5; cf. Tuchman 1978, 116–20). In visual media, the represented physical distance between the observed and the observer often reflects attempts to encourage feelings of emotional involvement or critical detachment in the viewer. The cultural variability of the degree of formality signified by different zones of proximity was highlighted in relation to face-to-face interaction in an influential book by Edward T. Hall – *The Hidden Dimension* (Hall 1966). Proximity is not the only marker of social distance in the visual media: *angles of view* are also significant. High angles (looking down on a depicted person from above) are widely interpreted as making that person look small and insignificant, and low angles (looking up at them from below) are said to make them look powerful and superior (Messaris 1997, 34–5 and 1994, 158; Kress and van Leeuwen 1996, 146).

Note that while the significations such as those listed in relation to photographic and filmic modes of address may represent the currently dominant, conventional or 'default' linkages of signifiers and signifieds, no programmatic decoding based on a 'dictionary' of one-to-one correspondences is possible – in analogue codes in particular there is a sliding relationship between signifiers and signifieds which the codes of the particular textual systems in which they are employed may function to anchor in various ways (Nichols 1981, 108).

Textual codes construct possible reading positions for the addresser and addressee. Building upon Jakobson's model Thwaites *et al.* define 'the functions of address' in terms of the construction of such subjects and of relationships between them.

- *expressive function*: the construction of an addresser (authorial persona);
- *conative function*: the construction of an addressee (ideal reader);
- *phatic function*: the construction of a relationship between these two.

(Thwaites *et al.* 1994, 14–15)

A textual code can be defined as a set of ways of reading which its producers and readers share. Not everyone has access to the relevant codes for reading (or writing) a text. The phatic function excludes as well as includes certain readers. Those who share the code are members of the same 'interpretative community' (Fish 1980, 167ff., 335–6, 338). Familiarity with particular codes is related to social position, in terms of such factors as class, ethnicity, nationality, education, occupation, political affiliation, age, gender and sexuality.

Reading positions

Stuart Hall stressed the role of social positioning in the interpretation of mass media texts by different social groups. In a model deriving from Frank Parkin's 'meaning systems', Hall suggested three hypothetical interpretative codes or positions for the reader of a text (Parkin 1972; Hall 1973 and 1980, 136–8; Morley 1980, 20–21, 134–7 and 1983, 109–10):

- *dominant (or 'hegemonic') reading*: the reader fully shares the text's code and accepts and reproduces the *preferred reading* (a reading which may not have been the result of any conscious intention on the part of the author(s)) – in such a stance the code seems 'natural' and 'transparent';
- *negotiated reading*: the reader partly shares the text's code and broadly accepts the preferred reading, but sometimes resists and modifies it in a way which reflects their own position, experiences and interests (local and personal conditions may be seen as exceptions to the general rule) – this position involves contradictions;
- *oppositional ('counter-hegemonic') reading*: the reader, whose social situation places them in a directly oppositional relation to the dominant code, understands the preferred reading but does not share the text's code and rejects this reading, bringing to bear an alternative frame of reference (radical, feminist etc.) (e.g. when watching a television broadcast produced on behalf of a political party they normally vote *against*).

This framework is based on the assumption that the latent meaning of the text is encoded in the dominant code. This is a stance which tends to reify the medium and to downplay conflicting tendencies within texts. Also, some critics have raised the question of how a 'preferred reading' can be established. Poststructuralist social semioticians would urge us not to seek such a reading within the form and structure of the text. Just as a reductive reading of Hall's model could lead to the reification of a medium or genre, it could also encourage the essentializing of readers (e.g. as 'the resistant reader') whereas reading positions are multiple, dynamic and contradictory. Despite the various criticisms, Hall's model has been very influential, particularly among British theorists.

The British sociologist David Morley employed this model in his studies of how different social groups interpreted a television programme (Morley 1980). Morley demonstrated differential access to the textual codes of a programme in the 'news magazine' genre (Morley 1980). He insisted that he did *not* take a *social determinist* position in which individual 'decodings' of a text are reduced to a direct consequence of social class position. 'It is always a question of how social position, as it is articulated through particular discourses, produces specific kinds of readings or decodings. These readings can then be seen to be patterned by the way in which the structure of access to different discourses is determined by social position' (Morley 1983, 113; cf. Morley 1992, 89–90). Different interpretative communities have access to different textual and interpretative codes (which offer them the potential to understand and sometimes also to produce texts which employ them). Morley added that any individual or group might operate different decoding strategies in relation to different *topics* and different *contexts*. A person might make 'oppositional' readings of the same material in one context and 'dominant' readings in other contexts (Morley 1981, 9 and 1992, 135). He noted that in interpreting viewers' readings of mass media texts attention should be paid not only to the issue of *agreement* (acceptance/rejection) but to *comprehension*, *relevance* and *enjoyment* (Morley 1981, 10 and 1992, 126–7, 136). There is thus considerable scope for variety in the ways in which individuals engage with such codes.

The interpretation of signs by their users can be seen from a semiotic perspective as having three levels, loosely related to C. W. Morris's framework for branches of semiotics (Morris 1938, 6–7).

1. *syntactic*: recognition of the sign (in relation to other signs);
2. *semantic*: comprehension of the intended meaning of the sign;
3. *pragmatic*: interpretation of the sign in terms of relevance, agreement, etc.

The most basic task of interpretation involves the identification of what a sign represents (denotation) and may require some degree of familiarity with the medium and the representational codes involved. This is particularly obvious in the case of language, but may also apply in the case of visual media such as photographs and films. Some would not grant this low-level process the label of 'interpretation' at all, limiting this term to such processes as the extraction of a 'moral' from a narrative text. However, some theorists take the stance that comprehension and interpretation are inseparable (e.g. Mick and Politi 1989, 85).

Semiotics has not been widely applied to the practice of decoding. While social semiotics stakes a claim to the study of situated semiotic practices, research in this area is dominated by ethnographic and phenomenological methodologies and is seldom closely allied to semiotic perspectives (though there is no necessary incompatibility). A notable exception is the research of David Mick in the field of advertising (Mick and Politi 1989, McQuarrie and Mick 1992, Mick and Buhl 1992).

Having explored some of the theoretical issues concerning the interactions between makers, texts and users we turn now to theories of *intertextuality* – which concern interactions between texts.

Intertextuality

Although Saussure stressed the importance of the relationship of signs to each other, one of the weaknesses of structuralist semiotics is the tendency to treat individual texts as discrete, closed-off entities and to focus exclusively on internal structures. Even where texts are studied as a 'corpus' (a unified collection), the overall generic structures tend themselves to be treated as strictly bounded. The structuralist's first analytical task is often described as being to delimit the boundaries of the system (what is to be included and what excluded), which is logistically understandable but ontologically problematic. Even remaining within the structuralist paradigm, we may note that codes transcend structures. The semiotic notion of 'intertextuality' introduced by Julia Kristeva is associated primarily with *poststructuralist* theorists. Kristeva referred to texts in terms of two axes: a *horizontal axis* connecting the author and reader of a text, and a *vertical axis*, which connects the text to other texts (Kristeva 1980, 69). Uniting these two axes are shared codes: every text and every reading depends on prior codes. Kristeva declared that 'every text is from the outset under the jurisdiction of other discourses which impose a universe on it' (cited in Culler 1981, 105). She argued that rather than confining our attention to the structure of a text we should study its 'structuration' (how the structure came into being). This involved siting it 'within the totality of previous or synchronic texts' of which it was a 'transformation' (*Le texte du roman*, cited by Coward and Ellis 1977, 52).

Intertextuality refers to far more than the 'influences' of writers on each other. For structuralists, language has powers which not only exceed individual control but also determine subjectivity. Structuralists sought to counter what they saw as a deep-rooted bias in literary and aesthetic thought which emphasized the uniqueness of both texts and authors. The ideology of individualism (with its associated concepts of authorial 'originality', 'creativity' and 'expressiveness') is a post-Renaissance legacy which reached its peak in Romanticism but which still dominates popular discourse. 'Authorship' was a historical invention. Concepts such as 'authorship' and 'plagiarism' did not exist in the Middle Ages. Saussure emphasized that language is a system which pre-exists the individual speaker. For structuralists and poststructuralists alike we are (to use the stock Althusserian formulation) 'always already' positioned by semiotic systems – and most clearly by language. Contemporary theorists have referred to the subject as being *spoken by* language. Barthes declares that 'it is language which speaks, not the author; to write is . . . to

reach the point where only language acts, "performs", and not "me"'
(Barthes 1977, 143). When writers write they are also *written*. To
communicate we must utilize existing concepts and conventions.
Consequently, while our intention to communicate and *what* we
intend to communicate are both important to us as individuals, meaning cannot be reduced to authorial 'intention'. To define meaning in
terms of authorial intention is the so-called 'intentional fallacy' identified by W. K. Wimsatt and M. C. Beardsley of the 'new critical'
tendency in literary criticism (Wimsatt and Beardsley 1954). We may,
for instance, communicate things without being aware of doing so.
As Michael de Montaigne wrote in 1580, 'the work, by its own force
and fortune, may second the workman, and sometimes out-strip
him, beyond his invention and knowledge' (*Essays*, trans. Charles
Cotton: 'Of the art of conferring' III, 8). Furthermore, in conforming
to any of the conventions of our medium, we act as a medium for
perpetuating such conventions.

Problematizing authorship

Theorists of intertextuality problematize the status of 'authorship',
treating the writer of a text as the orchestrator of what Roland
Barthes refers to as the 'already-written' rather than as its originator
(Barthes 1974, 21). 'A text is . . . a multidimensional space in which
a variety of writings, none of them original, blend and clash. The
text is a tissue of quotations . . . The writer can only imitate a gesture
that is always anterior, never original. His only power is to mix writings, to counter the ones with the others, in such a way as never to
rest on any one of them' (Barthes 1977, 146). In his book *S/Z*,
Barthes deconstructed Balzac's short story *Sarrasine*, seeking to 'de-
originate' the text – to demonstrate that it reflects many voices, not
just that of Balzac (Barthes 1974). It would be pure idealism to
regard Balzac as 'expressing himself' in language since we do not
precede language but are *produced* by it. For Barthes, writing did
not involve an instrumental process of recording pre-formed thoughts
and feelings (working from signified to signifier) but was a matter
of working with the signifiers and letting the signifieds take care of
themselves (Chandler 1995, 60ff.).

One of the founding texts of semiotics, the *Cours de linguistique générale*, itself problematizes the status of authorship. While the text published by Payot in Paris bears the name of Ferdinand de Saussure as its author, it was in fact not the work of Saussure at all. Saussure died in 1913 without leaving any detailed outline of his theories on general linguistics or on what he called semiology. The *Cours* was first published posthumously in 1916 and was assembled by Charles Bally and Albert Sechehaye ('with the collaboration of Albert Riedlinger') on the basis of the notes which had been taken by at least seven students, together with a few personal notes which had been written by Saussure himself. The students' notes referred to three separate courses on general linguistics which Saussure had taught at the University of Geneva over the period of 1906–11. Saussure thus neither wrote nor read the book which bears his name, although we continually imply that he did by attaching his name to it. It is hardly surprising that various contradictions and inconsistencies and a lack of cohesion in the text have often been noted. Indeed, some commentators have suggested that the *Cours* does not always offer 'a faithful reflection' of Saussure's ideas – a hardly unproblematic notion (Saussure 1983, xii). On top of all this, English readers have two competing translations of the *Cours* (Saussure 1974; Saussure 1983). Each translation is, of course, a re-authoring. No 'neutral' translation is possible, since languages involve different value systems – as is noted in the *Cours* itself. Nor can specialist translators be expected to be entirely disinterested. Furthermore, anyone who treats the *Cours* as a founding text in semiotics does so by effectively 'rewriting' it, since its treatment of semiology is fragmentary. Finally, we are hardly short of commentaries to bring both this foundational text and us as readers into line with the interpreter's own theories (e.g. Harris 1987; Thibault 1997).

Reading as rewriting

This rather extreme but important example thus serves to highlight that every reading is always a rewriting. It is by no means an isolated example. The first critique of the ideas outlined in the *Cours* was in a book entitled *Marxism and the Philosophy of Language* which was published in Russian in 1929 under the name Valentin Voloshinov, but it has subsequently been claimed that this book had in fact been written by Mikhail Bakhtin, and the authorship of this text is still contested (Morris 1994, 1). Readers, in any case, construct authors. They perform a kind of amateur archaeology, reconstructing them from textual shards while at the same time feeling able to say about anyone whose writings they have read, 'I *know* her (or him).' The reader's 'Roland Barthes' (for example) never existed. If one had total access to everything he had ever written throughout his life it would be marked by contradiction. The best we can do to reduce such contradictions is to construct yet more authors, such as 'the early Barthes' and 'the later Barthes'. Barthes died in 1981, but every invocation of his name creates another Barthes.

In 1968 Barthes announced 'the death of the author' and 'the birth of the reader', declaring that 'a text's unity lies not in its origin but in its destination' (Barthes 1977, 148). The framing of texts by other texts has implications not only for their *writers* but also for their *readers*. Fredric Jameson argued that 'texts come before us as the always-already-read; we apprehend them through the sedimented layers of previous interpretations, or – if the text is brand-new – through the sedimented reading habits and categories developed by those inherited interpretive traditions' (cited in Rodowick 1994, 286, where it was, with delicious irony in this context, cited from Tony Bennett). A famous text has a history of readings. 'All literary works . . . are "rewritten", if only unconsciously, by the societies which read them' (Eagleton 1983, 12). No one today – even for the first time – can read a famous novel or poem, look at a famous painting, drawing or sculpture, listen to a famous piece of music or watch a famous play or film without being conscious of the contexts in which the text had been reproduced, drawn upon, alluded to, parodied and so on. Such contexts constitute a primary frame which the reader cannot avoid drawing upon in interpreting the text.

No text is an island

The concept of intertextuality reminds us that each text exists in relation to others. In fact, texts owe more to other texts than to their own makers. Michel Foucault declared that:

> The frontiers of a book are never clear-cut: beyond the title, the first lines and the last full stop, beyond its internal configuration and its autonomous form, it is caught up in a system of references to other books, other texts, other sentences: it is a node within a network ... The book is not simply the object that one holds in one's hands ... Its unity is variable and relative.

> (Foucault 1974, 23)

Texts are framed by others in many ways. Most obvious are formal frames: a television programme, for instance, may be part of a series and part of a *genre* (such as *soap* or *sitcom)*. Our understanding of any individual text relates to such framings. Texts provide contexts within which other texts may be created and interpreted. The art historian Ernst Gombrich goes further, arguing that all art, however 'naturalistic' is 'a manipulation of vocabulary' rather than a reflection of the world (Gombrich 1982, 70, 78, 100). Texts draw upon multiple codes from wider contexts – both textual and social. The assignment of a text to a genre provides the interpreter of the text with a key intertextual framework. Genre theory is an important field in its own right, and genre theorists do not necessarily embrace semiotics. Within semiotics genres can be seen as sign-systems or codes – conventionalized but dynamic structures. Each example of a genre utilizes conventions which link it to other members of that genre. Such conventions are at their most obvious in 'spoof' versions of the genre. But intertextuality is also reflected in the fluidity of genre boundaries and in the blurring of genres and their functions which is reflected in such recent coinages as 'advertorials', 'infomercials', 'edutainment', 'docudrama' and 'faction' (a blend of 'fact' and 'fiction').

The debts of a text to other texts are seldom acknowledged (other than in the scholarly apparatus of academic writing). This serves to further the mythology of authorial 'originality'. However, some texts allude directly to each other – as in 'remakes' of films, extra-diegetic references to the media in the animated cartoon *The Simpsons*, and many amusing contemporary TV ads (in the UK, perhaps most notably in the ads for Boddington's beer). This is a particularly self-conscious form of intertextuality: it credits its audience with the necessary experience to make sense of such allusions and offers them the pleasure of recognition. By alluding to other texts and other media this practice reminds us that we are in a mediated reality, so it can also be seen as an 'alienatory' mode which runs counter to the dominant 'realist' tradition which focuses on persuading the audience to believe in the ongoing reality of the narrative. It appeals to the pleasures of critical detachment rather than of emotional involvement.

In order to make sense of many contemporary advertisements (notably cigarette ads such as for Silk Cut) one needs to be familiar with others in the same series. Expectations are established by reference to one's previous experience in looking at related advertisements. Modern visual advertisements make extensive use of intertextuality in this way. Sometimes there is no direct reference to the product at all. Instant identification of the appropriate interpretative code serves to identify the interpreter of the advertisement as a member of an exclusive club, with each act of interpretation serving to renew one's membership.

Links also cross the boundaries of formal frames, for instance, in sharing topics with treatments within other genres (the theme of war is found in a range of genres such action-adventure film, documentary, news, current affairs). Some genres are shared by several media: the genres of *soap*, *game show* and *phone-in* are found on both television and radio; the genre of the *news report* is found on TV, radio and in newspapers; the *advertisement* appears in all mass media forms. Texts in the genre of the *trailer* are directly tied to specific texts within or outside the same medium. The genre of the *programme listing* exists within the medium of print (listings magazines, newspapers) to support the media of TV, radio and film. TV soaps generate substantial coverage in popular newspapers, magazines and books; the 'magazine' format was adopted by TV and radio. And so on.

The notion of intertextuality problematizes the idea of a text having boundaries and questions the dichotomy of 'inside' and 'outside': where does a text 'begin' and 'end'? What is 'text' and what is 'context'? The medium of television highlights this issue: it is productive to think of television in terms of a concept which Raymond Williams called 'flow' rather than as a series of discrete texts. Much the same applies to the World Wide Web, where hypertext links on a page can link it directly to many others. However, texts in any medium can be thought of in similar terms. The boundaries of texts are permeable. Each text exists within a vast 'society of texts' in various genres and media: no text is an island entire of itself. A useful semiotic technique is comparison and contrast between differing treatments of similar themes (or similar treatments of different themes), *within* or *between* different genres or media.

Intratextuality

While the term intertextuality would normally be used to refer to allusions to other texts, a related kind of allusion is what might be called 'intratextuality' – involving internal relations within the text. Within a single code (e.g. a photographic code) these would be simply syntagmatic relationships (e.g. the relationship of the image of one person to another within the same photograph). However, a text may involve several codes: a newspaper photograph, for instance, may have a caption (indeed, such an example serves to remind us that what we may choose to regard as a discrete 'text' for analysis lacks clear-cut boundaries: the notion of intertextuality emphasizes that texts have contexts).

Roland Barthes introduced the concept of *anchorage* (Barthes 1977, 38ff.). Linguistic elements can serve to 'anchor' (or constrain) the preferred readings of an image: 'to *fix* the floating chain of signifieds' (ibid., 39). Barthes employed this concept primarily in relation to advertisements, but it applies of course to other genres such as captioned photographs, maps, narrated television and film documentaries, and cartoons and comics ('comic books' to North Americans) with their speech and thought 'balloons'. Barthes argued that the principal function of anchorage was ideological (ibid., 40). This is perhaps most obvious when photographs are used in contexts such as newspapers. Photograph captions typically present themselves as neutral labels for what self-evidently exists in the depicted world while actually serving to define the terms of reference and point of view from which it is to be seen. For instance, 'It is a very common practice for the captions to news photographs to tell us, in words, exactly how the subject's expression *ought to be read*' (Hall 1981, 229). You may check your daily newspaper to verify this claim. Such textual anchorages can have a more subversive function, however. For instance, in the 1970s, the photographer Victor Burgin exhibited posters in the form of images appropriated from print advertisements together with his own printed text which ran counter to the intended meaning of the original ads.

Barthes used the term *relay* to describe text–image relationships which were 'complementary', instancing cartoons, comic strips and narrative film (ibid., 41). He did not coin a term for 'the paradoxical case where the image is constructed according to the text' (ibid., 40). Even if it were true in the 1950s and early 1960s that the verbal text was primary in the relation between texts and images, in contemporary society visual images have acquired far more importance in contexts such as advertising, so that what he called 'relay' is far more common. There are also many instances where the 'illustrative use' of an image provides anchorage for ambiguous text – as in assembly instructions for flat-pack furniture (note that when we talk about 'illustrating' and 'captioning' we logocentrically imply the primacy of verbal text over images). Awareness of the importance of intertextuality should lead us to examine the functions of those images and written or spoken text used in close association within a text, not only in terms of their respective codes, but in terms of their overall rhetorical orchestration.

In media such as film, television and the World Wide Web, multiple codes are involved. As the film theorist Christian Metz put it, codes 'are not . . . added to one another, or juxtaposed in just any manner; they are organized, articulated in terms of one another in accordance with a certain order, they contract unilateral hierarchies . . . Thus a veritable *system of intercodical relations* is generated which is itself, in some sort, another code' (Metz 1974, 242). The interaction of film and soundtrack in chart music videos offers a good example of the dynamic nature of their modes of relationship and patterns of relative dominance. The codes involved in such textual systems clearly cannot be considered in isolation: the dynamic patterns of dominance between them contribute to the generation of meaning. Nor need they be assumed to be always in complete accord with each other – indeed, the interplay of codes may be particularly revealing of incoherences, ambiguities, contradictions and omissions which may offer the interpreter scope for deconstructing the text.

Bricolage

Claude Lévi-Strauss's notion of the *bricoleur* who creates improvized structures by appropriating pre-existing materials which are ready to hand is now fairly well known within cultural studies (Lévi-Strauss 1974, 16–33, 35–6, 150n.; cf. Lévi-Strauss 1964). Lévi-Strauss saw 'mythical thought' as 'a kind of bricolage' (Lévi-Strauss 1974, 17): 'it builds ideological castles out of the debris of what was once a social discourse' (ibid., 21n.). The *bricoleur* works with signs, constructing new arrangements by adopting existing signifieds as signifiers and 'speaking' 'through the medium of things' – by the choices made from 'limited possibilities' (ibid., 20, 21). 'The first aspect of bricolage is . . . to construct a system of paradigms with the fragments of syntagmatic chains', leading in turn to new syntagms (ibid., 150n.). 'Authorship' could be seen in similar terms. Lévi-Strauss certainly saw artistic creation as in part a dialogue with the materials (ibid., 18, 27, 29). Logically (following Quintilian), the practice of *bricolage* can be seen as operating through several key transformations: addition, deletion, substitution and transposition (Nöth 1990, 341).

Types and degrees of intertextuality

Gérard Genette proposed the term 'transtextuality' as a more inclusive term than 'intertextuality' (Genette 1997). He listed five subtypes:

1. *intertextuality*: quotation, plagiarism, allusion;
2. *paratextuality*: the relation between a text and its 'paratext' – that which surrounds the main body of the text – such as titles, headings, prefaces, epigraphs, dedications, acknowledgements, footnotes, illustrations, dustjackets, etc.;
3. *architextuality*: designation of a text as part of a genre or genres (Genette refers to designation by the text itself, but this could also be applied to its framing by readers);
4. *metatextuality*: explicit or implicit critical commentary of one text on another text (metatextuality can be hard to distinguish from the following category);
5. *hypotextuality* (Genette's term was *hypertextuality*): the relation between a text and a preceding 'hypotext' – a text or genre on which it is based but which it transforms, modifies, elaborates or extends (including parody, spoof, sequel, translation).

To such a list, computer-based *hypertextuality* should be added: text which can take the reader directly to other texts (regardless of authorship or location). This kind of intertextuality disrupts the conventional 'linearity' of texts. Reading such texts is seldom a question of following standard sequences predetermined by their authors.

It may be useful to consider the issue of 'degrees of intertextuality'. Would the 'most intertextual' text be an indistinguishable copy of another text, or would that have gone beyond what it means to be intertextual? Would the 'most intratextual' text be one which approached the impossible goal of referring only to itself? Even if no specific text is referred to, texts are written within genres and use language in ways which their authors have seldom 'invented'. Intertextuality does not seem to be simply a continuum on a single dimension and there does not seem to be a consensus about what dimensions we should be looking for. Intertextuality is not a feature of the text alone but of the 'contract' which reading it forges between its author(s) and reader(s). Since the dominant mode of producing texts seems to involve masking their debts, *reflexivity* seems to be an important issue – we need to consider how *marked* the intertextuality is. Some defining features of intertextuality might include the following:

- *reflexivity*: how reflexive (or self-conscious) the use of inter-textuality seems to be (if reflexivity is important to what it means to be intertextual, then presumably an indistinguish-able copy goes beyond being intertextual);
- *alteration*: the alteration of sources (more *noticeable* alter-ation presumably making it more reflexively intertextual);
- *explicitness*: the specificity and explicitness of reference(s) to other text(s) (e.g. direct quotation, attributed quotation) (is *assuming* recognition more reflexively intertextual?);
- *criticality to comprehension*: how important it would be for the reader to *recognize* the intertextuality involved;
- *scale of adoption*: the overall scale of allusion/incorpora-tion within the text; and
- *structural unboundedness*: to what extent the text is pre-sented (or understood) as part of or tied to a larger structure (e.g. as part of a genre, of a series, of a serial, of a maga-zine, of an exhibition, etc.) – factors which are often not under the control of the author of the text.

Confounding the realist agenda that 'art imitates life,' intertextuality suggests that art imitates art. Oscar Wilde (typically) took this notion further, declaring provocatively that 'life imitates art'. Texts are instrumental not only in the construction of other texts but in the construction of experiences. Much of what we 'know' about the world is derived from what we have read in books, newspapers and magazines, from what we have seen in the cinema and on television and from what we have heard on the radio. Life is thus lived through texts and framed by texts to a greater extent than we are normally aware of. As the sociologist Scott Lash observes, 'We are living in a society in which our *perception* is directed almost as often to repre-sentations as it is to "reality"' (Lash 1990, 24). Intertextuality blurs the boundaries not only between texts but between texts and the world of lived experience. Indeed, we may argue that we know no pre-textual experience. The world as we know it is merely its current representation.

Chapter 7

Limitations
and strengths

Other than as 'the study of signs' there is relatively
little agreement among semioticians themselves as to
the scope and methodology of semiotics. Although
Saussure had looked forward to the day when semiotics would become part of the social sciences,
semiotics is still a relatively loosely defined critical
practice rather than a unified, fully-fledged analytical
method or theory. At worst, what passes for 'semiotic analysis' is little more than a pretentious form of
literary criticism applied beyond the bounds of literature and based merely on subjective interpretation
and grand assertions. This kind of abuse has earned
semiotics an unenviable reputation in some quarters
as the last refuge for academic charlatans. Criticisms
of structuralist semiotics have led some theorists to
abandon semiotics altogether, while others have
sought to merge it with new perspectives. It is difficult to offer a critique of a shifting target which
changes its form so fluidly as it moves.

Imperialism

Semiotics is often criticized as 'imperialistic', since some semioticians appear to regard it as concerned with, and applicable to, anything and everything, trespassing on almost every academic discipline. Semiotic analysis is just one of many techniques which may be used to explore sign practices. Signs in various media are not alike – different types may need to be studied in different ways. As with any other process of mediation, semiotics suits some purposes better than others. It does not, for instance, lend itself to quantification, a function for which *content analysis* is far better adapted (which is not to suggest that the two techniques are incompatible, as many semioticians seem to assume). The empirical testing of semiotic claims requires other methods. Semiotic approaches make certain kinds of questions easier to ask than others: they do not in themselves shed light on how people in particular social contexts actually interpret texts, which may require ethnographic and phenomenological approaches (see McQuarrie and Mick 1992).

Semioticians do not always make explicit the limitations of their techniques, and semiotics is sometimes uncritically presented as a general-purpose tool. Structuralist semiotics is based on a linguistic model but not everyone agrees that it is productive to treat photography and film, for instance, as 'languages'. Paul Messaris, for instance, disputes that we need to learn to 'read' the formal codes of photographic and audio-visual media, arguing that the resemblance of their images to observable reality is not merely a matter of cultural convention: 'to a substantial degree the formal conventions encountered in still or motion pictures should make a good deal of sense even to a first-time viewer' (Messaris 1994, 7). Others have criticized the way in which some semioticians have treated almost anything as a code, while leaving the details of such codes inexplicit (particularly in the case of ideological codes) (e.g. Corner 1980).

Sometimes semioticians present their analyses as if they were purely objective 'scientific' accounts rather than subjective interpretations. Yet few semioticians seem to feel much need to provide empirical evidence for particular interpretations, and much semiotic analysis is loosely impressionistic and highly unsystematic (or alternatively, generates elaborate taxonomies with little evident practical application). Some semioticians seem to choose examples which illustrate the points they wish to make rather than applying semiotic analysis to an extensive random sample. Semiotic analysis requires a highly skilled analyst if it is not to leave readers feeling that it merely buries the obvious in obscurity. In some cases, it seems little more than an excuse for interpreters to display the appearance of mastery through the use of jargon which excludes most people from participation. In practice, semiotic analysis invariably consists of individual readings. We are seldom presented with the commentaries of several analysts on the same text, to say nothing of evidence of any kind of consensus among different semioticians. Few semioticians make their analytical strategy sufficiently explicit for others to apply it either to the examples used or to others. Structuralist semioticians tend to make no allowance for alternative readings, assuming either that their own interpretations reflect a general consensus or a meaning which resides within the text. Semioticians who reject the investigation of other people's interpretations privilege what has been called the 'élite interpreter' – though socially oriented semioticians would insist that the exploration of people's interpretive practices is fundamental to semiotics.

Form and function

Some semiotic analysis has been criticized as nothing more than an abstract and 'arid formalism' which is preoccupied with classification. Semiotic analysis often shows a tendency to downplay the *affective* domain – though the study of connotations ought to include the sensitive exploration of highly variable and subjective emotional nuances. In structuralist semiotics the focus is on *langue* rather than *parole* (Saussure's terms), on formal systems rather than on social practices. Structuralist studies have tended to be purely textual analyses, and critics complain that the social dimension (such as how people interpret texts) tends to be dismissed as (or reduced to) 'just another text'. Semiotics can appear to suggest that meaning is purely explicable in terms of determining textual structures. Such a stance is subject to the same criticisms as linguistic determinism. In giving priority to the determining power of the system it can be seen as fundamentally conservative. Purely structuralist semiotics does not address processes of production, audience interpretation or authorial intentions. It ignores particular practices, institutional frameworks and the cultural, social, economic and political context. Even Roland Barthes, who argued that texts are codified to encourage a reading which favours the interests of the dominant class, confined his attention to internal textual organization and did not engage with the social context of interpretation. It cannot be assumed that preferred readings will go unchallenged (Hall 1980; Morley 1980). The failure of structuralist semiotics to relate texts to social relations has been attributed to its functionalism (Slater 1983, 259). We must consider not only *how* signs signify (structurally) but also *why* (socially); structures are not causes. The creation and interpretation of texts must be related to social factors outside the structures of texts. Furthermore, the relationships between signifiers and their signifieds may be ontologically arbitrary but they are not socially arbitrary. We should beware of allowing the notion of the sign as arbitrary to foster the myth of the neutrality of the medium.

Dominic Strinati, a sociologist of popular culture, notes:

> How can we know that a bunch of roses signifies passion unless we also know the intention of the sender and the reaction of the receiver, and the kind of relationship they are involved in? If they are lovers and accept the conventions of giving and receiving flowers as an aspect of romantic, sexual love, then we might accept . . . [this] interpretation. But if we do this, we do so on the basis not of the sign but of the social relationships in which we can locate the sign . . . The roses may also be sent as a joke, an insult, a sign of gratitude, and so on. They may indicate passion on the part of the sender but repulsion on the part of the receiver; they may signify family relations between grandparents and grandchildren rather than relations between lovers, and so on. They might even connote sexual harassment.
>
> (Strinati 1995, 125)

Feminist theorists have suggested that despite its usefulness to feminists in some respects, structuralist semiotics 'has often obscured the significance of power relations in the constitution of difference, such as patriarchal forms of domination and subordination' (Franklin *et al.* 1996, 263).

Synchronic analysis studies a phenomenon as if it were frozen at one moment in time; *diachronic* analysis focuses on change over time. Insofar as semiotics tends to focus on synchronic rather than diachronic analysis (as it does in Saussurean semiotics), it underplays the dynamic nature of media conventions (for instance, television conventions change fairly rapidly compared to conventions for written English). It can also underplay dynamic changes in the cultural myths which signification both alludes to and helps to shape. Purely structuralist semiotics ignores process and historicity – unlike historical theories like Marxism.

Structuralist approaches tend to deny the specificity of texts. Critics object to an over-emphasis on the similarities between texts (e.g. Coward and Ellis 1977, 5). The focus on 'underlying structures' which characterizes the structural formalism of theorists such as Propp, Greimas and Lévi-Strauss neglects distinctive features which may be important in themselves. This is particularly vexatious for literary critics, for whom issues of stylistic difference are a central concern.

Inescapable frames

There can be no 'exhaustive' semiotic analyses because every analysis is located in its own particular social and historical circumstances (Hodge and Tripp 1986, 27). Semioticians seek to distance themselves from dominant codes by strategies aimed at *denaturalization*. The notion of 'making the familiar strange, and the strange familiar' is now a recurrent feature of artistic and photographic manifestos and of creative 'brainstorming' sessions in many fields. The phrase itself has been attributed to the German poet Novalis (1772–1801, a.k.a. Friedrich von Hardenberg), who declared that the essence of Romanticism was 'to make the familiar strange, and the strange familiar'. The concept is found among other Romantic theorists such as Wordsworth and Coleridge. The notion is also closely associated with Surrealism and with Brechtian 'alienation'. However, its adoption by semioticians probably owes most to Russian formalist criticism (Lemon and Reis 1965). Victor Shklovsky of the Moscow school argued in 1916 that the key function of art was *estrangement*, *defamiliarization* or 'making strange' (*ostranenie*) – i.e. renewing our perception of everyday things and events which are so familiar that our perception of them has become routinized (Hawkes 1977, 62–7). Russian formalism was a key influence on the development of semiotics in Eastern Europe, and the legacy of 'making the familiar strange' is an important one for semiotics. However, the strategy of *defamiliarization* is itself ideological and has been associated with the myth that the tactic of surprise may serve to banish 'distortions' so that we may 'objectively' perceive 'reality' (Watney 1982, 173–4). Clearly the strategy of 'making the familiar strange' needs to be coupled with an awareness that while we may be able to bypass one set of conventions we may never escape the framing of experience by convention.

There is a tendency for some semioticians to represent semiotic analysis as a process of 'decoding', as in the title of Judith Williamson's widely cited book, *Decoding Advertisements* (Williamson 1978). Theorists such as Mikhail Bakhtin and Roland Barthes have used semiotics for the 'revelatory' political purpose of 'demystifying' society. This approach involves the assumption that there is a 'literal truth' or pre-given reality underlying the coded version, which can be 'revealed' by the skilled analyst. Poststructuralist theorists have argued that the structuralist enterprise is impossible – we cannot stand outside our sign-systems. Contemporary Marxist theorists emphasize 'the politics of signification' – signification cannot be neutral ('value-free'). In his widely cited essays on the history of photographic practices, John Tagg comments that he is 'not concerned with exposing the manipulation of a pristine "truth", or with unmasking some conspiracy, but rather with the analysis of the specific "political economy" within which the "mode of production" of "truth" is operative' (Tagg 1988, 174–5).

Poststructuralist semiotics

Some contemporary theorists have rejected a purely structuralist semiotics. But such a rejection need not involve a wholesale rejection of semiotics. Influential as it has been, structuralist analysis is but one approach to semiotics. Many of the criticisms of semiotics are directed at a form of semiotics to which few contemporary semioticians adhere. While some semioticians have retained a structuralist concern with formal systems (mainly focusing on detailed studies of narrative, film and television editing and so on), many have become more concerned with 'social semiotics' (Hodge and Kress 1988). A key concern of social semioticians is with what are often called 'specific signifying practices'. Such 'reformed' semioticians practise 'poststructuralist' semiotics, focusing on what one has called 'situated social semiosis' (Jensen 1995, 57). This at least is the rhetoric of social semioticians, but the extent to which social semiotics has so far met the concerns of sociologists is debatable. However, it is early days: 'social semiotics' is still under construction. Contemporary theorists who have associated themselves with this development include: Gunther Kress, Robert Hodge, Theo van Leeuwen, Klaus Bruhn Jensen, Paul J. Thibault and Jay Lemke (Hodge and Kress 1988; Jensen 1995; Lemke 1995; Kress and van Leeuwen 1996; Thibault 1997).

It is only fair to note that much of the criticism of semiotics has taken the form of self-criticism by those within the field. The theoretical literature of semiotics reflects a constant attempt by many semioticians to grapple with the implications of new theories for their framing of the semiotic enterprise. Seeking to account for the role of social change and the role of the subject, poststructuralist semiotics has adopted Marxist and psychoanalytical inflections. Another inflection derives from Foucault – emphasizing power relations in discursive practices. Such shifts of direction are not an abandonment of semiotics but of the limitations of purely structuralist semiotics. Contemporary apologists have noted that there is nothing new about the emphasis on the social dimension of semiotics. The roots of social semiotics can be traced to the early theorists. Neither Saussure nor Peirce studied the social use of signs. However,

213

Saussure did envisage semiotics as 'a science which studies the role of signs as part of social life'. As for Peirce, the notion of semiosis as a dialogic process is central to his thinking. Signs do not exist without interpreters, and semiotic codes are of course social conventions. However, it has to be acknowledged that an emphasis on the social dimension of semiotics in the form of the study of specific meaning-making *practices* is relatively recent outside of specialized academic journals and it is not yet much in evidence at the heart of the activities of many semiotic researchers.

Strengths of semiotic analysis

Semiotics can help to denaturalize theoretical assumptions in academia just as in everyday life; it can thus raise new theoretical issues. While this means that many scholars who encounter semiotics find it unsettling, others find it exciting. Semiotics is not, never has been, and seems unlikely ever to be, an academic discipline in its own right. It is now widely regarded primarily as one mode of analysis among others rather than as a 'science' of cultural forms. However, it does offer a focus of enquiry, with a central concern for meaning-making practices which conventional academic disciplines treat as peripheral. Specific semiotic modalities are addressed by such specialists as linguists, art historians and anthropologists, but we must turn to semioticians if we wish to study meaning-making and representation across modalities. Semiotics provides us with a potentially unifying conceptual framework and a set of methods and concepts for use across the full range of signifying practices, which include gesture, posture, dress, writing, speech, photography, the mass media and the Internet.

Traditional structural semiotics was primarily applied to textual analysis but it is misleading to identify contemporary semiotics with structuralism. The turn to social semiotics has been reflected in an increasing concern with the role of the reader. In either form, semiotics is invaluable if we wish to look beyond the manifest content of texts. Structuralist semiotics seeks to look behind or beneath the surface of the observed in order to discover the underlying organization of phenomena. The more obvious the structural organization of a text or code may seem to be, the more difficult it may be to see beyond such surface features. Searching for what is 'hidden' beneath the 'obvious' can lead to fruitful insights. Semiotics is also well adapted to exploring connotative meanings. Social semiotics alerts us to how the same text may generate different meanings for different readers.

Mediation

Whereas both 'commonsense' and positivist realism involve an insistence that reality is independent of the signs that refer to it, socially oriented semioticians tend to adopt constructionist stances, emphasizing the role of sign-systems in the construction of reality. They argue that there is nothing 'natural' about our values: they are social constructions which are peculiar to our location in space and time. Assertions which seem to us to be 'obvious', 'natural', universal, given, permanent and incontrovertible may be generated by the ways in which sign-systems operate in our discourse communities. Acknowledging the mediation of signs need not involve a denial of external physical reality – we may argue that although things may exist independently of signs we know them only through the mediation of signs and see only what our sign-systems allow us to see.

While structuralist semioticians have sometimes been criticized for seeking to impose verbal language as a model on media which are non-verbal or not solely or primarily verbal, the virtue of adopting a linguistic model lies in treating all signs as being to some extent arbitrary and conventional – thus fostering an awareness of the ideological forces that seek to naturalize signs. Semioticians argue that signs are related to their signifieds by social conventions which we learn. We become so used to such conventions in our use of various media that they seem 'natural', and it can be difficult for us to realize the conventional nature of such relationships. When we take these relationships for granted we treat the signified as unmediated or 'transparent', as when we interpret television or photography as 'a window on the world'. Semiotics demonstrates that the 'transparency' of the 'medium' is illusory.

The semiotic stance which problematizes 'reality' and emphasizes mediation and representational convention in the form of codes is criticized as relativism (or conventionalism) by those veering towards realism. Such critics often fear an extreme relativism in which every representation of reality is regarded as being as good as any other. There are understandable objections to any apparent sidelining of referential concerns such as truth, facts, accuracy, objectivity, bias and distortion. Socially oriented semioticians tend to be very much aware that representations are far from equal. Valentin Voloshinov declared that 'whenever a sign is present, ideology is present too' (Voloshinov 1973, 10). There are no ideologically 'neutral' sign-systems: signs function to persuade as well as to refer. Sign-systems help to naturalize and reinforce particular framings of 'the way things are', although the operation of ideology in signifying practices is typically masked. Consequently, semiotic analysis always involves ideological analysis. If signs do not merely reflect reality but are involved in its construction then those who control the sign-systems control the construction of reality. However, 'commonsense' involves incoherences, ambiguities, inconsistencies, contradictions, omissions, gaps and silences which offer leverage points for potential social change. The role of ideology is to suppress these in the interests of dominant groups. Consequently, reality construction occurs on 'sites of struggle'. Dominant social groups seek to limit the meanings of signs to those which suit their interests and to naturalize such meanings. For Roland Barthes, various codes contribute to reproducing bourgeois ideology, making it seem natural, proper and inevitable. One need not be a Marxist to appreciate that it can be liberating to become aware of whose view of reality is being privileged in the process. Many semioticians see their primary task as being to *denaturalize* signs, texts and codes. Semiotics can thus show ideology at work and demonstrate that 'reality' can be challenged.

While processes of mediation tend to retreat to transparency in our routine everyday practices, adopting a semiotic approach can help us to attend to specific textual practices. This has made it a particularly attractive approach for media educators, for instance. In the study of the mass media, semiotic approaches can draw our attention to such taken-for-granted practices as the classic Hollywood convention of 'invisible editing' which is still the dominant editing style in popular cinema and television. Semiotic treatments can make us aware that this is a manipulative convention which we have learned to accept as 'natural' in film and television. In relation to the mass media, semiotics has made distinctive theoretical contributions. In association with psychoanalysis, semiotics also introduced the theory of 'the positioning of the subject' (the spectator) in relation to the filmic text. While this structuralist stance may have reinforced the myth of the irresistibility of media influence, the emphasis of social semioticians on diversity of interpretation (within social parameters) has countered the earlier tendency to equate meaning with 'message' (or content) and to translate this directly to 'media effects'.

The construction of meanings and subjects

As an approach to communication which focuses on meaning and interpretation, semiotics challenges the reductive transmission model. Signs do not just 'convey' meanings, but constitute a medium in which meanings are *constructed*. Semiotics helps us to realize that meaning is not passively absorbed but arises only in the active process of interpretation. Even within the structuralist paradigm, someone has to relate signs to each other and to the codes within which they make sense. Semiotics highlights the richness of interpretation which signs generate (Voloshinov 1973, 23).

The romantic mythology of individual creativity and of the 'originality' of 'the author' (e.g. the *auteur* in film) has been undermined by various strands in semiotics: by the structuralist emphasis on the primacy of the semiotic system and of ourselves as produced by language; by the social semiotic emphasis on the role of the interpreters of a text; and by the poststructuralist semiotic notion of intertextuality (highlighting what texts owe to other texts). Individuals are not unconstrained in their construction of meanings. As the sociologist Stuart Hall puts it, our 'systems of signs . . . *speak us* as much as we speak in and through them' (Hall 1977, 328). 'Commonsense' suggests that 'I' am a unique individual with a stable, unified identity and ideas of my own. Semiotics can help us to realize that such notions are created and maintained by our engagement with sign-systems: our sense of identity is established through signs. We derive a sense of 'self' from drawing upon conventional, pre-existing repertoires of signs and codes which we did not ourselves create. We are thus the *subjects* of our sign-systems rather than being simply instrumental 'users' who are fully in control of them. While we are not *determined* by semiotic processes we are *shaped* by them far more than we realize. The postmodernist notion of fragmented and shifting identities may provide a useful corrective to the myth of the unified self. But unlike those postmodernist stances which simply celebrate radical relativism, semiotics can help us to focus on *how* we make sense of ourselves, while social semiotics anchors us to the study of situated practices in the construction of identities and the part that our engagement with sign-systems plays in such processes.

Feminist theorists note that structuralist semiotics has been important as a tool for critiques of reductionism and essentialism and has 'facilitated the analysis of contradictory meanings and identities' (Franklin *et al.* 1996, 263). Semiotics has sought to study cultural artifacts and practices of whatever kind on the basis of unified principles, at its best counteracting cultural chauvinism and bringing some coherence to communication and cultural studies. While semiotic analysis has been widely applied to the literary, artistic and musical canon, it has also been applied to the 'decoding' of a wide variety of popular cultural phenomena. It has thus helped to stimulate the serious study of popular culture.

Semiotic modes

While all verbal language is communication, most communication is non-verbal. In an increasingly visual age, an important contribution of semiotics from Roland Barthes onwards has been a concern with imagistic as well as linguistic signs, particularly in the context of advertising, photography and audio-visual media. Semiotics may encourage us not to dismiss a particular medium as of less worth than another: literary and film critics often regard television as of less worth than prose fiction or 'artistic' film. To élitist literary critics, of course, this would be a weakness of semiotics. Potentially, semiotics could help us to realize differences as well as similarities between various media. It could help us to avoid the routine privileging of one semiotic mode over another, such as the spoken over the written or the verbal over the non-verbal. We need to realize the affordances and constraints of different semiotic modes – visual, verbal, gestural and so on. Such a realization could lead to the recognition of the importance of new literacies in a changing semiotic ecology. At present, 'with regard to images, most people in most societies are mostly confined to the role of spectator of other people's productions' (Messaris 1994, 121). Most people feel unable to draw or paint, and even among those who own video-cameras not everyone knows how to make effective use of them. This is a legacy of an educational system which still focuses almost exclusively on the acquisition of one kind of symbolic literacy (that of verbal language) at the expense of most other semiotic modes (in particular the iconic mode). This institutional bias disempowers people not only by excluding many from engaging in those representational practices which are not purely linguistic but by handicapping them as critical readers of the majority of texts to which they are routinely exposed throughout their lives. A working understanding of key concepts in semiotics – including their practical application – can be seen as essential for everyone who wants to understand the complex and dynamic communication ecologies within which we live. As Peirce put it, 'the universe . . . is perfused with signs, if it is not composed exclusively of signs' (Peirce 1931–58, 5.449n.). There is no escape from signs. Those who cannot understand them and the systems of which they are a part are in the greatest danger of being manipulated by those who can. In short, semiotics cannot be left to semioticians.

Going further

By far the most useful general reference book covering much of the field is Nöth's *Handbook of Semiotics* (1990), available since 1995 in paperback. A socially oriented perspective is outlined in *Social Semiotics* by Hodge and Kress (1988). As for 'the semiotics of . . .', consult the relevant references listed in this book. For media semiotics, for instance, you might begin with Bignell's *Media Semiotics* (1997) and Jensen's *Social Semiotics of Mass Communication* (1995). For literary semiotics, start with Culler's *Structuralist Poetics* (1975) and *The Pursuit of Signs* (1981).

Consulting the foundational theorists, Saussure and Peirce, is wise since they are frequently misrepresented in popular texts. There are two English translations of Saussure – that by Wade Baskin dating from 1959 (Saussure 1974) and a later British translation by Roy Harris (Saussure 1983). Watch out for Harris's quirky substitution of 'signal' and 'signification' for what are still invariably known as the signifier and the signified. There are various useful commentaries (e.g. Culler 1985; Harris 1987; Holdcroft 1991;

Thibault 1997). Peirce's writings are voluminous and the references to semiotics are scattered. There is an eight-volume edition (Peirce 1931–58) which may be available in libraries, the most useful volume perhaps being volume two. A CD-ROM version is available from InteLex. A new printed edition is underway (Peirce 1998–). Useful selections are also available (e.g. Peirce 1966, 1998). A recent commentary is Merrell (1997).

The main works of the leading semioticians are listed here in the references. Two collections of Barthes' essays offer a fairly gentle introduction to his version of cultural semiotics – *Mythologies* (1957/1987) and *Image–Music–Text* (1977). The work of Jakobson (e.g. 1960) and Lévi-Strauss (e.g. 1972) is an essential foundation for structuralist theory. There is now a lively illustrated guide to Lévi-Strauss (Wiseman and Groves 2000). Greimas's *On Meaning* (1987) is not for beginners. Metz's *Film Language* (1974) is important for film theory. Jean-Marie Floch's *Visual Identities* has just appeared in English translation (Floch 2000). Eco's *Theory of Semiotics* (Eco 1976) is widely cited but difficult – it should be read in conjunction with his more recent *Kant and the Platypus* (Eco 1999). The writings of the key poststructuralists, Derrida (1976, 1978), Foucault (1970, 1974) and Lacan (1977), are initially daunting, and a beginner's guide may be helpful (e.g. Sarup 1993). Readers offering affordable selections are available for some of the key theorists (e.g. Barthes 1983, Foucault 1991, Derrida 1998).

The online version of the text of this present volume includes further suggestions and gateways to additional resources. This is currently at:

http://www.aber.ac.uk/media/Documents/S4B/

Glossary

addresser and addressee   Jakobson used these terms
to refer to what, in transmission models of
communication, are called the 'sender' and the
'receiver' of a message. Other commentators
have used them to refer more specifically to
constructions of these two roles within the text,
so that *addresser* refers to an authorial persona,
while *addressee* refers to an 'ideal reader'. *See
also* **codes, functions of signs**.

analogue oppositions (antonyms)   Pairs of oppositional signifiers in a paradigm set representing
categories with comparative grading on the
same implicit dimension, e.g. good–bad where
'not good' is not necessarily 'bad' and vice
versa. *See also* **binary oppositions**.

analogue signs   Analogue signs are signs in a form
in which they are perceived as involving graded
relationships on a continuum rather than as
discrete units (in contrast to digital signs). Note,
however, that digital technology can transform
analogue signs into digital reproductions which

may be perceptually indistinguishable from the 'originals'. *See also* **digital signs**.

anchorage Roland Barthes introduced the concept of *anchorage*. Linguistic elements in a text (such as a caption) can serve to 'anchor' (or constrain) the preferred readings of an image (conversely the illustrative use of an image can anchor an ambiguous verbal text). *See also* **preferred reading**.

arbitrariness Saussure emphasized that the relationship between the linguistic signifier and signified is *arbitrary*: the link between them is not necessary, intrinsic or 'natural'. Many subsequent theorists apply this also to the relation between the signifier and any real-world referent. Peirce noted that the relationship between signifiers and their signifieds varies in arbitrariness – from the radical arbitrariness of symbolic signs, via the perceived similarity of signifier to signified in iconic signs, to the minimal arbitrariness of indexical signs. Many semioticians argue that *all* signs are to some extent arbitrary and conventional (and thus subject to ideological manipulation). *See also* **conventionality**, **motivation and constraint**, **primacy of the signifier**, **relative autonomy**.

articulation of codes *Articulation* refers to structural levels within semiotic codes. Semiotic codes have either single articulation, double articulation or no articulation. *See also* **double articulation**, **relative autonomy**, **single articulation**, **unarticulated codes**.

binary oppositions (or digital oppositions) Pairs of mutually exclusive signifiers in a paradigm set representing categories which are logically opposed, e.g. alive–not-alive. *See also* **analogue oppositions (antonyms)**, **markedness**.

bricolage Lévi-Strauss's term for the appropriation of pre-existing materials which are ready to hand is widely used to refer to the intertextual authorial practice of adopting and adapting signs from other texts. *See also* **intertextuality**.

broadcast codes Fiske's term for codes which are shared by members of a mass audience and which are learned informally through experience rather than deliberately or institutionally. In contrast to narrowcast codes, broadcast codes are structurally simpler, employing standard conventions and 'formulas'. They are more repetitive and predictable – 'overcoded' – having a high degree of *redundancy*. In such codes several elements serve to emphasize and reinforce preferred meanings. Broadcast codes are heavily intertextual, although the intertextuality is normally transparent. *See also* **codes**, **intertextuality**, **narrowcast codes**.

channel A sensory mode utilized by a medium (e.g. visual, auditory, tactile). Available channel(s) are dictated by the technical features of the medium in which a text appears. The sensory bias of the channel limits the codes for which it is suitable. *See also* **medium**.

codes One of the fundamental concepts in semiotics. Semiotic codes are procedural systems of related conventions for correlating signifiers and signifieds in certain domains. Codes provide a framework within which signs make sense: they are interpretative devices which are used by interpretative communities. Some codes are fairly explicit; others (dubbed 'hermeneutics' by Guiraud) are much looser. *See also* **articulation of codes**, **broadcast codes**, **codification**, **dominant code and reading**, **interpretative community**, **narrowcast codes**, **negotiated code and reading**, **oppositional code and reading**, **unarticulated codes**.

codification A historical social process whereby the conventions of a particular code (e.g. for a genre) become widely established (Guiraud).

commutation test A structuralist analytical technique used in the paradigmatic analysis of a text to determine whether a change on the level of the signifier leads to a change on the level of the signified. To apply this test, a particular signifier in a text is selected. Then meaningful alternatives taken from the same paradigm set are considered. The effects of each substitution are assessed in terms of how this might affect the sense made of the sign. *See also* **markedness**, **paradigmatic analysis**, **transformation, rules of**.

connotation The socio-cultural and 'personal' associations produced as a reader decodes a text. The term also refers to the relationship between the signifier and its signified. For Barthes, connotation was a second 'order of signification' which uses the denotative sign (signifier and signified) as its signifier and attaches to it an additional signified. In this framework, connotation is a sign which derives from the signifier of a denotative sign (so denotation leads to a chain of connotations). *See also* **denotation**.

constitution of the subject *See* **subject**, **interpellation**.

constraint *See* **motivation and constraint**.

conventionality A term often used in conjunction with the term *arbitrary* to refer to the relationship between the signifier and the signified. In the case of a symbolic system such as verbal language this relationship is purely conventional – dependent on social and cultural conventions (rather than in any sense 'natural'). The conventional nature of codes means that they have to be *learned* (not necessarily formally). Thus some semioticians speak of learning to 'read' photographs, television or film, for instance. *See also* **arbitrariness**, **primacy of the signifier**, **relative autonomy**.

Copenhagen school This was a structuralist and formalist group of linguists founded by the Danish linguists Louis Hjelmslev (1899–1966) and Viggo Brøndal (1887–1953). Roman Jakobson (1896–1982) was associated with this group from 1939–49. Influenced by Saussure, its most distinctive contribution was a concern with 'glossematics'. While Hjelmslev did accord a privileged status to language, his glossematics included both linguistics and 'non-linguistic languages' – which Hjelmslev claimed could be analysed independently of their material substance. It is a formalist approach in that it considers semiotic systems without regard for their social context. Hjelmslev's theories strongly influenced Algirdas Greimas (1917–92), and to a lesser extent the French cultural theorist Roland Barthes (1915–80) and the film theorist Christian Metz (1931–93). *See also* **Moscow school**, **Paris school**, **structuralism**.

decoding The comprehension and interpretation of texts by decoders with reference to relevant codes. Most commentators assume that the reader actively constructs meaning rather than simply 'extracting' it from the text. *See also* **codes**, **encoding**.

deconstruction This is a poststructuralist strategy for textual analysis, which was developed by Jacques Derrida. Practitioners seek to dismantle the rhetorical structures within a text to demonstrate how key concepts within it depend on their unstated oppositional relation to absent signifiers (this involved building on the structuralist method of paradigmatic analysis). Deconstructionists have also exposed culturally embedded conceptual oppositions in which the initial term is privileged, leaving 'Term B' negatively 'marked'. Radical deconstruction is not simply a *reversal* of the valorization in an opposition but a demonstration of the instability of such oppositions. *See also* **denaturalization, markedness, analogue oppositions, binary oppositions, paradigmatic analysis, poststructuralism**.

denaturalization, defamiliarization One of the goals of semioticians is *denaturalization*: revealing the socially coded basis of phenomena which are taken for granted as 'natural'. The concept was borrowed from Shklovsky's formalist notion of *defamiliarization*, according to which a key function of art is to 'make the familiar strange'. A feature of many postmodern texts is a parodic use of intertextual references which functions to denaturalize the normally transparent representational conventions of 'realistic' textual codes. The semiotician seeks to *denaturalize* signs and codes in order to make more explicit the underlying rules for encoding and decoding them, and often also with the intention of revealing the usually invisible operation of ideological forces. *See also* **deconstruction, naturalization**.

denotation The term refers to the relationship between the signifier and its signified. *Denotation* is routinely treated as the definitional, 'literal', 'obvious' or 'commonsense' meaning of a sign, but semioticians tend to treat it as a signified about which there is a relatively broad *consensus*. For Barthes, a denotative sign existed within what he called the first 'order of signification'. In this framework, connotation is a further sign (or signs) deriving from the signifier of a denotative sign.

However, no clear distinction can be made between denotation and connotation. *See also* **connotation**.

diachronic analysis Diachronic analysis studies change in a phenomenon (such as a code) over time (in contrast to synchronic analysis). Saussure saw the development of language in terms of a series of synchronic states. Critics argue that this fails to account for how change occurs. *See also* **langue and parole**, **synchronic analysis**.

digital signs Digital signs involve discrete units such as words and numerals, in contrast to analogue signs. Note, however, that digital technology can transform analogue signs into digital reproductions which may be perceptually indistinguishable from the 'originals', and that texts generated in a digital medium can be 'copies without originals' (e.g. a word-processed text). *See also* **tokens and types**.

discourse community *See* **interpretative community**.

dominant (or 'hegemonic') code and reading Within Stuart Hall's framework, this is an ideological code in which the decoder fully shares the text's code and accepts and reproduces the preferred reading (a reading which may not have been the result of any conscious intention on the part of the author(s)) – in such a stance the textual code seems 'natural' and 'transparent'. *See also* **preferred reading**, **negotiated code and reading**, **oppositional code and reading**

double articulation A semiotic code which has 'double articulation' (as in the case of verbal language) can be analysed into two abstract structural levels. At the *level of first articulation* the system consists of the smallest meaningful units available (e.g. morphemes or words in a language). These meaningful units are complete signs, each consisting of a signifier and a signified. At the *level of second articulation*, a semiotic code is divisible into minimal functional units which lack meaning in themselves (e.g. phonemes in speech or graphemes in writing). They are not signs in themselves (the code must have a first level of articulation for these lower units to be combined into meaningful signs). Theoretical linguists have largely abandoned the use of the term *articulation* in the structural sense, preferring to refer to 'duality of patterning'. *See also* **articulation of codes**, **single articulation**.

elaborated codes *See* **narrowcast codes**.

empty signifier An 'empty' or 'floating' signifier is variously defined as a signifier with a vague, highly variable, unspecifiable or non-existent signified. Such signifiers mean different things to different people: they may stand for many or even *any* signifieds; they may mean whatever their interpreters want them to mean. Those who posit the existence of such signifiers argue that there is a radical disconnection between signifier and signified. For a Saussurean semiotician, no signifier can exist without a corresponding signified – to qualify as a sign *something* must be signified. *See also* **signifier**, **transcendent(al) signified**.

encoding The production of texts by encoders with reference to relevant codes. Encoding involves foregrounding some meanings and backgrounding others. *See also* **codes**, **decoding**.

formalism *See* **Moscow school**.

functions of signs In Jakobson's model of linguistic communication, the dominance of any one of six factors within an utterance reflects a different linguistic function: *referential*, oriented towards the *context*; *expressive*, oriented towards the *addresser*; *conative*, oriented towards the *addressee*; *phatic*, oriented towards the *contact*; *metalingual*, oriented towards the *code*; *poetic*, oriented towards the *message*. In any given situation one of these factors is 'dominant', and this dominant function influences the general character of the 'message'.

glossematics *See* **Copenhagen school**.

hegemonic code *See* **dominant code and reading**.

homology *See* **isomorphism**.

iconic A mode in which the signifier is perceived as resembling or imitating the signified (recognizably looking, sounding, feeling, tasting or smelling like it) – being similar in possessing some of its qualities (e.g. a portrait, a diagram, a scale-model, onomatopoeia, metaphors, 'realistic' sounds in music, sound effects in radio drama, a dubbed film soundtrack, imitative gestures). *See also* **indexical**, **isomorphism**, **symbolic**.

indexical   A mode in which the signifier is *not* purely arbitrary but is directly connected in some way (physically or causally) to the signified – this link can be observed or inferred (e.g. smoke, thermometer, fingerprint). *See also* **iconic**, **symbolic**.

interpellation   Interpellation is Althusser's term to describe a mechanism whereby the human subject is 'constituted' (constructed) by pre-given structures or texts (a structuralist stance). Such framings reflect a stance of structural or textual determinism which has been challenged by contemporary social semioticians who tend to emphasize the 'polysemic' and 'multiaccentual' nature of texts, together with the diversity of their uses. *See also* **subject**.

interpretant   In Peirce's model of the sign, the *interpretant* is *not* an interpreter but rather the sense made of the sign. Peirce doesn't feature the interpreter directly in his triad, although he does highlight the interpretative process of semiosis. *See also* **unlimited semiosis**.

interpretative community   Those who share the same codes are members of the same 'interpretative community' – a term introduced by the literary theorist Stanley Fish to refer to both 'writers' and 'readers' of particular genres of texts (but which can be used more widely to refer to those who share any code). Linguists tend to use the logocentric term, 'discourse community'. Constructionists argue that interpretative communities are involved in the construction and maintenance of reality within the ontological domain which defines their concerns. The conventions within the codes employed by such communities become naturalized among its members. Individuals belong simultaneously to several interpretative communities. *See also* **code**, **signifying practices**.

intertextuality   The semiotic notion of intertextuality introduced by Kristeva is associated primarily with poststructuralist theorists. Intertextuality refers to the various links in form and content which bind a text to other texts. Each text exists in relation to others. Texts owe more to other texts than to their own makers. Texts provide contexts such as genre within which other texts may be created and interpreted. *See also* **bricolage**, **intratextuality**.

intratextuality   While the term intertextuality would normally be used to refer to links to other texts, a related kind of link is what might be called 'intratextuality' – involving internal relations *within* the text. Within a single code (e.g. a photographic code) these would be simply syntagmatic relationships (e.g. the relationship of the image of one person to another within the same photograph). However, a text may involve several codes: a newspaper photograph, for instance, may have a caption. *See also* **anchorage**, **intertextuality**.

irony   Irony is a rhetorical trope. It is a kind of double sign in which the 'literal sign' combines with another sign typically to signify the opposite meaning. However, understatement and overstatement can also be ironic. *See also* **metaphor**, **metonymy**, **synecdoche**, **trope**.

isomorphism   The term is used to refer to correspondences, parallels, or similarities in the properties, patterns or relations of (a) two *different structures*; (b) structural *elements* in two *different structures* and (c) structural *elements* at different levels *within the same structure*. Some theorists use the term *homology* in much the same way. Structuralists seek to identify such patterns and note homologies between structures at all levels within a system because all structural units are generated from the same basic rules of transformation. *See also* **iconic**, **structuralism**, **transformation**, **rules of**.

langue and parole   These are Saussure's terms. *Langue* refers to the abstract system of rules and conventions of a signifying system – it is independent of, and pre-exists, individual users. *Parole* refers to concrete instances of its use. *See also* **diachronic analysis**, **synchronic analysis**.

logocentrism   Derrida used this term to refer to the 'metaphysics of presence' in Western culture – in particular its phonocentrism, and its foundation on a mythical 'transcendent signified'. Logocentrism can also refer to a typically unconscious interpretative bias which privileges linguistic communication over the revealingly named 'non-verbal' forms of communication and expression, and over unverbalized feelings; logocentrism privileges both the eye and the ear over other sensory modalities such as touch. *See also* **channel**, **phonocentrism**.

markedness The concept of markedness introduced by Jakobson can be applied to the poles of a paradigmatic opposition (e.g. male–female). Paired signifiers (such as *male–female*) consist of an 'unmarked' form (in this case, the word *male*) and a 'marked' form (in this case the word *female*). The 'marked' signifier is distinguished by some special semiotic feature (in this case the addition of an initial *fe-*). A marked or unmarked status applies not only to signifiers but also to their signifieds. With many of the familiarly paired terms, the two signifieds are valorized – accorded different values. The marked form (typically the second term) is presented as 'different' and is (implicitly) negative. The unmarked form is typically dominant (e.g. statistically within a text or corpus) and therefore seems to be 'neutral', 'normal' and 'natural'. *See also* **deconstruction**, **analogue oppositions**, **binary oppositions**, **paradigm**, **transcendent(al) signified**.

medium The term 'medium' is used in a variety of ways by different theorists, and may include such broad categories as speech and writing, or print and broadcasting or relate to specific technical forms within the media of mass communication or the media of interpersonal communication. Signs and codes are always anchored in the material form of a medium – each of which has its own constraints and affordances. A medium may be digital or analogue. Marshall McLuhan famously declared that 'the medium is the message'. A medium is typically treated instrumentally as a transparent vehicle of representation by readers of texts composed within it, but the medium used may itself contribute to meaning. *See also* **channel**, **sign vehicle**.

message This term variously refers either to a text or to the meaning of a text – referents which literalists tend to conflate. *See also* **text**.

metaphor   Metaphor expresses the unfamiliar (known in literary jargon as the 'tenor') in terms of the familiar (the 'vehicle'). In semiotic terms, a metaphor involves one signified acting as a signifier referring to a rather different signified. Since metaphors apparently disregard 'literal' or denotative resemblance they can be seen as symbolic as well as iconic. Metaphoric signifiers tend to foreground the signifier rather than the signified. Deconstructionists have sought to demonstrate how dominant metaphors function to privilege unmarked signifieds. *See also* **irony**, **metonymy**, **synecdoche**, **trope**.

metonymy   A metonym is a figure of speech that involves using one signified to stand for another signified which is directly related to it or closely associated with it in some way, notably the substitution of effect for cause. It is sometimes considered to include the functions ascribed by some to synecdoche. Metonymy simulates an indexical mode. Metonymic signifiers foreground their signifieds and background themselves. *See also* **irony**, **synecdoche**, **metaphor**, **trope**.

modality   Modality refers to the reality status accorded to or claimed by a sign, text or genre. Peirce's classification of signs in terms of the mode of relationship of the sign vehicle to its referent reflects their modality – their apparent transparency in relation to 'reality' (the symbolic mode, for instance, having low modality). In making sense of a text, its interpreters make 'modality judgements' about it. They assess what are variously described as the plausibility, reliability, credibility, truth, accuracy or facticity of texts within a given genre as representations of some recognizable reality. In doing so, they draw upon their knowledge of the world (and social codes) and of the medium (and textual codes). Such judgements are made in part with reference to cues within texts which semioticians (following linguists) call 'modality markers', which include features of form and content.

modelling systems, primary and secondary   'Secondary modelling systems' are described, following Lotman, as semiotic superstructures built upon 'primary modelling systems'. Within this framework, writing is a secondary modelling system and written texts are built upon a primary modelling system which consists of verbal language. Since this stance grants primacy to the spoken form, it has been criticized as phonocentric. Other theorists have extended this notion to 'texts' in other media, seeing them as secondary modelling systems built out of a primary 'language'. Cinematic texts, for instance, have sometimes been seen as built upon a primary modelling system of 'graphic language'. However, whether such a 'language' has basic building blocks and what these might be has been hotly disputed.

modes of address Implicit and explicit ways in which aspects of the style, structure and/or content of a text function to 'position' readers as subjects ('ideal readers') (e.g. in relation to class, age, gender and ethnicity). Aspects of this include degrees of directness and of formality, narrative point of view and the markedness of one form of address compared with another. *See also* **functions of signs**.

Moscow school The Moscow Linguistics Circle was co-founded in 1915 by the Russian linguists Roman Jakobson (1896–1982) and Pjotr Bogatyrev (1893–1971). Together with the Petrograd Society for the Study of Poetic Language (*Opoyaz*) – which included Victor Shklovsky (1893–1984), Yuri Tynyanov (1894–1943) and Boris Eikhenbaum (1886–1959) – the Moscow school was the origin of Russian formalism (a term initially used pejoratively by critics). Formalism represented a linguistic focus on literary and aesthetic practices. The primary focus of the formalists was on form, structure, technique or medium rather than on content. They saw literary language as language 'made strange' and their model was poetry rather than prose. They were particularly interested in literary 'devices' such as rhyme, rhythm, metre, imagery, syntax and narrative techniques – favouring writing which 'laid bare' its devices. Formalism evolved into structuralism in the late 1920s and 1930s. When formalist criticism was suppressed in the early 1930s by the Russian government, Jakobson emigrated to Czechoslovakia and became part of the Prague Linguistic Circle. *See also* **Prague school**.

motivation and constraint The term 'motivation' (used by Saussure) is sometimes contrasted with 'constraint' in describing the extent to which the signified determines the signifier. The more a signifier is constrained by the signified, the more 'motivated' the sign is: iconic signs are highly motivated; symbolic signs are unmotivated. The less motivated the sign, the more learning of an agreed code is required. *See also* **arbitrariness**.

multiaccentuality of the sign Voloshinov's term is used to refer to the diversity of the use and interpretation of texts by different audiences.

myth Barthes argues that the 'orders of signification' called denotation and connotation combine to produce ideology in the form of *myth* – which has been described as a *third* order of signification. Myths operate through codes and serve the ideological function of naturalization.

narrowcast codes In contrast to broadcast codes, narrowcast codes are aimed at a limited audience, structurally more complex, less repetitive and tend to be more subtle, original and unpredictable. Following Bernstein, they are controversially described by some theorists as 'elaborated codes'. *See also* **broadcast codes**, **codes**.

naturalization Codes which have been naturalized are those which are so widely distributed in a culture and which are learned at such an early age that they appear not to be constructed but to be 'naturally' given. Myths serve the ideological function of naturalization – making the cultural seem 'natural', 'normal', 'self-evident', 'commonsense', and thus 'taken for granted'. *See also* **denaturalization**.

negotiated code and reading Within Stuart Hall's framework, this is an ideological code in which the reader partly shares the text's code and broadly accepts the preferred reading, but sometimes resists and modifies it in a way which reflects their own social position, experiences and interests (local and personal conditions may be seen as exceptions to the general rule). *See also* **dominant code and reading**, **oppositional code and reading**.

object Term used in Peirce's triadic model of the sign to describe the referent of the sign – what the sign 'stands for'. Note that unlike Saussure's abstract signified, the referent is an object in the world. This need not exclude the reference of signs to abstract concepts and fictional entities as well as to physical objects, but Peirce's model allocates a place for a physical reality which Saussure's model did not feature.

oppositional code and reading Within Stuart Hall's framework, this is an ideological code in which the reader, whose social situation places them in a directly oppositional relation to the dominant code, understands the preferred reading but does not share the text's code and rejects this reading, bringing to bear an alternative ideological code. *See also* **dominant code and reading**, **negotiated code and reading**, **oppositional code and reading**.

oppositions, semantic *See* **analogue oppositions**, **binary oppositions**.

paradigm A paradigm is a set of associated signifiers which are all members of some defining category, but in which each signifier is significantly different. In natural language there are grammatical paradigms such as verbs or nouns. In a given context, one member of the paradigm set is structurally replaceable with another. *See also* **paradigmatic analysis**, **syntagm**.

paradigmatic analysis Paradigmatic analysis is a structuralist technique which seeks to identify the various paradigms which underlie the 'surface structure' of a text. This aspect of structural analysis involves a consideration of the positive or negative connotations of each signifier (revealed through the use of one signifier rather than another), and the existence of 'underlying' thematic paradigms (e.g. binary oppositions such as *public/private*). *See also* **analogue oppositions**, **binary oppositions**, **commutation test**, **markedness**, **paradigm**, **syntagmatic analysis**.

Paris school This is a school of structuralist semiotic thinking established by Algirdas Greimas (1917–92), a Lithuanian by origin. Strongly influenced by Louis Hjelmslev (1899–1966), it seeks to identify basic structures of signification. Greimas focused primarily on the semantic analysis of textual structures but the Paris school has expanded its rigorous (critics say arid) structural analysis to cultural phenomena such as gestural language, legal discourse and social science. It is formalist in treating semiotic systems as autonomous rather than exploring the importance of social context. *See also* **Copenhagen school**, **structuralism**.

parole *See* **langue**.

phonocentrism Phonocentrism is a typically unconscious interpretative bias which privileges speech over writing (and consequently the oral–aural over the visual). *See also* **channel**, **logocentrism**.

positioning of the subject *See* **subject.**

poststructuralism While poststructuralism is often interpreted simply as 'anti-structuralism', it is worth noting that the label refers to a school of thought which developed *after*, out of, and in relation to structuralism. Poststructuralism built on and adapted structuralist notions in addition to problematizing many of them. Both schools of thought are built on the assumption that we are the subjects of language rather than being simply instrumental 'users' of it, and poststructuralist thinkers have developed further the notion of 'the constitution of the subject'. Poststructuralist semiotics involves a rejection of Saussure's hopes for semiotics as a systematic 'science' which could reveal some fundamental 'deep structures' underlying forms in an external world. Poststructuralist semioticians engage in deconstruction, emphasizing the instability of the relationship between the signifier and the signified and the way in which the dominant ideology seeks to promote the illusion of a transcendental signified. Poststructuralist theorists include Derrida, Foucault, Lacan, Kristeva and the later Barthes. *See also* **deconstruction**, **intertextuality**, **primacy of the signifier**, **semiotics**, **transcendental signified**, **structuralism**.

Prague school This influential structuralist and functionalist group of linguists/semioticians was established in 1926 in Prague by Czech and Russian linguists, although the term 'Prague school' was not used until 1932. Principal members of this group included: Vilem Mathesius (1882–1946), Bohuslav Havránek (1893–1978), Jan Mukarovsky (1891–1975), Nikolai Trubetzkoy (1890–1938) and Roman Jakobson (1896–1982). It was functionalist in analysing semiotic systems in relation to social functions such as communication rather than treating them purely as autonomous forms (in contrast to Saussure and Hjelmslev). While they are known for their identification of the 'distinctive features' of language, these theorists also explored culture and aesthetics. With the emergence of Nazism, some, including Jakobson, emigrated to the USA. *See also* **Moscow school**, **structuralism**.

preferred reading   This is a term which Stuart Hall originally used in relation to television news and current affairs programmes but which is often applied to other kinds of text. Readers of a text are guided towards a preferred reading and away from 'aberrant decoding' through the use of codes. A preferred reading is not necessarily the result of any conscious intention on the part of the producer(s) of a text. The term is often used as if it refers to a meaning which is in some way 'built into' the form and/or content of the text – a notion which is in uneasy accord with a textual determinism which Hall rejected. *See also* **dominant code and reading**.

primacy of the signifier   The argument that 'reality' or 'the world' is at least partly created by the language (and other media) we use insists on *the primacy of the signifier* – suggesting that the signified is shaped by the signifier rather than *vice versa*. Some theorists stress the materiality of the signifier. Others note that the same signifier can have different signifieds for different people or for the same person at different times. Poststructuralist theorists such as Lacan, Barthes, Derrida, Foucault have developed the notion of the primacy of the signifier, but its roots can be found in Saussure and structuralism. *See also* **arbitrariness, conventionality, poststructuralism, relative autonomy**.

reading, dominant, negotiated and oppositional   *See* **dominant code and reading, negotiated code and reading, oppositional code and reading**.

referent   What the sign 'stands for'. In Peirce's triadic model of the sign this is called the *object*. In Saussure's dyadic model of the sign a referent in the world is not explicitly featured – only the *signified* – a concept which may or may not refer to an object in the world. This is sometimes referred to as 'bracketing the referent'. Note that referents can include ideas, events and material objects. Anti-realist theorists such as Foucault reject the concreteness of referents, regarding them as products of language. *See also* **representation**.

relative autonomy   Saussure's model of the sign assumes the relative autonomy of language in relation to 'reality' (it does not directly feature a 'real world' referent); there is no essential bond between words and things. In a semiotic system with double articulation the levels of the signifier and of the signified are relatively autonomous. The signifier and the signified in a sign are autonomous to the extent that their relationship is arbitrary (commentators also speak of 'relative arbitrariness' or 'relative conventionality'). *See also* **arbitrariness**, **articulation of codes**, **conventionality**, **primacy of the signifier**.

representamen   The *representamen* is one of the three elements of Peirce's model of the sign and it refers to the form which the sign takes (not necessarily material). When it refers to a *non-material form* it is comparable to Saussure's *signifier*; whereas when it refers to *material form* it is what some commentators refer to as the *sign vehicle*. *See also* **signifier**.

representation   Standard dictionaries note that a representation is something which stands for or in place of something else – which is of course what semioticians call a sign. Semiotics foregrounds and problematizes the process of representation. Representation always involves 'the construction of reality'. All texts, however 'realistic' they may seem to be, are constructed representations rather than simply transparent 'reflections', recordings, transcriptions or reproductions of a pre-existing reality. Whether through 'direct' perception or mediated texts, what we experience as realities always involve representational codes. Representations which become familiar through constant re-use come to feel 'natural' and unmediated. Representation is unavoidably selective, fore-grounding some things and backgrounding others. Both structuralist and poststructuralist theories lead to 'reality' and 'truth' being regarded as the products of particular systems of representation. *See also* **referent**.

restricted codes *See* **broadcast codes**.

semiology Saussure's term *sémiologie* dates from a manuscript of 1894. 'Semiology' is sometimes used to refer to the study of signs by those within the Saussurean tradition (e.g. Barthes, Lévi-Strauss, Kristeva and Baudrillard), while 'semiotics' sometimes refers to those working within the Peircean tradition (e.g. Morris, Richards, Ogden and Sebeok). Sometimes 'semiology' refers to work concerned primarily with textual analysis while 'semiotics' refers to more philosophically oriented work. Nowadays the term 'semiotics' is widely used as an umbrella term to include 'semiology' and (to use Peirce's term) 'semiotic'. *See also* **semiotics**.

semiosis This term was used by Peirce to refer to the *process* of 'meaning-making'. *See also* **signification**, **signifying practices**, **unlimited semiosis**.

semiosphere The Russian cultural semiotician Yuri Lotman coined this term to refer to 'the whole semiotic space of the culture in question' – it can be thought of as a semiotic ecology in which different languages and media interact.

semiotic square Greimas introduced the semiotic square as a means of mapping the key semantic oppositions in a text or practice. If we begin by drawing a horizontal line linking two familiarly paired terms such as 'beautiful' and 'ugly', we turn this into a semiotic square by making this the upper line of a square in which the two other logical possibilities – 'not ugly' and 'not beautiful' occupy the lower corners. The semiotic square reminds us that this is not simply a binary opposition because something which is not beautiful is not necessarily ugly and that something which is not ugly is not necessarily beautiful.

semiotics, definition of Semiotics is 'the study of signs'. Semiotics has not become widely institutionalized as a formal academic discipline and it is not really a science. It is not purely a method of textual analysis, but involves both the theory and analysis of signs, codes and signifying practices. Beyond the most basic definition, there is considerable variation among leading semioticians as to what semiotics involves, although a distinctive concern is with *how* things signify. *See also* **poststructuralism**, **semiology**, **sign**, **structuralism**.

sign   A sign is a meaningful unit which is interpreted as 'standing for' something other than itself. Signs are found in the physical form of words, images, sounds, acts or objects (this physical form is sometimes known as the sign vehicle). Signs have no *intrinsic* meaning and become signs only when signusers invest them with meaning with reference to a recognized code. *See also* **analogue signs**, **digital signs**, **functions of signs**, **signification**.

sign vehicle   A term sometimes used to refer to the physical or material form of the sign (e.g. words, images, sounds, acts or objects). For some commentators this means the same as the *signifier* (which for Saussure himself did *not* refer to *material* form). The Peircean equivalent is the *representamen*: the form which the sign takes, but even for Peirce this was not necessarily a material form. *See also* **medium**, **representamen**, **signifier**, **tokens and types**.

signification   In Saussurean semiotics, the term *signification* refers to the relationship between the signifier and the signified. It is also variously used to refer to: the defining function of signs (i.e. that they signify, or 'stand for'; something other than themselves); the *process* of signifying (semiosis); signs as part of an overall semiotic *system*; *what* is signified (*meaning*); the reference of language to reality; a representation. *See also* **semiosis**, **value**.

signified (signifié)   For Saussure, the signified was one of the two parts of the sign (which was indivisible except for analytical purposes). Saussure's *signified* is the mental *concept* represented by the signifier (and is *not* a material thing). This does not exclude the reference of signs to physical objects in the world as well as to abstract concepts and fictional entities, but the signified is not itself a referent in the world (which Peirce's *object* can be). It is common for subsequent interpreters to equate the *signified* with 'content' (matching the *form* of the signifier in the familiar dualism of 'form and content'). *See also* **referent, signifier, transcendent(al) signified**.

signifier (signifiant) For Saussure, this was one of the two parts of the sign (which was indivisible except for analytical purposes). In the Saussurean tradition, the signifier is the *form* which a sign takes. For Saussure himself, in relation to linguistic signs, this meant a non-material form of the spoken word. Subsequent semioticians have treated it as the material (or physical) form of the sign – something which can be seen, heard, felt, smelt or tasted (also called the sign vehicle). *See also* **empty signifier, primacy of the signifier, representamen, sign vehicle, signified**.

signifying practices These are the meaning-making behaviours in which people engage (including the production and reading of texts) following particular conventions or rules of construction and interpretation. *See also* **interpretative community**.

single articulation, codes with Codes with single articulation have either first articulation or second articulation only. Codes with *first articulation only* (e.g. traffic signs) consist of signs – meaningful elements which are systematically related to each other – but there is no second articulation to structure these signs into minimal, non-meaningful elements. Other semiotic codes lacking double articulation have *second articulation only*. These consist of signs which have specific meanings which are not derived from their elements (e.g. binary code). They are divisible only into *figurae* (minimal functional units). *See also* **articulation of codes, double articulation, unarticulated codes**.

structuralism The primary concern of the Structuralists is with systems or structures rather than with referential meaning or the specificities of usage (*see* **langue and parole**). Structuralists regard each language as a relational system or structure and give priority to the *determining* power of the language system (a principle shared by poststructuralists). They seek to describe the overall organization of all sign-systems as 'languages'. Structuralists search for 'deep structures' underlying the surface features of phenomena (such as language, society, thought and behaviour). Their textual analysis is synchronic, seeking to delineate the codes and rules which underlie the production of texts by comparing those perceived as belonging to the same system (e.g. a genre) and identifying invariant constituent units. *See also* **commutation test, Copenhagen school, langue and parole, paradigmatic analysis, poststructuralism, Paris school, Prague school, semiotics, synchronic analysis, syntagmatic analysis, Tartu school, transformation, rules of**.

subject   In theories of subjectivity a distinction is made between 'the subject' and 'the individual'. While the individual is an actual person, the *subject* is a set of *roles* constructed by dominant cultural and ideological values. The structuralist notion of the *'positioning of the subject'* refers to the 'constitution' (construction) of subjects as 'ideal readers' by the text. According to this theory of textual (or discursive) positioning, the reader is obliged to adopt a 'subject-position' which already exists within the structure and codes of the text. Contemporary theorists contend that there may be several alternative (even contradictory) subject-positions from which a text may make sense, and these are not necessarily built into the text itself (or intended). Poststructuralist theorists critique the concept of the unified subject. *See also* **addresser and addressee, interpellation, preferred reading**.

symbolic   A mode in which the signifier does *not* resemble the signified but which is arbitrary or purely conventional – so that the relationship must be learnt (e.g. the word 'stop', a red traffic light, a national flag, a number). *See also* **arbitrariness, iconic, indexical**.

synchronic analysis   Synchronic analysis studies a phenomenon (such as a code) as if it were frozen at one moment in time. Structuralist semiotics focuses on synchronic rather than diachronic analysis and is criticized for ignoring historicity. *See also* **langue and parole, structuralism**.

synecdoche A figure of speech involving the substitution of part for whole, genus for species or vice versa. Some theorists do not distinguish it from metonymy. *See also* **irony**, **metaphor**, **metonymy**, **trope**.

syntagm A syntagm is an orderly combination of interacting signifiers which forms a meaningful whole (sometimes called a 'chain'). In language, a sentence, for instance, is a syntagm of words. *Syntagmatic relations* are the various ways in which constituent units within the same text may be structurally related to each other. Syntagmatic relationships exist both between *signifiers* and between *signifieds*. Relationships between *signifiers* can be either *sequential* (e.g. in film and television narrative sequences), or *spatial* (e.g. montage in posters and photographs). Relationships between *signifieds* are *conceptual* relationships (such as in argument). *See also* **paradigmatic analysis**, **syntagmatic analysis**.

syntagmatic analysis Syntagmatic analysis is a structuralist technique which seeks to establish the 'surface structure' of a text and the relationships between its parts. *See also* **paradigmatic analysis**, **syntagm**.

Tartu school What is sometimes called the 'Moscow–Tartu school of semiotics' was founded in the 1960s by Yuri Lotman (1922–93), who worked in Tartu University, Estonia. Lotman worked within the tradition of formalist structuralist semiotics but broadened his semiotic enterprise by establishing 'cultural semiotics', his goal being to develop a unified semiotic theory of culture. *See also* **structuralism**.

text Most broadly, this term is used to refer to anything which can be 'read' for meaning; to some theorists, 'the world' is 'social text'. Although the term appears to privilege written texts (it seems *graphocentric* and *logocentric*), to most semioticians a 'text' is an system of signs (in the form of words, images, sounds and/or gestures). It is constructed and interpreted with reference to the conventions associated with a genre and in a particular medium of communication. The term is often used to refer to *recorded* (e.g. written) texts which are independent of their users (used in this sense the term excludes unrecorded speech). A text is the product of a process of representation and 'positions' both its makers and its readers (*see* **subject**). Typically, readers tend to focus mainly on what is represented in a text rather than on the processes of representation involved (which usually seem to be transparent). *See also* **representation**.

tokens and types Peirce made a distinction between *tokens* and *types*. In relation to words in a text, a count of the tokens would be a count of the total number of words used (regardless of type), while a count of the types would be a count of the *different* words used (ignoring any repetition). The medium used may determine whether a text is a type which is its own sole token (unique original) or simply one token among many of its type ('a copy without an original'). *See also* **digital signs**.

transcendent(al) signified Derrida argued that dominant ideological discourse relies on the metaphysical illusion of a transcendental signified – an ultimate referent at the heart of a signifying system which is portrayed as 'absolute and irreducible', stable, timeless and transparent – as if it were *independent of* and *prior to* that system. All other signifieds within that signifying system are subordinate to this dominant central signified which is the final meaning to which they point. Without such a foundational term to provide closure for meaning, every signified functions as a signifier in an endless play of signification. *See also* **deconstruction**, **empty signifier**, **markedness**, **poststructuralism**.

transformation, rules of Lévi-Strauss argued that new structural patterns within a culture are generated from existing ones through formal 'rules of transformation' based on systematic similarities, equivalences, parallels, or symmetrical inversions. The patterns on different levels of a structure (e.g. within a myth) or in different structures (e.g. in different myths) are seen as logical transformations of each other. Rules of transformation enable the analyst to reduce a complex structure to some more basic constituent units. *See also* **commutation test**, **isomorphism**, **structuralism**.

trope   Tropes are rhetorical 'figures of speech' such as metaphor, metonymy, synecdoche and irony. Poststructuralist theorists such as Derrida, Lacan and Foucault have accorded considerable importance to tropes. *See also* **irony**, **metaphor**, **metonymy**, **synecdoche**.

types and tokens   *See* **tokens and types**.

unarticulated codes   Codes without articulation consist of a series of signs bearing no direct relation to each other. These signs are not divisible into recurrent compositional elements (e.g. the folkloristic 'language of flowers'). *See also* **articulation of codes**.

unlimited semiosis   While Saussure established the general principle that signs always relate to other signs, within his model the relationship between signifier and signified was stable and predictable. Umberto Eco coined the term 'unlimited semiosis' to refer to the way in which, for Peirce (via the 'interpretant'), for Barthes (via connotation), for Derrida (via 'freeplay') and for Lacan (via 'the sliding signified'), the signified is endlessly commutable – functioning in its turn as a signifier for a further signified. *See also* **interpretant**, **transcendent(al) signified**.

value   For Saussure language was a relational system of 'values'. He distinguished the value of a sign from its signification or referential meaning. A sign does not have an 'absolute' value in itself – its value is dependent on its relations with other signs within the signifying system as a whole. Words in different languages can have equivalent referential meanings but different values since they belong to different networks of associations. There is some similarity here to the distinction between denotation ('literal' meaning) and connotation (associations). *See also* **signification**, **structuralism**.

Note: A more extensive glossary is available in the online version of this text, currently at: http://www.aber.ac.uk/media/Documents/S4B/

References

Abrams, Meyer H. (1971) *The Mirror and the Lamp: Romantic Theory and the Critical Tradition*. London: Oxford University Press.

Alberti, Leon Battista (1966) *On Painting* (trans. John R. Spencer). New Haven, CT: Yale University Press.

Alcoff, Linda and Elizabeth Potter (eds) (1993) *Feminist Epistemologies*. London: Routledge.

Allen, Robert C. (ed.) (1992) *Channels of Discourse, Reassembled*. London: Routledge.

Allport, Gordon W. and Leo J. Postman (1945) 'The basic psychology of rumour', *Transactions of the New York Academy of Sciences*, Series II 8: 61–81. Reprinted in Eleanor E. Maccoby, Theodore M. Newcomb and Eugene L. Hartley (eds) (1959) *Readings in Social Psychology* (3rd edn). London: Methuen, pp. 54–65.

Althusser, Louis (1971) *Lenin and Philosophy* (trans. Ben Brewster). London: New Left Books.

Altman, Rick (1992) 'The material heterogeneity of recorded sound', in Rick Altman (ed.) (1992) *Sound Theory, Sound Practice*. New York: Routledge, pp. 15–31.

—— (1999) *Film/Genre*. London: BFI.

Ang, Ien (1985) *Watching 'Dallas': Soap Opera and the Melodramatic Imagination*. London: Methuen.

Argyle, Michael (1969) *Social Interaction*. London: Tavistock/Methuen.

—— (1983) *The Psychology of Interpersonal Behaviour* (4th edn). Harmondsworth: Penguin.

—— (1988) *Bodily Communication* (2nd edn). London: Methuen.

Baggaley, Jon and Steve Duck (1976) *Dynamics of Television*. Farnborough: Saxon House.

Barthes, Roland (1953/1967) *Writing Degree Zero* (trans. Annette Lavers and Colin Smith). London: Cape.

—— (1957/1987) *Mythologies*. New York: Hill & Wang.

—— (1964/1967). *Elements of Semiology* (trans. Annette Lavers and Colin Smith). London: Jonathan Cape.

—— (1973/1974) *S/Z*. London: Cape.

—— (1977) *Image–Music–Text*. London: Fontana.

—— (1982) *Empire of Signs* (trans. Richard Howard). New York: Hill & Wang.

—— (1983) *A Barthes Reader* (ed. Susan Sontag). New York: Hill & Wang.

—— (1985) *The Fashion System* (trans. Matthew Ward and Richard Howard). London: Jonathan Cape.

Baudrillard, Jean (1984) 'The precession of simulacra', in Brian Wallis (ed.) (1984) *Art After Modernism: Rethinking Representations*, vol. 1. New York: Museum of Contemporary Art (reprinted from *Art and Text* 11 (September 1983): 3–47.

—— (1988) *Selected Writings* (ed. Mark Poster). Cambridge: Polity Press.

—— (1995) *The Gulf War Did Not Take Place* (trans. Paul Patton). Bloomington, IN: Indiana University Press.

Bazin, André (1974) *Jean Renoir*. London: W. H. Allen.

Belsey, Catherine (1980) *Critical Practice*. London: Methuen.

Benjamin, Walter (1992) *Illuminations* (ed. Hannah Arendt, trans. Harry Zohn). London: Fontana.

Berger, Peter and Thomas Luckmann (1967) *The Social Construction of Reality*. New York: Anchor/Doubleday.

Bernstein, Basil (1971) *Class, Codes and Control*, vol. 1: *Theoretical Studies towards a Sociology of Language*. London: Routledge & Kegan Paul.

Bignell, Jonathan (1997) *Media Semiotics: An Introduction*. Manchester: Manchester University Press.

Birdwhistell, Ray L. (1971) *Kinesics and Context: Essays on Body–Motion Communication*. London: Allen Lane.

Bolter, Jay David (1991) *Writing Space: The Computer, Hypertext and the History of Writing*. Hillsdale, NJ: Lawrence Erlbaum.

Boorstin, Daniel J. (1961) *The Image, or What Happened to the American Dream*. London: Weidenfeld & Nicolson.

Bordwell, David, Janet Staiger and Kristin Thompson (1988) *The Classical Hollywood Cinema: Film Style and Mode of Production to 1960*. London: Routledge.

Bordwell, David and Kristin Thompson (1993) *Film Art: An Introduction* (4th edn). New York: McGraw-Hill.

Brooks, Cleanth and Robert Penn Warren (1972) *Modern Rhetoric* (shorter 3rd edn). New York: Harcourt Brace Jovanovich.

Bruner, Jerome S., Jacqueline S. Goodnow and George A. Austin ([1956] 1962) *A Study of Thinking*. New York: Wiley.

Bruner, Jerome S. (1966) 'Culture and cognitive growth', in J. S. Bruner, R. R. Olver and P. M. Greenfield (eds) (1966) *Studies in Cognitive Growth*. New York: Wiley.

Bruner, Jerome S. (1990) *Acts of Meaning*. Cambridge, MA: Harvard University Press.

Burgin, Victor (ed.) (1982a) *Thinking Photography*. London: Macmillan.

—— (1982b) 'Photographic practice and art theory', in Burgin (ed.) (1982a), pp. 39–83.

Burke, Kenneth (1969) *A Grammar of Motives*. Berkeley, CA: University of California Press.

Burr, Vivien (1995) *An Introduction to Social Constructionism*. London: Routledge.

Butler, Judith (1999) *Gender Trouble: Feminism and the Subversion of Identity*. London: Routledge.

Chandler, Daniel (1995) *The Act of Writing: A Media Theory Approach*. Aberystwyth: University of Wales, Aberystwyth.

—— (1998) *Semiótica para Principiantes* (trans. Vanessa Hogan Vega and Iván Rodrigo Mendizábal). Quito, Ecuador: Ediciones Abya-Yala/ Escuela de Comunicación Social de la Universidad Politécnica Salesiana.

Chase, Stuart (1938) *The Tyranny of Words*. New York: Harcourt, Brace & World.

Cherry, Colin (1966) *On Human Communication* (2nd edn). Cambridge, MA: MIT Press.

Clark, Herbert H. and Eve V. Clark (1977) *Psychology and Language: An Introduction to Psycholinguistics*. New York: Harcourt Brace Jovanovich.

Cook, Guy (1992) *The Discourse of Advertising*. London: Routledge.

Coren, Stanley, Lawrence M. Ward and James T. Enns (1994) *Sensation and Perception* (4th edn; International edn). Fort Worth, TX: Harcourt Brace.

Corner, John (1980) 'Codes and Cultural Analysis', *Media, Culture and Society* 2: 73–86.

Corner, John and Jeremy Hawthorne (eds) (1980) *Communication Studies: An Introductory Reader*. London: Edward Arnold.

Coward, Rosalind and John Ellis (1977) *Language and Materialism: Developments in Semiology and the Theory of the Subject*. London: Routledge & Kegan Paul.

Crystal, David (1987) *The Cambridge Encyclopedia of Language*. Cambridge: Cambridge University Press.

Culler, Jonathan (1975) *Structuralist Poetics: Structuralism, Linguistics and the Study of Literature*. London: Routledge & Kegan Paul.

—— (1981) *The Pursuit of Signs: Semiotics, Literature, Deconstruction*. London: Routledge & Kegan Paul.

—— (1985) *Saussure*. London: Fontana.

Davis, Desmond (1960) *The Grammar of Television Production* (revised by John Elliot). London: Barrie & Rockliff.

Davis, Howard and Paul Walton (eds) (1983a) *Language, Image, Media*. Oxford: Basil Blackwell.

—— (1983b) 'Death of a premier: consensus and closure in international news', in Davis and Walton (eds), (1983a), pp. 8–49.

Deregowski, Jan B. (1980) *Illusions, Patterns and Pictures: A Cross-Cultural Perspective*. New York: Academic Press.

Derrida, Jacques (1974) 'White Mythology: Metaphor in the Text of Philosophy', *New Literary History* 6(1): 5–74.

—— (1976) *Of Grammatology* (trans. Gayatri Chakravorty Spivak). Baltimore, MD: Johns Hopkins University Press.

—— (1978) *Writing and Difference* (trans. Alan Bass). London: Routledge & Kegan Paul.

—— (1981) *Positions* (trans. Alan Bass). London: Athlone Press.

—— (1998) *A Derrida Reader* (ed. Peggy Kamuf). New York: Columbia University Press.

Dyer, Richard (1992) *Only Entertainment*. London: Routledge.

—— (1997) *White*. London: Routledge.

Eagleton, Terry (1983) *Literary Theory: An Introduction*. Oxford: Basil Blackwell.

Easthope, Antony (1990) *What a Man's Gotta Do*. Boston, MA: Unwin Hyman.

Eaton, Mick (ed.) (1981) *Cinema and Semiotics* (*Screen* Reader 2). London: Society for Education in Film and Television.

Eco, Umberto (1965) 'Towards a semiotic enquiry into the television message', in Corner and Hawthorn (eds) (1980), pp. 131–50.

—— (1976) *A Theory of Semiotics*. Bloomington, IN: Indiana University Press/London: Macmillan.

—— (1981) *The Role of the Reader*. London: Hutchinson.

—— (1982) 'Critique of the image', in Burgin (ed.) (1982a), pp. 32–8.

—— (1984) *Semiotics and the Philosophy of Language*. Bloomington, IN: Indiana University Press.

—— (1999) *Kant and the Platypus: Essays on Language and Cognition*. London: Secker and Warburg.

Edgerton, Samuel Y. (1975) *The Renaissance Rediscovery of Linear Perspective*. New York: Harper & Row.

Fairclough, Norman (1995) *Media Discourse*. London: Edward Arnold.

Fish, Stanley (1980) *Is There A Text In This Class? The Authority Of Interpretive Communities*. Cambridge, MA: Harvard University Press.

Fiske, John (1982) *Introduction to Communication Studies*. London: Routledge.

—— (1987) *Television Culture*. London: Routledge.

—— (1989) 'Codes', in Tobia L. Worth (ed.) *International Encyclopedia of Communications*, vol. 1. New York: Oxford University Press, pp. 312–16.

Fiske, John and John Hartley (1978) *Reading Television*. London: Methuen.

Fleming, Dan (1996) *Powerplay: Toys as Popular Culture*. Manchester: Manchester University Press.

Floch, Jean-Marie (2000) *Visual Identities* (trans. Pierre Van Osselaer and Alec McHoul). London: Continuum.

Forceville, Charles (1996) *Pictorial Metaphor in Advertising*. London: Routledge.

Foucault, Michel (1970) *The Order of Things*. London: Tavistock.

—— (1974) *The Archaeology of Knowledge*. London: Tavistock.

—— (1991) *The Foucault Reader* (ed. Paul Rabinow). Harmondsworth: Penguin.

Franklin, Sarah, Celia Lury and Jackie Stacey (1996) 'Feminism and cultural studies: pasts, presents, futures', in Storey (ed.) (1996), pp. 255–72.

Freud, Sigmund (1938) *The Basic Writings of Sigmund Freud*. New York: Modern Library.

Fuss, Diane (ed.) (1991) *Inside/Out: Lesbian Theories, Gay Theories*. London: Routledge.

Gallie, W. B. (1952) *Peirce and Pragmatism*. Harmondsworth: Penguin.

Galtung, Johan and Eric Ruge (1981) 'Structuring and selecting news', in Cohen and Young (eds) (1981), pp. 52–63.

Gardiner, Michael (1992) *The Dialogics of Critique: M M Bakhtin and the Theory of Ideology*. London: Routledge.

Gelb, I. J. (1963) *A Study of Writing*. Chicago: University of Chicago Press.

Genette, Gérard (1997) *Palimpsests* (trans. Channa Newman and Claude Doubinsky). Lincoln, NB: University of Nebraska Press.

Genosko, Gary (1994) *Baudrillard and Signs: Signification Ablaze*. London: Routledge.

Glasgow University Media Group (1980) *More Bad News*. London: Routledge & Kegan Paul.

Goffman, Erving (1969) *Behaviour in Public Places*. Harmondsworth: Penguin.

—— (1979) *Gender Advertisements*. New York: Harper & Row/London: Macmillan.

Gombrich, Ernst H. (1977) *Art and Illusion: A Study in the Psychology of Pictorial Representation*. London: Phaidon.

—— (1982) *The Image and the Eye: Further Studies in the Psychology of Pictorial Representation*. London: Phaidon.

Goodman, Marcia (1990) 'Innocent impostors: gender, genre and the teaching of writing', *Visions and Revisions: Research for Writing Teachers* 2 (1): 37–51.

Goodman, Nelson (1968) *Languages of Art: An Approach to a Theory of Symbols*. London: Oxford University Press.

Grayson, Kent (1998) 'The icons of consumer research: using signs to represent consumers' reality', in Stern (ed.) (1998), pp. 27–43.

Greenberg, J. H. (1966) *Language Universals*. The Hague: Mouton.

Greimas, Algirdas (1966/1983) *Structural Semantics*. Lincoln, NB: University of Nebraska Press.

—— (1987) *On Meaning: Selected Writings in Semiotic Theory* (trans. Paul J. Perron and Frank H. Collins). London: Frances Pinter.

Grosz, Elizabeth (1993) 'Bodies and knowledges: feminism and the crisis of reason', in Alcoff and Potter (eds) (1993), pp. 187–215.

Guiraud, Pierre (1975) *Semiology* (trans. George Gross). London: Routledge & Kegan Paul.

Gumpert, Gary and Robert Cathcart (1985) 'Media grammars, generations and media gaps', *Critical Studies in Mass Communication* 2: 23–35.

Hall, Edward T. (1959) *The Silent Language*. Greenwich, CT: Fawcett.

—— (1966) *The Hidden Dimension*. New York: Doubleday.

Hall, Stuart (1977) 'Culture, the media and the "ideological effect"', in James Curran, Michael Gurevitch and Janet Woollacott (eds) (1977)

Mass Communication and Society. London: Edward Arnold, pp. 315–48.

—— (1973/1980) 'Encoding/decoding', in Centre for Contemporary Cultural Studies (ed.) *Culture, Media, Language: Working Papers in Cultural Studies, 1972–79,* London: Hutchinson, pp. 128–38.

—— (1981) 'The determinations of news photographs', in Cohen and Young (eds) (1981), pp. 226–43.

—— (1996) 'Cultural studies: two paradigms', in Storey (ed.) (1996), pp. 31–48.

Harris, Roy (1987) *Reading Saussure: A Critical Commentary on the 'Cours de linguistique générale'*. London: Duckworth.

Hawkes, Terence (1972) *Metaphor*. London: Methuen.

—— (1977) *Structuralism and Semiotics*. London: Routledge.

Hayakawa, S. I. (1941) *Language in Action*. New York: Harcourt, Brace.

Higgins, Patrick (1993) *A Queer Reader*. London: Fourth Estate.

Hjelmslev, Louis (1961) *Prolegomena to a Theory of Language* (trans. Francis J. Whitfield). Madison: University of Wisconsin Press.

Hockett, Charles F. (1958) *A Course in Modern Linguistics*. New York: Macmillan.

Hodge, Robert and Gunther Kress (1988) *Social Semiotics*. Cambridge: Polity.

Hodge, Robert and David Tripp (1986) *Children and Television: A Semiotic Approach*. Cambridge: Polity Press.

Holdcroft, David (1991) *Saussure: Signs, Systems and Arbitrariness*. Cambridge: Cambridge University Press.

Innis, Robert E. (ed.) (1986) *Semiotics: An Introductory Reader*. London: Hutchinson.

Ivins, William (1938/1975) *On the Rationalization of Sight*. New York: Da Capo Press.

Jakobson, Roman (1960) 'Closing statement: linguistics and poetics', in Sebeok (ed.) (1960), pp. 350–77.

—— (1971) 'Language in relation to other communication systems', in Roman Jakobson: *Selected Writings*, vol. 2. Mouton: The Hague, pp. 570–9.

Jakobson, Roman and Morris Halle (1956) *Fundamentals of Language*. The Hague: Mouton.

James, William (1890/1950) *The Principles of Psychology*, vol. 1. New York: Dover.

Jameson, Fredric (1972) *The Prison-House of Language*. Princeton, NJ: Princeton University Press.

Jensen, Klaus Bruhn (1995) *The Social Semiotics of Mass Communication*. London: Sage.

Johnson, Richard (1996) 'What is cultural studies anyway?', in Storey (ed.) (1996), pp. 75–114.

Keller, Helen (1945) *The Story of My Life*. London: Hodder & Stoughton.

Kennedy, John (1974) *A Psychology of Picture Perception*. San Francisco, CA: Jossey-Bass.

Kipling, Rudyard (1977) *Selected Verse* (ed. James Cochrane). Harmondsworth: Penguin.

Kitses, Jim (1970) *Horizons West*. London: Secker & Warburg/BFI.

Korzybski, Alfred (1933) *Science and Sanity: An Introduction to Non-Aristotelian Systems and General Semantics*. Lancaster, PA: Science Press.

Kress, Gunther and Theo van Leeuwen (1996) *Reading Images: The Grammar of Visual Design*. London: Routledge.

—— (1998) 'Front pages: (the critical) analysis of newspaper layout', in Allan Bell and Peter Garrett (eds) (1998) *Approaches to Media Discourse*. Oxford: Blackwell, pp. 186–219.

Kristeva, Julia (1980) *Desire in Language: A Semiotic Approach to Literature and Art*. New York: Columbia University Press.

Kubovy, Michael (1986) *The Psychology of Perspective and Renaissance Art*. Cambridge: Cambridge University Press.

Lacan, Jacques (1977) *Écrits* (trans. Alan Sheridan). London: Routledge.

Lakoff, George and Mark Johnson (1980) *Metaphors We Live By*. Chicago: University of Chicago Press.

Langer, Susanne K. (1951) *Philosophy in a New Key: A Study in the Symbolism of Reason, Rite and Art*. New York: Mentor.

Lanham, Richard A. (1969) *A Handlist of Rhetorical Terms*. Berkeley: University of California Press.

Larrucia, Victor (1975) 'Little Red Riding-Hood's metacommentary: paradoxical injunction, semiotics and behaviour', *Modern Language Notes* 90(4): 517–34.

Lash, Scott (1990) *Sociology of Postmodernism*. London: Routledge.

Leach, Edmund (1970) *Lévi-Strauss* (Fontana Modern Masters). London: Fontana.

—— (1982) *Social Anthropology* (Fontana Masterguides). London: Fontana.

Lechte, John (1994) *Fifty Key Contemporary Thinkers: From Structuralism to Postmodernity*. London: Routledge.

Leiss, William, Stephen Kline and Sut Jhally (1990) *Social Communication in Advertising: Persons, Products and Images of Well-Being* (2nd edn). London: Routledge.

Lemke, Jay (1995) *Textual Politics: Discourse and Social Dynamics*. London: Taylor & Francis.

Lemon, Lee T. and Marion J. Reis (1965) *Russian Formalist Criticism*. Lincoln, NE: University of Nebraska Press.

Lévi-Strauss, Claude (1961) *Tristes Tropiques* (trans. John Russell). New York: Criterion.

—— (1964) *Totemism* (trans. Rodney Needham). Harmondsworth: Penguin.

—— (1972) *Structural Anthropology* (trans. Claire Jacobson and Brooke Grundfest Schoepf). Harmondsworth: Penguin.

—— (1962/1974) *The Savage Mind*. London: Weidenfeld and Nicolson.

—— (1950/1987) *Introduction to the Work of Marcel Mauss* (trans. Felicity Baker). London: Routledge & Kegan Paul.

Lewis, Justin (1991) *The Ideological Octopus: An Exploration of Television and its Audience*. New York: Routledge.

Leymore, Varda Langholz (1975) *Hidden Myth: Structure and Symbolism in Advertising*. New York: Basic Books.

Lodge, David (1977/1996) *The Modes of Modern Writing: Metaphor, Metonymy and the Typology of Modern Literature*. London: Arnold.

Lotman, Yuri (1976) *Analysis of the Poetic Text*. Ann Arbor: University of Michigan Press.

—— (1990) *Universe of the Mind: A Semiotic Theory of Culture* (trans. Ann Shukman). Bloomington, IN: Indiana University Press.

Lovell, Terry (1983) *Pictures of Reality: Aesthetics, Politics and Pleasure*. London: BFI.

Lyons, John (1977) *Semantics*, vol. 1. Cambridge: Cambridge University Press.

Malkiel, Yakov (1968) *Essays on Linguistic Themes*. Oxford: Blackwell.

MacCabe, Colin (1974) 'Realism and the cinema', *Screen* 15(2), pp. 7–27.

McKim, Robert H. (1972) *Experiences in Visual Thinking*. Monterey, CA: Brooks/Cole.

McLuhan, Marshall (1962) *The Gutenberg Galaxy*. Toronto: University of Toronto Press.

—— (1970) *Counterblast*. London: Rapp & Whiting.

McLuhan, Marshall and Quentin Fiore (1967) *The Medium is the Message*. New York: Bantam.

McQuarrie, Edward F. and David Glen Mick (1992) 'On resonance: a critical pluralistic inquiry into advertising rhetoric', *Journal of Consumer Research* 19: 180–97.

Merrell, Floyd (1997) *Peirce, Signs, and Meaning*. Toronto: University of Toronto Press.

Messaris, Paul (1982) 'To what extent does one have to learn to interpret movies?' in Sari Thomas (ed.) (1982) *Film/Culture*. Metuchen, NJ: Scarecrow Press, pp. 168–83.

Messaris, Paul (1994) *Visual 'Literacy': Image, Mind and Reality*. Boulder, CO: Westview Press.

Messaris, Paul (1997) *Visual Persuasion: The Role of Images in Advertising*. London: Sage.

Metz, Christian (1974) *Film Language: A Semiotics of the Cinema* (trans. Michael Taylor). New York: Oxford University Press.

—— (1981) 'Methodological propositions for the analysis of film', in Eaton (ed.) (1981), pp. 86–98.

—— (1982) *The Imaginary Signifier* (trans. Celia Britton, Annwyl Williams, Ben Brewster and Alfred Guzzetti). Bloomington: Indiana University Press.

Mick, David Glen and Claus Buhl (1992) 'A meaning-based model of advertising experiences', *Journal of Consumer Research* 19: 317–38.

Mick, David Glen and Laura G. Politi (1989) 'Consumers' interpretations of advertising imagery: a visit to the hell of connotation', in Elizabeth C. Hirschman (ed.) (1989) *Interpretive Consumer Research*. Provo, UT: Association for Consumer Research, pp. 85–96.

Monaco, James (1981) *How to Read a Film*. New York: Oxford University Press.

Morley, David (1980) *The 'Nationwide' Audience: Structure and Decoding*. London: BFI.

—— (1981) '"The *Nationwide* Audience" – a critical postscript', *Screen Education* 39: 3–14.

—— (1983) 'Cultural transformations: the politics of resistance', in Davis and Walton (eds) (1983), pp. 104–17.

—— (1992) *Television, Audiences and Cultural Studies*. London: Routledge.

Morris, Charles W. (1938/1970) *Foundations of the Theory of Signs*. Chicago: Chicago University Press.

Morris, Pam (ed.) (1994) *The Bakhtin Reader: Selected Writings of Bakhtin, Medvedev, Voloshinov*. London: Edward Arnold

Murray, Donald M. (1978) 'Internal revision – a process of discovery', in C. R. Cooper and L. Odell (eds) *Research on Composing*. Urbana, IL: NCTE.

Newcomb, Theodore M. (1952) *Social Psychology*. London: Tavistock.

Nichols, Bill (1981) *Ideology and the Image: Social Representation in the Cinema and Other Media*. Bloomington, IN: Indiana University Press.

Nöth, Winfried (1990) *Handbook of Semiotics*. Bloomington, IN: Indiana University Press.

Ogden, Charles K. (1930/1944) *Basic English* (9th edn). London: Kegan Paul, Trench, Trubner & Co.

Ogden, Charles K. and Ivor A. Richards (1923) *The Meaning of Meaning*. London: Routledge & Kegan Paul.

Olson, David (1994) *The World on Paper: The Conceptual and Cognitive Implications of Writing and Reading*. Cambridge: Cambridge University Press.

Osgood, Charles E., George J. Suci and Percy H. Tannenbaum (1957) *The Measurement of Meaning*. Urbana, IL: University of Illinois Press.

O'Sullivan, Tim, John Hartley, Danny Saunders, Martin Montgomery and John Fiske (1994) *Key Concepts in Communication and Cultural Studies*. London: Routledge.

Panofsky, Erwin (1970) *Meaning in the Visual Arts*. Harmondsworth: Penguin.

Parkin, Frank (1972) *Class Inequality and Political Order*. London: Granada.

Peirce, Charles Sanders (1998–) *Writings of Charles S. Peirce: A Chronological Edition* (6 vols so far) (ed. Nathan Houser, Peirce Edition Project). Bloomington, IN: Indiana University Press.

—— (1931–58) *Collected Writings* (8 vols) (ed. Charles Hartshorne, Paul Weiss and Arthur W. Burks). Cambridge, MA: Harvard University Press.

—— (1966) *Selected Writings*. New York: Dover.

—— (1998) *The Essential Peirce: Selected Philosophical Writings* (2 vols). Bloomington, IN: Indiana University Press.

Pepper, Stephen C. (1942) *World Hypotheses: A Study in Evidence*. Berkeley, CA: University of California Press.

Piaget, Jean (1929) *The Child's Conception of the World*. New York: Humanities Press.

—— (1971) *Structuralism* (trans. Chaninah Maschler). London: Routledge & Kegan Paul.

Pollio, Howard, J. Barrow, H. Fine and M. Pollio (1977) *The Poetics of Growth: Figurative Language in Psychology, Psychotherapy and Education*. Hillsdale, NJ: Lawrence Erlbaum.

Pranger, Brian (1990) *The Arena of Masculinity*. London: GMP.

Propp, Vladimir I. (1928/1968) *Morphology of the Folktale* (trans. Laurence Scott, 2nd edn). Austin: University of Texas Press.

Reddy, Michael J (1979) 'The conduit metaphor – a case of frame conflict in our language about language', in Andrew Ortony (ed.) (1979) *Metaphor and Thought*. Cambridge: Cambridge University Press, pp. 284–324.

Reisz, Karel and Gavin Millar (1972) *The Technique of Film Editing*. London: Focal Press.

Richards, Ivor A. (1932) *The Philosophy of Rhetoric*. London: Oxford University Press.

Rodowick, David N. (1994) *The Crisis of Political Modernism: Criticism and Ideology in Contemporary Film Theory*. Berkeley, CA: University of California Press.

Romanyshyn, Robert D. (1989) *Technology as Symptom and Dream*. London: Routledge.

Rosenblum, Ralph and Robert Karen (1979) *When the Shooting Stops . . . The Cutting Begins: A Film Editor's Story*. New York: Da Capo.

Ryan, T. A. and C. B. Schwartz (1956) 'Speed of perception as a function of mode of representation', *American Journal of Psychology* 96: 66–9.

Sapir, Edward (1958) *Culture, Language and Personality* (ed. D. G. Mandelbaum). Berkeley, CA: University of California Press.

—— (1921/1971) *Language*. London: Rupert Hart-Davis.

Sarup, Madan (1993) *An Introductory Guide to Post-Structuralism and Postmodernism*. Athens, GA: University of Georgia Press.

Saussure, Ferdinand de (1916/1974) *Course in General Linguistics* (trans. Wade Baskin). London: Fontana/Collins.

—— (1916/1983) *Course in General Linguistics* (trans. Roy Harris). London: Duckworth.

Scribner, Sylvia and Michael Cole (1981) *The Psychology of Literacy*. Cambridge, MA: Harvard University Press.

Sebeok, Thomas A. (ed.) (1960) *Style in Language*. Cambridge, MA: MIT Press.

—— (1994) *Signs: An Introduction to Semiotics*. Toronto: University of Toronto Press.

Seiter, Ellen (1992) 'Semiotics, structuralism and television', in Allen (ed.) (1992), pp. 31–66.

Shannon, Claude E. and Warren Weaver (1949) *A Mathematical Model of Communication*. Urbana, IL: University of Illinois Press.

Silverman, Kaja (1983) *The Subject of Semiotics*. New York: Oxford University Press.

Silverman, David and Brian Torode (1980) *The Material Word: Some Theories of Language and its Limits*. London: Routledge & Kegan Paul.

Slater, Don (1983) 'Marketing mass photography', in Davis and Walton (eds) (1983), pp. 245–63.

Smith, Frank (1982) *Writing and the Writer*. London: Heinemann.

—— (1988) *Understanding Reading*. Hillsdale, NJ: Erlbaum.

Snyder, J. and N. W. Allen (1982) 'Photography, vision and representation', in T. Barrow, S. Armitage and W. Tydeman (eds) (1982) *Reading into Photography*. Albuquerque: University of New Mexico Press.

Stam, Robert (2000) *Film Theory*. Oxford: Blackwell.

Stern, Barbara B. (ed.) (1998) *Representing Consumers: Voices, Views and Visions*. London: Routledge.

Storey, John (ed.) (1996) *What is Cultural Studies?* London: Arnold.

Strinati, Dominic (1995) *An Introduction to Theories of Popular Culture*. London: Routledge.

Sturrock, John (1979) (ed.) *Structuralism and Since: From Lévi-Strauss to Derrida*. Oxford: Oxford University Press.

—— (1986) *Structuralism*. London: Paladin.

Swales, John (1990) *Genre Analysis: English in Academic and Research Settings*. Cambridge: Cambridge University Press.

Tagg, John (1988) *The Burden of Representation: Essays on Photographies and Histories*. Basingstoke: Macmillan.

Thibault, Paul J. (1997) *Re-reading Saussure: The Dynamics of Signs in Social Life*. London: Routledge.

Thwaites, Tony, Lloyd Davis and Warwick Mules (1994) *Tools for Cultural Studies: An Introduction*. South Melbourne: Macmillan.

Tuchman, Gaye (1978) *Making News: A Study in the Construction of Reality*. New York: Free Press.

Tudor, Andrew (1974) *Image and Influence: Studies in the Sociology of Film*. London: George Allen and Unwin.

Vico, Gianbattista (1744/1968) *The New Science* (trans. Thomas Goddard Bergin and Max Harold Finch). Ithaca, NY: Cornell University Press.

Voloshinov, Valentin N (1973) *Marxism and the Philosophy of Language* (trans. Ladislav Matejka and I. R. Titunik). New York: Seminar Press.

Watney, Simon (1982) 'Making strange: the shattered mirror', in Burgin (ed.) (1982a), pp. 154–76.

White, Hayden (1973) *Metahistory: The Historical Imagination in Nineteenth-Century Europe*. Baltimore, MD: Johns Hopkins University Press.

—— (1978) *Tropics of Discourse: Essays in Cultural Criticism*. Baltimore, MD: Johns Hopkins University Press.

—— (1987) *The Content of the Form: Narrative Discourse and Historical Representation*. Baltimore, MD: Johns Hopkins University Press.

White, John (1967) *The Birth and Rebirth of Pictorial Space*. London: Faber & Faber.

Whorf, Benjamin Lee (1956) *Language, Thought and Reality* (ed. John B. Carroll). Cambridge, MA: MIT Press.

Wilden, Anthony (1987) *The Rules Are No Game: The Strategy of Communication*. London: Routledge & Kegan Paul.

Willemen, Paul (1994) *Looks and Frictions: Essays in Cultural Studies and Film Theory*. London: BFI/Bloomington, IN: Indiana University Press.

Williamson, Judith (1978) *Decoding Advertisements*. London: Marion Boyars.

Wimsatt, William K. and Monroe C. Beardsley (1954) *The Verbal Icon: Studies in the Meaning of Poetry*. Lexington, KY: University of Kentucky Press.

Wiseman, Boris and Judy Groves (2000) *Introducing Lévi-Strauss and Structural Anthropology*. Cambridge: Icon.

Wollen, Peter (1969) *Signs and Meaning in the Cinema*. London: Secker & Warburg/BFI.

Wright, Lawrence (1983) *Perspective in Perspective*. London: Routledge & Kegan Paul.

Young, Brian M. (1990) *Television Advertising and Children*. Oxford: Clarendon Press.

Index

aberrant decoding (Eco)
158, 179, 238

Abrams, Meyer H. 108,
133

absent signifiers xvi, 68, 80,
98–101, 110–12, 119–20,
126, 134, 156, 227

address, modes of *see*
modes of address

addresser and addressee *see*
(Jakobson) 61, 177–9,
180, 190–1, 223, 229

aesthetic codes 63–4, 74,
107–8, 120, 136, 149,
161–73

Alberti, Leon Battista 183,
185–6

Alcoff, Linda 134

Allen, N. W. 187

Allport, Gordon W. 101

Althusser, Louis 30, 141,
181, 195, 230

Altman, Rick 170

'always-already given' 115,
150, 195, 198

analogue oppositions 104,
223

analogue signs and codes
45–7, 140, 148, 164, 191,
223, 228, 232

anchorage (Barthes) 66,
201–2, 224

Ang, Ien 63

arbitrariness 23, 25–32,
36–7, 38, 39, 43, 44–5, 58,
64, 68–71, 74–5, 76, 129,
141, 145, 147, 163, 166,
169, 210, 215, 224, 226,
230, 239, 243

Argyle, Michael 155, 156

Aristotle 26, 102

articulation of codes 9,
10–11, 224, 228–9, 239,
242, 246

associative relations
(Saussure) 79–81, 99, 143

authorial intention *see* intentional fallacy

axes of selection and combination *see* selection and combination

Baggaley, Jon 54

Bakhtin, Mikhail 13, 34, 198, 212

bar, the 19, 21, 28

Barthes, Roland 6, 7, 9, 11, 52, 75, 82, 83, 90, 92, 100, 104, 125, 134, 140–6, 163–5, 171–2, 195–6, 198, 201–2, 210, 212, 216, 218, 222, 224, 225, 226, 227, 235, 237, 238, 240, 246

Baskin, Wade xviii, 221

Baudrillard, Jean 76–7, 240

Bazin, André 63

Beardsley, Monroe C. 196

Belsey, Catherine 72, 161

Benjamin, Walter 48

Bennett, Tony 198

Benveniste, Emile 3, 9

Berger, John 162, 163

Berger, Peter 156

Bernstein, Basil 154–5, 171, 235

Bignell, Jonathan 162, 221

binarism or dualism 46, 53, 95, 98, 101–7, 110–11, 113, 119–21, 139, 144, 159, 242

binary oppositions 46, 95, 98, 101–10, 117–21, 134, 144, 159, 224, 236, 240

Birdwhistell, Ray L. 155

Bogatyrev, Pjotr 234

Bolter, Jay David 52

Boorstin, Daniel J. 76

Bordwell, David 167

bracketing the referent 20, 27, 29, 239

bricolage 203, 224

broadcast codes 170–1, 224–5

Brøndal, Viggo 226

Brooks, Cleanth 84, 159

Bruner, Jerome S. 47, 69, 91, 117, 164

Buhl, Claus 194

Burgin, Victor 62, 202

Burke, Kenneth 137

Burr, Vivien 156

Butler, Judith 78, 106

Carroll, Lewis 21, 74

Cathcart, Robert 173

chain *see* syntagm

Chandler, Daniel 52, 53, 76, 108, 196

channel 3, 148, 170, 177, 225

Chase, Stuart 66

Cherry, Colin 45

cinematic signs and codes *see* filmic signs and codes

circles, linguistic/semiotic *see* Copenhagen school, Moscow school, Paris school, Prague school, Tartu school

Clark, Eve V. and Herbert H. 110–12

classification of signs *see* modes of relationship

codes 8, 10, 12, 14–15, 31, 46–7, 52, 61, 64, 68, 80, 82, 90, 99, 100, 106–7, 117, 124, 140–3, 145–6, 147–73, 175–9, 180, 182, 184–7, 188–9, 191–3, 194, 195, 199, 200–3, 208, 211, 212, 214, 215–16, 217, 218, 224, 225, 226, 227, 228, 229, 230, 231, 232, 233, 235, 236, 238, 239, 241, 242, 243, 246 codes of textual production and interpretation 84, 117, 147, 149, 229, 243

codification 172–3, 183, 210, 225

Cole, Michael 70

commonsense 21, 27, 69, 73, 140, 145, 164, 215, 216, 217, 227, 235

communication 3, 5, 9, 10, 31, 56, 68, 83, 112, 129, 147–9, 175–9, 189, 217–19, 223, 229, 231–2, 238

commutation test 99–101, 225

complex sign 83

conative function 191, 229

condensation (Freud) 51

connotation 8, 31, 50, 63, 88, 98, 99, 111–12, 123, 140–4, 145–6, 160, 162, 164, 173, 209–10, 215, 225–6, 227–8, 235, 236, 246

constitution of the subject 91, 105, 156, 182–3, 187, 191, 217–18, 223, 237, 243

constraint see motivation and constraint

constructivism, (social) constructionism xvi-xvii, 14–15, 27, 55, 59, 60–1, 66, 73, 76, 105, 125–6, 154, 156–7, 182–3, 191, 205, 215–16, 217–18, 230, 239, 243

content analysis 8–9, 208

content, plane of see planes of content and expression

contextual meaning 9, 13, 23, 29, 43, 48, 80, 113, 141, 154–6, 158, 169, 176–9, 188, 193, 198–9, 210, 226, 230–1, 237

contiguity 42, 130–2, 139

conventionalism 166, 216

conventionality 3, 8, 12, 14, 17, 30–2, 36–43, 45, 50, 62–4, 71, 73, 77, 81, 84–6, 99, 105, 117, 124, 127, 147–8, 156, 158, 160, 161–2, 166–9, 170, 172–3, 182, 183–5, 188–91, 196, 199, 204, 208, 210–12, 214, 215–18, 224, 225, 226, 227, 230, 231, 239, 242, 243, 244

Cook, Guy 40

Copenhagen school 6, 7, 226

Coren, Stanley 151

Corner, John 208

Coward, Rosalind 13, 26, 28, 44, 52, 181, 195, 211

Crystal, David 155

Culler, Jonathan 32, 43, 59, 74, 79, 95, 96–7, 111, 121, 137, 195, 221

cultural relativism/relativity see relativism/relativity, cultural

Davis, Desmond 190

Davis, Howard 42, 97

deconstruction 15, 52, 75, 115, 146, 173, 196, 203, 227, 233, 237

deep structure 9, 89, 93, 119, 137, 237, 242

denaturalization, defamiliarization 15, 66, 126, 146, 173, 211–12, 214, 216, 227

denotation 27, 38, 63, 123–4, 127, 140–5, 164, 194, 226, 227–8, 233, 235, 246

Deregowski, Jan B. 162

Derrida, Jacques 7, 51–2, 75–6, 111–12, 115, 126, 150, 222, 227, 231, 237, 238, 245, 246

design features of language 4, 10, 26, 70

determination of meaning 2, 14, 25, 43, 44, 58, 75, 80, 90, 142, 154,

158, 172, 179, 181, 193, 195, 209, 230, 238

diachronic analysis 12, 44, 98, 117, 211, 228, 243

Dickens, Charles 120, 188

differential meaning 24–5

digital signs and codes 42, 45–7, 104, 140, 148, 163, 223–4, 228, 232

directness of address 188–90, 234

discourse 8, 9, 64, 72, 83, 84–6, 91, 105, 114–15, 123–4, 126, 145, 148, 159, 161, 179, 180, 193, 195, 203, 213, 215, 230, 237, 243, 245

displacement (linguistic) 69–70

displacement (Freud) 51

dominant (or 'hegemonic') code and reading (Hall) 64, 108, 149–50, 183, 192, 228

double articulation 10, 224, 228–9, 239, 242

dualism *see* binarism

duality of patterning *see* double articulation

Duck, Steve 54

dyadic model of sign 18, 32, 35, 238–9

Dyer, Richard 30, 156

Eagleton, Terry 171, 198

Easthope, Antony 84–5

Eco, Umberto 2, 6, 7, 33, 47–8, 53, 59, 61–2, 134, 149, 158, 161, 166, 171, 179, 222, 246

Edgerton, Samuel Y. 183, 184

Eikhenbaum, Boris 234

elaborated codes *see* narrowcast codes

élite interpreter 209

Ellis, John 13, 26, 28, 44, 52, 181, 195, 211

empty signifier 74–7

encoding 106, 149, 175–9, 193, 227, 229

encoding and decoding model of communication 175–9

enunciation/énonciation 126

epistemology 70, 91, 126

essentialism 58, 193, 218

expression, plane of *see* planes of content and expression

expressive function 191, 229

Fairclough, Norman 159

figurae (Hjelmslev) 7, 242

filmic signs and codes 10, 12, 38, 42, 43, 52–3, 61, 62, 64, 73, 81, 82, 87, 97–8, 100, 128, 131, 133, 149, 159–60, 161–2, 165–70, 172, 182, 187–8, 189–91, 194, 200, 201–3, 208, 217, 226, 234, 244

Fiore, Quentin 186

first articulation 228, 242

Fish, Stanley 123–4, 192, 230

Fiske, John 12, 108, 141, 143–4, 171, 224

Fleming, Dan 120–1

floating signifier *see* empty signifier

Floch, Jean-Marie 108–9, 121, 222

Forceville, Charles 128

foregrounding 64, 74, 89, 112, 132, 135, 141, 161, 168, 178, 182, 188, 190, 229, 233, 239

form and content 52, 53, 62, 64, 82, 86, 90–1, 104, 124–5, 158, 160, 182–3, 230, 233, 234, 238, 242

form and substance *see* plane of content, plane of expression

formalism 66, 90, 135, 209, 211, 212, 226, 227, 234, 237, 244
formality of address 85–6, 154, 188, 190–1, 234
Foucault, Michel 7, 71, 91, 115, 126, 199, 213, 222, 237, 238, 239, 245–6
Franklin, Sarah 211, 218
Freud, Sigmund 51, 69, 105
functionalism 4, 5, 15, 24, 49, 57, 79, 80, 82, 92, 93, 96, 130, 134, 187, 191, 210, 228, 237–8, 242
functions of signs 56–7, 178–9, 191–2, 216, 229, 238
Fuss, Diane 112

Gallie, W. B. 75
Galtung, Johan 76
Gardiner, Michael 29
Gelb, I. J. 45
Genette, Gérard 203–4
Genosko, Gary 3
genre 2, 3, 60–1, 63–4, 81, 82, 89, 108, 111, 113, 117, 134, 138, 149, 150, 158–60, 165, 167, 173, 179, 182–3, 188–90, 193, 199, 200–1, 204–5, 225, 230, 233, 243, 244
gestalt psychology 57, 89, 150–2
Glasgow University Media Group 9, 97
glossematics 226
Goffman, Erving 88, 156
Gombrich, Ernst H. 47, 77, 86, 161, 162, 166, 199
Goodman, Marcia 84
Goodman, Nelson 162–3, 166
'grammar' of a medium 190
graphocentrism 244
grande syntagmatique 98
Grayson, Kent 40, 59

Greenberg, J. H. 110
Greimas, Algirdas 6, 9, 68, 93, 95–7, 118–21, 211, 222, 226, 236–7, 240
Grosz, Elizabeth 106
Guiraud, Pierre 150, 172, 225
Gumpert, Gary 173

Hall, Edward T. 155, 191
Hall, Stuart 7, 141, 148, 149, 150, 157, 158, 170–1, 179, 180, 192, 193, 202, 210, 217, 228, 235, 236, 238
Halle, Morris 101, 125, 131, 132, 133, 134, 140, 177
Harris, Roy xviii, 27, 80, 177, 197, 221
Hartley, John 12, 144
Havránek, Bohuslav 238
Hawkes, Terence 9, 36, 43, 72, 95, 124, 165, 212
Hayakawa, S. I. 66, 67
hegemonic code see dominant code
hermeneutics 225
Higgins, Patrick 156
historicity 4, 13, 30–1, 44–5, 58, 76–7, 90, 107, 113, 115, 126, 141–3, 152, 162, 164, 172, 183–4, 195, 211, 243
Hjelmslev, Louis 3, 6, 7, 9, 10, 23, 53–4, 74, 140, 142, 144, 226, 236, 238
Hobbes, Thomas 126
Hockett, Charles F. 10, 26, 70
Hodge, Robert 8, 14, 37, 52, 59, 60, 61, 63, 83, 91, 98, 115–17, 211, 213, 221
homology see isomorphism
homo significans 17
humanism 180–1, 185

iconic mode 37–45, 61–2, 76, 127, 131, 150, 163, 166, 219, 224, 229, 233, 235
'ideal readers' 160, 179, 181, 191, 223, 234, 243
idealism (subjectivism) 50–2, 58–9, 76, 77, 126, 196
ideological codes 46, 125, 129, 149, 195, 208, 228, 236
ideology 12, 15, 28, 46, 91, 99, 108, 113, 125, 129, 138, 140–1, 143–5, 148–50, 159, 164–5, 173, 180–3, 187–8, 190, 195, 201, 203, 208, 212, 215–16, 224, 227, 228, 235, 236, 237, 243, 245
idiolect 148–9
illusionism 187
Imaginary, the (Lacan) 91, 105, 188
imaginary signifier (Metz) 62
immanent or intrinsic meaning 14, 17, 75, 32, 35, 53, 135
indexical mode 37, 39–45, 65, 76, 130–1, 133–4, 163, 184, 224, 230, 233
Innis, Robert E. 3, 9
intentional fallacy 65, 196
interpellation (Althusser) 181, 230
interpersonal communication 3, 177, 179, 232
interpretant (Peirce) 32–3, 35, 59, 230, 246
interpretative codes 149–50, 157–9, 169, 172–3, 175, 192–3, 200, 225, 226, 230, 242, 244
interpretative community 192, 225, 230
intertextuality 80, 172, 194–205, 217, 224, 225, 227, 230–1
intratextuality 80, 201–3, 204, 231
irony 52, 115, 134–7, 231, 245

isomorphism or homology 56, 107, 138, 231
Ivins, William 184, 186

Jakobson, Roman 6–7, 9, 13, 43, 74, 80, 100, 101, 103–4, 110, 118, 125, 131, 132, 133–4, 139–40, 147, 177–9, 191, 222, 223, 226, 229, 232, 234, 238
James, Henry 188
James, William 152
Jameson, Fredric 23, 68, 92–3, 96, 118, 120, 137, 150, 198
Jensen, Klaus Bruhn 213, 221
Johnson, Mark 87, 88, 124, 125, 127, 129–31, 132, 145
Johnson, Richard 180, 181

Karen, Robert 162, 167
Keller, Helen 70
Kennedy, John 61
Kipling, Rudyard 104–5
Kitses, Jim 108
Korzybski, Alfred 66–9
Kress, Gunther 14, 37, 53, 59, 60, 63, 83, 87–9, 91, 115–17, 187, 190, 191, 213, 221
Kristeva, Julia 7, 9, 195, 230, 237, 240
Kubovy, Michael 184

Lacan, Jacques 7, 9, 28, 51, 74, 75, 91, 105, 112, 140, 180, 188, 222, 237, 238, 245, 246
Lakoff, George 87, 88, 124, 125, 127, 129–31, 132, 145
Langer, Susanne K. 10–11, 20, 38, 39
'language' of a medium 9, 11–12, 93, 97–8, 150, 162

langue and parole 12–14, 23, 117, 209, 231

Lanham, Richard A. 132

Larrucia, Victor 93–5

Lash, Scott 205

latent meaning 8, 121, 193

Leach, Edmund 69, 102, 106

Lechte, John 30, 74, 110

Leiss, William 9

Lemke, Jay 213

Lemon, Lee T. 212

levels of signification see orders of signification

Lévi-Strauss, Claude 7, 9, 13, 30–1, 45, 51, 68, 75, 83, 90, 93, 106–7, 138, 140, 144–5, 203, 211, 222, 224, 240, 245

Lewis, Justin 29

Leymore, Varda Langholz 83, 104, 120

linguistic determinism 126, 154, 195, 210

linguistic relativism see relativism, linguistic

literal meaning 101, 115, 123–4, 126–7, 134–6, 140–2, 143–4, 146, 163–4, 212, 227, 231, 232, 233, 246

Little Red Riding-Hood 93–5

Locke, John 6, 126

Lodge, David 132

logocentrism 2, 86, 202, 230, 231–2, 244

Lotman, Yuri 5, 171, 172, 233, 240, 244

Lovell, Terry 63, 76, 112

Luckmann, Thomas 156

Lyons, John 26, 35, 41, 45, 47–8, 50, 57, 103, 104, 110, 111

MacCabe, Colin 180

making the familiar strange see denaturalization

Malkiel, Yakov 111

markedness 74, 110–18, 135, 204, 227, 232, 233, 234

mass communication 179, 232

materialism 18, 50, 52, 59, 76–7, 113, 115–16, 150

materiality of the sign 18–21, 32, 48–54, 63, 117, 226, 232, 238, 239, 241, 242

Mathesius, Vilem 238

McKim, Robert H. 67

McLuhan, Marshall 4, 81, 185, 186–7, 232

McQuarrie, Edward F. 9, 194, 208

meaning see connotation, contextual meaning, denotation, determination of meaning, differential meaning, immanent or intrinsic meaning, intentional fallacy, latent meaning, literal meaning, polysemy, relational meaning, structural meaning

meaning structures (Hall) 179

meaning systems (Parkin) 192

mediation 4, 14, 35, 41, 62, 66, 73, 76–7, 144, 161, 170, 200, 208, 215–17, 239

medium 2–5, 41–2, 52–3, 60–4, 72–3, 81, 89–91, 99, 123, 131, 141, 150, 158, 161, 163, 165, 172–3, 185, 187, 188, 193, 194, 196, 200, 201, 210, 215, 217, 218–19, 225, 228, 232, 233, 234, 244, 245

'medium is the message' (McLuhan) 4, 81, 91, 232

message 2, 4, 12, 60, 68, 81, 91, 163–5, 176–9, 182, 217, 223, 229, 232–3

'message without a code' (Barthes) 163–4

Messaris, Paul 162, 166, 169, 191, 208, 219

metalingual function 158, 178, 229

metaphor 37, 45, 53, 66, 67–8, 87–8, 106, 115, 124–9, 130, 131–4, 137, 139, 143, 145, 229, 233, 245

metonymic (synecdochic) fallacy 134

metonymy 125, 130–2, 134, 137, 139, 233, 244, 245

Metz, Christian 6, 53, 54, 62, 90, 97–8, 165, 172, 202, 222, 226

Mick, David Glen xix, 9, 121, 194, 208

Millar, Gavin 167, 169

mimesis 73, 161

mirror phase 105, 188

mise-en-scène 82

modality 37, 59, 60–4, 71, 73, 135, 150, 159, 233

modelling systems, primary and secondary 233–4

models of communication *see* encoding and decoding model, transmission model

models of the sign *see* Peircean model, Saussurean model

modes of address 160, 179–80, 182, 188–92, 234

modes of relationship 36, 43, 166

Monaco, James 62, 173

montage 82, 84, 97, 244

Morley, David 150, 192, 193, 210

Morris, Charles W. 6, 7, 194, 240

Morris, Pam 13, 198

Moscow school 6–7, 212, 234

motivation and constraint 29, 30, 37–8, 45–6, 235

Mukarovsky, Jan 238

multiaccentuality (Voloshinov) 181, 230, 235

Murray, Donald M. 85

myth 9, 76, 93, 106–7, 108, 129, 144–6, 157, 163–4, 200, 203, 210, 211, 217, 218, 235, 245

narration or narrative voice 91, 165, 188–90, 234

narrative 9, 61, 73, 83–4, 89–98, 159–60, 165, 167–9, 171–2, 180, 185, 188–90, 194, 200, 202, 234, 244

narratology 9, 89, 92–7

narrowcast codes 136, 170–1, 224, 235

naturalism 165, 199

naturalization 51, 64, 91, 107, 117, 126, 141, 145, 157, 169, 182, 215–16, 230, 235

negotiated code and reading (Hall) 150, 192, 235

Newcomb, Theodore M. 101

Nichols, Bill 47, 73, 91, 149, 150, 152–3, 156, 166, 182, 185, 187, 191

nomenclaturism 27, 56–8, 72

nominal realism 70–1

non-neutrality of medium, sign or representation 3, 30, 53, 64, 71, 77–8, 81, 87, 91, 112, 123, 141, 148, 159, 161, 165, 182, 187, 197, 202, 210, 212, 216, 232

Nöth, Winfried xix, 6, 34, 101, 165, 203, 221

object (referent) 20, 23, 32–4, 36, 37, 38–42, 45, 55–6, 58–9, 62, 67–9, 163–4, 236, 238–9, 241
objectivism *see* realism (objectivism)
Ogden, Charles K. 6, 29, 34, 68, 240
Olson, David 70, 71, 176
ontology 30, 31, 35, 60, 91, 113–14, 129, 195, 210, 230
open and closed signs and texts 47, 75, 140, 158
oppositional code and reading (Hall) 150, 192–3, 236
oppositions, semantic *see* analogue oppositions, binary oppositions
orders of signification 142–5, 226, 227, 235
Orwell, George 111
O'Sullivan, Tim 144
Osgood, Charles E 144
overcoding 171, 225
overdetermination 158, 172

Panofsky, Erwin 140, 184
paradigm 79, 80–3, 93, 98–101, 107–8, 110, 117, 139, 143, 165, 203, 223, 224, 225, 227, 232, 236
Paris school 6, 95, 236–7
Parkin, Frank 192
parole *see* langue
Peircean model of the sign 32–5, 59, 230, 236, 238, 239
parsimony, ontological 148
Peirce, Charles Sanders 5, 6–7, 8, 17, 32–5, 36, 37, 38–43, 44, 47, 50, 57, 59, 61, 75, 76, 86, 163,

166, 179, 213–14, 219, 221–2, 224, 230, 233, 236, 238, 239, 240, 241, 245, 246
Pepper, Stephen C. 133, 138
perceptual codes 57, 61, 89, 149, 150–3, 157, 165, 166, 184
phatic function of signs 191–2, 229
phenomenal reality 152–3, 168, 184–5
phonocentrism 20, 51, 115, 231, 234, 237
'photographic message' (Barthes) 141, 163–4
photographic signs and codes 10, 12, 37–8, 42, 43, 53, 61–2, 73, 82, 84, 87, 89, 99–100, 133, 141, 143, 149, 161–2, 163–6, 172, 182, 185, 187, 189, 191, 194, 201, 202, 208, 215, 226, 231, 244
Piaget, Jean 70, 164
planes of content and expression (Hjelmslev) 23, 53
planes of paradigm and syntagm (Jakobson) 80
planes of signifier (or sound) and signified (or thought) (Saussure) 23, 28, 53
Plato 26, 51
poetic or aesthetic function 124, 150, 159, 178–9, 229
Pollio, Howard 127
polysemy 120, 140, 181, 230
polyvocality 189
positioning of the subject 99, 180–2, 191, 243
Postman, Leo J. 101
postmodernism 14, 49, 52, 74, 75–7, 136, 218, 227
poststructuralism 7, 21, 33, 51, 75, 91, 108, 113, 124, 126, 195, 213,

222, 227, 230, 237, 238, 240, 242, 243, 245
Potter, Elizabeth 134
pragmatics 194
Prague school 7, 100, 234, 237–8
Pranger, Brian 156
preferred reading 81–2, 91, 106, 111, 158, 171, 192–3, 201, 210, 224, 225, 228, 235, 236, 238
primacy of the signifier 21, 28, 52, 58, 61–2, 74, 115, 238
Propp, Vladimir I. 90, 92, 93, 95, 96, 211

Quintilian 101, 203

real, the (Lacan) 64, 105
realism, aesthetic 40, 63–6, 72–3, 86, 90, 91, 107, 118, 120, 125, 132, 134, 139, 141, 149, 161–70, 180, 182, 185, 187, 189, 200, 205, 227, 239
realism (objectivism) xvii, 35, 55–7, 59, 66, 67, 70–1, 73, 76–7, 125, 215–16, 239
reality/realities xvii, 2, 12, 14–15, 23, 27–9, 34–5, 41–2, 51, 55–78, 86, 90, 102, 113, 114–15, 123–6, 131, 133–4, 152, 154, 156–7, 161, 163, 165–8, 181, 184–5, 187, 200, 205, 208, 212, 215–16, 230, 233, 236, 238, 239–40, 241
Reddy, Michael J. 124, 129, 176
reduction 53, 57, 68, 92–7, 121, 137, 139, 163, 178, 193, 217, 218
redundancy 171, 225
referent 20, 22, 25–7, 29, 32, 33–6, 37, 56–9, 64, 66, 69–71, 73, 74, 76–7, 91, 126, 130, 141, 157, 177–9, 216, 224, 229, 232, 233, 236, 238–9, 241, 242, 245, 246
referential function 57, 177–8, 229
reflexivity 136, 146, 204–5
reification 193
Reis, Marion J. 212
Reisz, Karel 167, 169
relational meaning 22, 24, 112, 246
relative autonomy 23, 30, 59, 71, 118, 141, 145, 147, 163, 166, 239
relativism/relativity, cultural 77, 216
relativism, epistemological 136, 138, 184, 216, 218
relativism/relativity, linguistic 154
representamen 32–3, 36, 239, 241
representation 2, 3, 14–15, 33, 35, 40, 46, 53, 55, 59, 60–67, 69, 71, 73, 74, 76–8, 86, 87, 107, 115, 140, 142, 145, 150, 161, 162, 163, 165–6, 173, 181, 183, 185–7, 189, 194, 205, 214, 216, 219, 227, 232, 233, 239–40, 241, 244, 245
representational codes and practices 55, 161, 166, 185, 189, 194, 216, 219, 227, 239
reproductive fallacy 63
restricted codes see broadcast codes
rhetoric 8, 99, 101, 102, 123–40, 146, 149, 159, 164, 202, 227, 231, 245
'rhetoric of the image' (Barthes) 141, 163, 165
Richards, Ivor A. 6, 26, 29, 34, 127, 240
Rodowick, David N. 198
Romanyshyn, Robert D. 183, 186
Rosenblum, Ralph 162, 166–7

Ruge, Eric 76
Ryan, T. A. 61

Sapir, Edward 86, 154
Sapir–Whorf hypothesis 58, 60, 129, 154, 179
Saussure, Ferdinand de 5–6, 7, 8, 9, 11, 12–14, 17, 18–32, 33–9, 44, 49, 50–1, 53, 54, 56–60, 66, 74, 75, 79–81, 82, 83, 98–9, 103, 108, 115–16, 140, 143, 145, 147, 176–7, 180, 194, 195, 197, 207, 209, 211, 213–14, 221, 224, 226, 228, 229, 231, 235, 236, 237, 238, 239, 240, 241, 242, 246
Saussurean model of the sign 18–32, 35–6, 58–60, 74, 241–2
schools of linguistics/semiotics *see* Copenhagen school, Moscow school, Paris school, Prague school, Tartu school
Schwartz, C. B. 61
Scribner, Sylvia 70
Sebeok, Thomas A. 6, 74, 240
second articulation 10, 228, 242
Seiter, Ellen 14
selection and combination, axes of 80, 139
semantic differential 144
semantics 47, 66–8, 73, 87, 101, 106, 111, 118, 144, 154, 194, 237, 240
semiology (Saussure, Barthes) 5–6, 9, 11, 24, 31–2, 77, 83, 197, 240
semiosis (Peirce) 5, 33–5, 60, 75, 213, 214, 230, 240, 241, 246
semiosphere 5, 240
semiotic economy 10, 21, 45, 182

semiotic square 118–21, 137, 240
semiotic triangle 34–5
semiotics, definition of 1–2, 5–6, 7, 8–9, 11–12, 17, 31, 55, 59, 116–17, 207, 240–1
'sender' and 'receiver' 2, 96, 176, 210, 223
sense 32, 35, 100, 127, 225
Shannon, Claude E. 176
sign, definition of 1–2, 8, 17–54, 241
sign vehicle 34, 35–6, 47–9, 52, 59, 233, 239, 241, 242
signification 9, 19, 24, 44, 47, 53, 54, 59, 68, 75–6, 117, 119, 134, 142, 144–5, 191, 211, 212, 221, 226–7, 235, 236, 241, 245, 246
signifier and signified xviii, 18–22, 25–31, 33, 36–8, 41, 44, 46, 49–53, 58, 62, 64, 66, 69–71, 73–5, 77, 80, 88, 100, 110–11, 115, 123, 125, 127–9, 132–3, 135, 140–3, 147, 158, 161, 163, 166, 191, 196, 203, 210, 221, 224, 225, 226, 227, 228, 229, 230, 232, 233, 235, 236, 237, 239, 241, 242, 243, 244, 245, 246
signifying practices 12, 42, 48, 55, 72, 79, 82, 99, 101, 106–7, 117, 120–1, 126, 136, 147–9, 161, 173, 179–80, 194, 203, 208–10, 213–14, 216–19, 224, 234, 240, 241, 242
Silverman, David 52, 95, 125
Silverman, Kaja 59, 80, 106, 141, 142
simulacrum (Baudrillard) 76–7
single articulation, codes with 224, 242

sites of struggle 13, 60, 216
Slater, Don 210
Smith, Frank 85, 176
Snyder, J. 187
social codes 149–50, 154–7, 169, 172, 176, 192–3, 199, 210, 227, 233
social construction of reality *see* constructivism
social determinism 13, 44, 193, 210
social semiotics 5–6, 8, 9, 12, 13–14, 29, 30–1, 35, 38, 49, 60, 83, 116–17, 141, 147, 154–7, 175–7, 179, 181, 188, 192–3, 194, 208, 209–11, 213, 214, 215, 216, 217, 218, 221, 226, 227, 230
sociolect 113
speech circuit 176
Sprat, Thomas 125, 126
Stam, Robert 29, 77, 170
Stern, Barbara B. 89, 126, 128
Strinati, Dominic 210
structural determinism 13, 27, 93, 102, 106, 108, 181, 195, 210, 230, 242, 243
structural meaning 22
structuralism 6–7, 8, 9, 12, 13, 14, 25, 32, 44, 79–80, 84, 92, 95, 99, 100, 101, 106, 121, 135, 143, 144, 147, 148, 158, 172, 179, 180, 181, 194–5, 207–18, 221, 222, 225, 226, 227, 230, 231, 234, 236, 237, 238, 239, 242–3, 244
structuration 195
Sturrock, John 25, 27, 29, 58
subject 13, 91, 96, 105, 113, 142, 157, 168, 179–83, 185–8, 189, 191, 195, 213, 217–18, 230, 234, 237, 243
subjectivism *see* idealism

subjectivity, theories of *see* subject
suture 188
Swales, John 84
symbolic mode 12, 20, 36–46, 59, 62, 73, 75–6, 91, 105, 131, 219, 224, 226, 233, 235, 243
symbolic order (Lacan) 72, 105, 112
synchronic analysis 12–13, 34, 44, 106–7, 143, 158, 172, 211, 228, 243
synecdoche 132–4, 137, 233, 243–4, 245
syntactics 10, 11, 27, 46, 47, 70, 81, 96, 149, 154–5, 164, 172, 194, 234
syntagm 79–98, 99, 100, 101, 139, 143, 165, 188, 201, 203, 231, 244

Tagg, John 30, 64, 163, 165, 212
Tartu school 5, 244
technological or media determinism 4, 173
televisual signs and codes 12, 37, 42, 43, 52–3, 61–2, 63–4, 73, 81, 82, 84, 87, 97–8, 117–18, 133, 149, 165–70, 172, 179, 188–90, 193, 199–201, 202, 211, 217, 226, 244
tenor (Richards) 127, 233
text 2–3, 8–9, 12, 52, 53, 63, 75, 79, 85–6, 92, 98, 107, 118, 120, 147–50, 152, 157–72, 175–6, 179, 188, 194–205, 209, 211, 230–1, 244–5
textual analysis 8–9, 54, 55, 79–121, 126, 149, 201, 214, 225, 227, 236, 237, 240, 243
textual codes 149, 157–72, 182, 191–3, 227, 228, 233

textual determinism 179, 181, 230, 238, 243
textual positioning *see* positioning of the subject
Thibault, Paul J. 35, 197, 213, 222
Thompson, Kristin 167
Thwaites, Tony 82, 182–3, 191
tokens and types 39, 47–50, 56, 245
Torode, Brian 52, 95, 125
transcendent(al) signified 75, 231, 237, 245
transformation, rules of 101, 107, 163, 203, 231, 245
translatability 3, 11, 47, 52, 57, 67–9, 90, 152, 161, 197
transmission model of communication 14, 176–7, 217, 233
transparency 3, 15, 21, 26, 30, 36, 40, 52, 59, 64, 68, 73, 74, 76, 78, 112, 124–5, 141, 155, 162, 165, 166, 173, 179, 182, 186–7, 192, 215–16, 225, 227, 228, 232, 233, 239, 245
triadic model of sign 32, 34, 35, 230, 236, 238
Tripp, David 8, 52, 61, 98, 211
tropes 101, 123–40, 143, 146, 231, 245–6
Trubetzkoy, Nikolai 238
Tuchman, Gaye 191
Tudor, Andrew 54
Tynyanov, Yuri 13, 234
types and tokens *see* tokens and types
unarticulated codes 246

univocality 86, 189
unlimited semiosis 33, 75, 246
unmarked categories *see* markedness
untranslatability *see* translatability

valorization 51, 52, 115–18, 227, 232
value of a sign (Saussure) 21, 23–5, 33, 80, 99, 111, 232, 246
vehicle in metaphor 127
vehicle, sign *see* sign vehicle
Vico, Giambattista 129, 137
Voloshinov, Valentin N. 13, 50–1, 141, 198, 216, 217, 235
Walton, Paul 42, 97
Warren, Robert Penn 84, 159
Watney, Simon 212
Weaver, Warren 176
White, Hayden 91, 137, 138–9, 159
White, John 184, 186
Whorf, Benjamin Lee 129, 154
Whorfianism or Whorfian hypothesis *see* Sapir-Whorf hypothesis
Wilden, Anthony 45, 46, 47, 65, 69, 130, 140
Willemen, Paul 143
Williamson, Judith 128–9, 212
Wimsatt, William K. 196
Wright, Lawrence 184

Young, Brian M. 121

zero sign (Jakobson) 74, 110